Remaining Relevant after Communism

Remaining Relevant after Communism

The Role of the Writer in Eastern Europe

ANDREW BARUCH WACHTEL

THE UNIVERSITY OF CHICAGO PRESS   CHICAGO AND LONDON

ANDREW BARUCH WACHTEL is the Bertha and Max Dressler Professor in the Humanities, dean of the Graduate School, and director of the Center for International and Comparative Studies at Northwestern University. He is the author of *Making a Nation, Breaking a Nation: Literature and Cultural Politics in Yugoslavia.*

The University of Chicago Press, Chicago 60637
The University of Chicago Press, Ltd., London
© 2006 by The University of Chicago
All rights reserved. Published 2006
Printed in the United States of America

15 14 13 12 11 10 09 08 07 06   1 2 3 4 5

ISBN: 0-226-86766-8 (cloth)

Library of Congress Cataloging-in-Publication Data

Wachtel, Andrew.
  Remaining relevant after communism : the role of the writer in Eastern Europe/
Andrew Baruch Wachtel.
     p. cm.
  Includes bibliographical references and index.
  ISBN 0-226-86766-8 (cloth : alk. paper)
     1. East European literaure—History and criticism.   2. Literature and society—Europe,
Eastern.   I. Title.
  PN849.E9W33 2006
  891.7'009–dc22

                                                                                        2005009972

⊗ The paper used in this publication meets the minimum requirements of the
American National Standard for Information Sciences—Permanence of Paper for
Printed Library Materials, ANSI Z39.48-1992.

Contents

Acknowledgments   vii

Introduction   1

CHAPTER 1. The Writer as National Hero   12

CHAPTER 2. 1989–2000: The End of the Golden Age   44

CHAPTER 3. Writers and Politics: Triumph, Tragedy, and Farce   73

CHAPTER 4. Writers and Nationalism   98

CHAPTER 5. The New Internationalism in East European Literature   119

CHAPTER 6. Writers and Journalism   140

CHAPTER 7. Dealing with Transition Head-On   166

CHAPTER 8. Learning to Love Popular Fiction   189

Conclusion   215

Bibliography   221

Index   229

Acknowledgments

A large-scale project succeeds only because of generous support from a variety of sources. This is particularly true for this project, which required extensive field research in multiple countries. I am grateful for the financial support I received from the National Council for Eurasian and East European Research (NCEEER) under the authority of a Title VIII grant from the U.S. Department of State. Further funding for the project came from ACTR/ACCELS through a grant provided by the National Endowment for the Humanities, and Northwestern University. The financial assitance these organizations provided allowed me to engage the services of a wonderful team of field researchers: in Bulgaria, Angelina Ilieva; in Croatia, Aleš Debeljak and Jadranka Pintarić; in the Czech Republic, Lea Hamrlíková and Lauren McConnell; in Hungary, Erzsébet Schiller, Andrea Reményi, and Éva Fodor; in Moldova, Irina Livezeanu, Liliana Armaşu, and Igor Caşu; in Poland, Piotr Nowak and Mihal Oklot; in Romania, Marius Lazar and Irina Livezeanu; in Russia, Mikhail Kolesnikov; in Slovenia, Aleš Debeljak and Ksenija Šabac; in Ukraine, Vitaly Kutik. Each researcher or research team provided a comprehensive account of the country on which he or she worked, and these reports were discussed at a conference held in Dubrovnik in 2001. At that event, the researchers and I had the good fortune to receive input and criticism from Mihai-Dinu Gheorghiu, Donald Sassoon, Nikolay Stoyanov, and Igor Štiks. I would like to thank them all for their excellent work and collegial help. They should not, however, be held responsible for any errors that have crept in or misinterpretation of their data, all of which should be attributed to the author.

In working on the manuscript, I was spurred by supportive conversation and advice from Northwestern colleagues including Clare Cavanagh, Ilya

Kutik, and Saul Morson. I would also like to acknowledge Jeffrey Brooks and Michael Heim, who provided enormously helpful and detailed criticism on drafts of the manuscript that were perhaps not as polished as either would have liked. Alan Thomas of the University of Chicago Press skillfully maneuvered the book through the publication process, for which I am grateful. Randolph Petilos and Erik Carlson from the University of Chicago Press turned a messy manuscript into a book, which I greatly appreciate.

Finally, I would like to thank my children, Samuel, Eleanor, and Elias, for putting up with my absences during the research phase of the project and, most of all, my wife, Elizabeth Calihan, to whom this book is dedicated.

Introduction

As the editor of a book series devoted to translations of contemporary East European literature, I am frequently asked, "Why has no new Milan Kundera appeared in Eastern Europe since the collapse of communist regimes?" Though the question seems simple, the answer is not. First of all there is a conceptual slippage within the question itself, whereby the words "Milan Kundera" stand for a writer who is simultaneously highly talented and world-renowned. If I take the liberty of disaggregating the query, the answer to the first part *is* fairly easy. Many talented writers have appeared in Eastern Europe since 1989. Indeed, one of the tasks of this study is to discuss a number of them, at least in part to encourage readers to recognize that work on the level of that produced in previous decades by writers such as Kundera, Alexander Solzhenitsyn, Wisława Szymborska, and Danilo Kiš continues to be created in Eastern Europe, even after the end of communism.

The answer to the second part of the question, however, is more complex, for it has less to do with literature per se than it does with the position and role of literature and those who produce it in society. Writers do not become as renowned as Kundera merely because they are talented (although a considerable amount of literary talent is undoubtedly required), but also because local and international cultural conditions allow and encourage their talent to be widely recognized and appreciated. Publishers must wish to make Kundera available, critics must decide to review him, state and privately funded groups must award him prizes, and readers (both in his own country and abroad) must choose to buy and, at least in some cases, to read his work. The phenomenon "Milan Kundera" is, therefore, as much sociocultural as literary.

I can say with some confidence that the sociocultural conditions that once allowed for the appearance of "Milan Kunderas" no longer exist in most of postcommunist Eastern Europe, and they are unlikely to return in the near future. The disappearance of these conditions was an indirect and unexpected consequence of the fall of the Berlin Wall in 1989, which ushered in the largest and the most successful experiment in democratization and the creation of free markets ever undertaken. In a fifteen-year rush, countries formerly hostile to Western Europe and the United States, governed for almost fifty years (more than eighty years in the case of the USSR) by an ideology that limited personal freedom in favor of the collective and that all but eliminated private enterprise in favor of state-controlled economies, were integrated into the Euro-Atlantic strategic alliance through membership in or partnership with NATO, and most became members of the European Union.[1] This transformation had broad repercussions in the cultural arena, although these have generally not been the subject of scholarly research or discussion. One key outcome is that, for a number of reasons to be considered in detail in this book, East European literature, at least in the traditional sense of serious fiction, drama, and poetry, is no longer perceived to be as important as it once was. As the Serbian critic Mihailo Pantić put it in a discussion of the changed role of literature in his own country: "From what had been an elite art form, which in a synthetic way recapitulated the general truths of people's experience and which deepened their understanding of reality . . . artistic literature in the postsocialist cultural model has become socially unnecessary, an almost completely private affair which lacks any social importance and which is interesting only to narrow academic circles, to writers, and to rare dedicated readers who nurture their passion as other marginal groups nurture theirs. Some people belong to satanic cults, some to the Society for Lovers of Bulldogs, and others, amazingly, read Serbian poetry."[2]

Pantić's wry assertion contains a number of important insights. Most crucial is that in socialist-era East European culture (and in presocialist

---

1. There is an enormous literature on what happened in the region in the course of the 1990s. For a good overall survey see J. F. Brown. To be sure, there are exceptions to this general story of Europeanization: while some former republics of the Soviet Union (Lithuania, Latvia, and Estonia) have been almost fully integrated, Ukraine, Belarus, and Russia itself have not, and the last may never be. In southeastern Europe, Serbia still remains for the most part outside this process as well, although it is likely eventually to be integrated into the European system.

2. Pantić (translation mine).

Eastern Europe as well, I might add), even such rarefied literary genres as lyric poetry were perceived to matter to a broad public. This does not mean that every member of society spent his or her leisure time reading Alexander Pushkin or Kundera. Nevertheless, it was indeed through literature that a good portion of society came to know itself, precisely because literary work was broadly believed to "recapitulate the general truths of people's experience." And even the portion of society that never read anything tended to point to the nation's literature, particularly its classical literature, as a source of pride. That is to say, in Eastern Europe literature was relevant.

There are many possible ways to define Eastern Europe as an integrated space.[3] In a provocative book, the historian Larry Wolff emphasized the role that West Europeans played in creating the concept of Eastern Europe, claiming baldly: "It was Western Europe that invented Eastern Europe as its complementary other half in the eighteenth century, the Age of Enlightenment.... Such was the invention of Eastern Europe. It has flourished as an idea of extraordinary potency since the eighteenth century, neatly dovetailing in our own times with the rhetoric and realities of the Cold War, but also certain to outlive the collapse of communism, surviving in the public culture and mental maps."[4] The problem with such a definition, however, is that in placing the onus on the mental mapping of Westerners, it implicitly denies that there are also objective reasons to see Eastern Europe as a unit, that there are factors shared by East European countries but absent or only minimally present in neighboring areas.

3. The term Eastern Europe itself cannot be used without creating controversy, particularly in the region. Beginning in the mid-1980s, as they attempted to pull themselves out of Soviet-imposed cold war isolation, many members of the East European elites preferred to use the term Central Europe to define those countries that lay between Russia and Germany. Kundera was especially articulate in this regard (see Kundera, "The Tragedy of Central Europe," in Stokes). European intellectuals, particularly British ones such as Timothy Garton Ash, began to use this terminology as well. Subsequently, however, even finer distinctions began to be made, with southeastern Europe being split off from Central Europe and the Baltic states recognizing their own distinctiveness. In this book I simply cannot use any term other than Eastern Europe. The primary reason is that pace Kundera, my research indicates that the literary and cultural developments described here are shared across all the former communist countries *including* Russia, so no geographical term that excludes Russia is acceptable. In this regard, I agree with J. F. Brown, who defends his use of the term Eastern Europe as follows: "It provides a suitable framework in which to discuss the abiding features of the region's modern history.... Many of the problems that these countries face are similar, the attempts to deal with them are comparable, their successes and failures are relevant and illustrative" (xiii).

4. Wolff, 1994, 4.

Students of politics, for example, have noted that the countries of Eastern Europe were, from the early modern period until the twentieth century, under the control of outside empires (though if this is the definition, then Russia is not an East European country). Economists, by contrast, can point to patterns of late industrial development in the context of the overall European market.

For those concerned with the study of culture, the situation is complicated. After all, the region, however defined, includes a bewildering variety of mutually incomprehensible languages belonging to the Indo-European (Slavic, Romance, Baltic), Finno-Ugric, and Turko-Altaic families. And until relatively recently, cultural cross-fertilization was often minimal or localized. However, scanning the cultural map of the region as a whole, I hazard to propose a cultural definition of Eastern Europe that, to my knowledge, has not been used before: Eastern Europe is that part of the world where serious literature and those who produce it have traditionally been overvalued. To be sure, as there is no Archimedean scale to measure the appropriate value of serious literature and of writers, I am really claiming only that in Eastern Europe writers and literature are overvalued in comparison with their counterparts in the rest of the world.

This can perhaps be most easily perceived by taking a stroll through any East European capital city. What immediately strikes a tourist from the United States or Western Europe is that on the pedestals generally reserved in our lands for political and military figures, here one finds poets and writers. Main streets and town squares are named for writers. Furthermore, as a result of the traditionally litero-centric educational system, every Russian taxi driver seems able to quote long passages from Pushkin's *Eugene Onegin*; every Polish shopkeeper knows some poems by Adam Mickiewicz; the lyrics to the new Slovenian national anthem are taken from the national poet France Prešeren, and so forth. Furthermore, at least until recently, the pronouncements of writers like Solzhenitsyn, Czesław Miłosz, and Václav Havel made national and international news. That is, literature and its most famous producers are in the air and on people's lips and minds to an extent that is different from their public position in other parts of the world.

A discussion of the historical reasons for the high level of prestige accorded to serious literature and its producers in Eastern Europe forms the topic of the first chapter of this book. For without an understanding of this phenomenon we will never be able to explain the conditions that allowed for the appearance of such figures as Kundera during the cold war period. Without going into detail here, I will simply say that serious literature and its producers began their rise to prominence in Eastern Europe during the so-called period of national revivals (beginning in the 1830s and, depending on the nation in question, continuing into the twentieth century). They were credited, usually posthumously, with being the founding fathers (almost always fathers, I am afraid, as few women writers in Eastern Europe were canonized as nation builders) of their countries, for these countries were seen as having been created on the basis of a shared national language and a literary corpus.[5]

Furthermore—and this sets East European nations apart from nations in other parts of the world where writers are perceived to have played a major role in national consolidation—serious literature and writers remained vitally important during the communist period, when national states already existed. The founding literary fathers of the nineteenth century were recast by communist critics as protocommunists, and the state also paid great attention to those contemporary writers willing to work at its behest as "engineers of human souls." Simultaneously, society (insofar as it was opposed to communist regimes) as well as Western critics took notice of dissident and semidissident writers who were willing to speak out against their governments. As a result, by the late communist period, serious literature and writers possessed an extraordinary level of relevance to their societies and a concomitant level of prestige and symbolic power.

The situation for writers and for literature changed dramatically in the wake of the collapse of communist states—that is, in the period 1989–1991. Most important, the creation of fledgling civil societies, democratic governments, and market economies in East European countries brought an end to the "objective conditions" that had placed writers on a pedestal for a century and a half. Writers were no longer needed to defend the nation's very right to exist (a role that had remained important especially in the Soviet and Yugoslav republics even as it had faded in the countries of Eastern Europe), and they were no longer in demand as the voice of conscience in oppressive regimes. At first, writers, like the majority of the population, were satisfied with the new situation. Rather quickly, however, they came to recognize that even if democratic societies and free markets

5. The Czech Božena Němcová is perhaps the only obvious example of a woman writer credited with an important nation-building role. This is not to say, however, that women writers were absent from literary life in Eastern Europe. For a good overview of women's writing in at least the central portions of this region, see Hawkesworth.

were in the main good for their countries (and, given the way the transition out of communism actually occurred and is still occurring in Eastern
Europe, not all of them would necessarily agree even with this assertion),
the new realities posed enormous difficulties for serious writers. Specifically, writers discovered that governments undergoing market reforms had
little money left for the generous subsidies that had been available under
communism. Book buying declined as the plunge in per capita income
typical of postcommunist Eastern Europe robbed consumers of their purchasing power. Worse, even when they could find spare cash for books,
potential readers suddenly had a wider range of choices. The advent of
market-driven private publishers and the disappearance of censorship led
to the appearance of previously forbidden forms of literature, particularly
translated and then native popular fiction. Finally, with the end of the cold
war, Western publishers and readers lost interest in writers from the no-
longer-dangerous postcommunist world. Writers quickly felt marginalized,
both intellectually and economically, and the prestige of serious literature
declined drastically in the first postcommunist decade. The second chapter
of this book is devoted to a detailed examination of these problems, which
are presented in the form of a comparison of the situation of writers and
institutions of writing in East European countries in 1985 (chosen as one
of the last years of "normal" communist existence) and 2000.

Nevertheless, the prestige of serious writing did not evaporate completely. On the one hand, a respect for literature and its producers had
been inculcated in the population at large for many years, and this did
not disappear quickly despite regime change. On the other, at least some
writers adapted quickly to the new situation and began to search for inno-
vative solutions. Some involved leaving the world of literature. Depending
on circumstance, education, and reputation, writers employed a variety of
strategies to convert their symbolic cultural capital into positions in politics,
journalism, or the private sphere. Others continued to write but adapted
by producing new kinds of work in response both to their own needs and
to those of the emerging literary markets in Eastern Europe. The bulk
of this book, chapters 3–8, presents an analysis of six broad strategies
(inevitably overlapping in some cases) that writers have followed. While
it would be difficult to prove that a given writer chose to produce one
or another kind of literary work in a conscious effort to retain relevance
and/or prestige in the conditions of postcommunism, the fact that similar
strategies were followed by significant numbers of writers in a variety of
countries is highly suggestive. Each chapter considers a given strategy in

a number of incarnations and a number of countries. I consider, in turn, nationalism, politics, internationalism, journalism, "literary transitology," and popular literature.

Some of these writers and their works have achieved significant recognition in their own countries, and a small number have, through translation into major European languages, broken out of the boundaries of their minor literatures (to use the famous term of Gilles Deleuze and Felix Guattari).[6] Beyond the occasional book review, however, there has been little or no scholarly work devoted to them. This book represents the first attempt at a comparative consideration of some of the strategies writers have employed to remain relevant for East European societies in general.[7] As we are speaking here of almost twenty countries and of a more or less equal number of languages, the reader can guess that I will make no attempt to provide an encyclopedic account of postcommunist literature, or even to consider all the strategies writers have employed in the region since 1989. Instead, I endeavor to describe what I perceive to be the most significant currents of literary development in Eastern Europe today and to analyze some key literary works.[8]

Terminology and Caveats

Before going further, I need to explain the terms used in the book's title. First the word "literature." As used here, "literature" when unmodified by any adjective refers to imaginative literature, to works of serious fiction, poetry, and drama. In an American context it would include the output of writers such as John Updike, Toni Morrison, or T. Coraghessan Boyle. It

6. They define the term in their seminal work *Kafka: Toward a Minor Literature.*

7. As I was completing the final revisions for this book, I received the first volume of what is announced as the four-volume *History of the Literary Cultures of East-Central Europe Junctures and Disjunctures in the 19th and 20th Centuries,* ed. Marcel Cornis-Pope and John Neubauer. While not without faults, this ambitious multiauthor project represents the first attempt to consider East European literature (excluding Russian, however) as a whole. The final, as-yet-unpublished volume is to contain an epilogue that considers the "outlook after 1989." The first analytic book in English devoted to a comparative analysis of contemporary East European fiction is Chitnis.

8. There is, of course, one postcommunist country where one might expect to find a different pattern of development: East Germany. Because the German transition took place through the absorption of the former communist country into a West European one, I felt that it would not make sense to compare postcommunist literary developments there with those in the rest of the region.

would not include fiction by Stephen King, Danielle Steel, or Tom Clancy, nor would it include such excellent nonfiction as that produced by authors like John McPhee or Alex Kotlowitz. This choice is not due to academic snobbery. In Eastern Europe, at least until the collapse of communism, popular or pulp literature was for the most part nonexistent, and serious nonfiction was rare.[9] For the most part, then, for the societies in question literature meant serious, highbrow literature. At the same time, both because of the absence of more popular fare and because the educational systems of Eastern Europe were more litero-centric than those of Western Europe or the United States, a surprisingly large percentage of the East European public actually read and appreciated literature in the sense it is used here.

What is more, they found it "relevant." By "relevance" I have in mind a shared belief on the part of writers and at least a reasonable-sized portion of society that what writers have to say in their literary work or, more broadly, in their self-presentation expresses truths to which society as a whole should attend. Relevance, thus, does not have to do, on the one hand, with sales or popularity or, on the other, with trenchant but unappreciated analysis. In this sense few American writers have ever been relevant. Certainly, Walt Whitman took himself as seriously as a spokesman for America as any of the nation-building writers of Eastern Europe did for their countries. The difference, however, is that average well-educated Americans cannot quote a line of Whitman's, while even poorly educated Poles will know a good chunk of Mickiewicz's verse by heart. And in our own day, serious writers such as Don DeLillo and Thomas Pynchon may well have important things to say about American society, but beyond a handful of literature professors few people are able and willing to recognize this. Instead, Americans turn to other types of people to tell them what they need and want to know about their society, be they politicians, television or radio personalities, preachers, or others. By contrast, what Solzhenitsyn wrote about the Gulag, what Miłosz had to say about Poland, or what Havel has to say about the Czech Republic *is* considered relevant by a broad audience. These and other writers may or may not employ exclusively literary forms to make their voices heard, but what is

9. There were exceptions. After having been mostly banned during the Stalin years, science fiction was permitted from the mid-1950s, and such writers as Stanisław Lem in Poland and the Strugatsky brothers in Russia made international reputations. And in Poland, writers like Ryszard Kapuściński produced successful literary journalism.

crucial is that each of them gained his authoritative position after initial success as a writer of serious literature. It remains to be seen whether any writer who began to publish in the conditions of postcommunism will be able to achieve the degree of relevance these giants possess, but as a result of these and other examples this level of relevance for a writer is at least considered possible in Eastern Europe.

Additionally, we need to consider the terms "communism" and "postcommunism." A great deal of ink has been spilled over these words, and I would like to try to avoid adding much more. Generally, in this work I use the word "communist" to describe regimes and societies in Eastern Europe (in the Soviet Union from 1917 to 1991 and in Eastern Europe from around 1948 until 1989). I generally use the word "socialist" to describe the economies of these countries. I use these terms in this way because they are the standard ones that have been employed in the scholarly literature, but I am, of course, well aware that none of these countries claimed to have achieved the creation of a communist society and that their economies were not, in fact, models of socialism. I am also aware that conditions varied enormously from one country to another as well as within individual countries at various times, so that to use one term to cover all of them is somewhat reckless. However, at least as far as the prestige and relevance of literature goes, it is my contention that the situation was similar enough throughout Eastern Europe to justify treating these countries as a coherent group. Similarly, although I use the term "postcommunist" to describe all East European societies since the fall of communist governments, I know that the situation in, say, Serbia, differs enormously from that in Hungary. Again, however, in the area on which I concentrate here—that is, the role and position of serious literature and its producers—I believe that the situation is similar enough to require a single term.

And this brings me to the first of my caveats. When I began discussing with my colleagues how best to present the material, I had to decide among three possible approaches. I could have focused on a single country taken to be more or less typical. I could have written a series of chapters on the current literary situation in a number of individual countries. Or I could have done what in the end I chose to do, which was to focus on broad literary strategies, more or less ignoring the differences between the various countries. As this approach is unusual, I would like to defend it here.

Perhaps the best studies of socialism or communism and postcommunism, at least to my mind, are those based on material drawn from a single country—I would cite here classic analyses of communism by Miłosz, György Konrád, and Iván Szelényi and the voluminous work of Katherine Verdery.[10] In the introduction to her study *What Was Socialism, and What Comes Next?* Verdery argues for the utility of such an approach: "Some might argue that Romania is not a 'typical' case and therefore is a poor guide for postsocialist studies, but I do not share this opinion. *No* socialist country was 'typical'; each had its specificities, and each shared certain features with some but not all other countries of the bloc. To assume that the conclusions drawn from one will apply to all would be unwise, but material from any of them can nevertheless raise questions that might prove fruitful elsewhere."[11]

Despite these precedents, however, I felt it would be unwise to focus this study exclusively on one country. In part, this was because of the way the information in this book was gathered. As opposed to the material considered by Verdery or the others cited above, my material was not based entirely on my own reading and knowledge. Rather, it drew on expertise from multiple individuals and from multiple countries. To choose only one for the purposes of analysis would have required sacrificing an enormous amount of excellent material and, worse, would have required me to claim to possess sufficient knowledge about the literary situation in one country to write this book about it. Another consideration was that, at least in part, the goal of chapters 3–8 is not merely descriptive but also persuasive, even missionary. I want readers of this book to become interested enough to want to read for themselves the best work that is being produced in Eastern Europe today. Since no one country's literature has a monopoly on the best work, it seemed more appropriate to analyze works drawn from a variety of traditions. Furthermore, in order to make such reading easier, whenever possible I tried to choose works that exist in English translation. Given the paucity of works that have been translated from any individual country, I could not achieve my goal by focusing on only one. Finally, drawing on works from multiple countries has allowed me to consider a broader spectrum within each category of writing than would have been possible had I limited myself to a single one.

As a result, then, chapters 3–8 have been organized in terms of literary and extraliterary strategies. This choice leads directly to a few more caveats. First, anyone who specializes in or lives in a particular East European

10. Miłosz, *The Captive Mind*; Konrád, *Antipolitics* and *The Melancholy of Rebirth*.
11. Verdery, 1996, 11.

country may feel that I fail to do justice to the specificities of the local situation. This is particularly true regarding the countries that were either not studied at all or on which less attention was focused—Albania, Macedonia, the Baltic states, and Belarus in particular. From what I have been able to discover, in many ways the situations in these countries overlap with those that have been considered. I hope that the general formulations put forward here will encourage scholars in these countries, as well as in the ones we focused on, to produce more specialized research that will allow us to see the nuances against the background of the overall pattern laid out here. Such future work may eventually require some adjustments to this broader pattern.

The other caveat concerns the specific strategies I have chosen to explore. Here I reiterate that this book is not meant to be an encyclopedic study of what has been produced in Eastern Europe since 1989. One can assume that there are many works, even excellent ones, from this period that do not fall into any of the categories I consider. I am sure that others will find whole categories of creative work I have overlooked. It is my hope that those who know the literatures of the region or of specific countries in it will be spurred by this effort to propose other possible categories or to question what is left out when one chooses to organize a study as I have done here. That is, I see this book as an introduction to a transnational consideration of postcommunist literature rather than as a valedictory summation of the results of more than a decade of writing in twenty countries.

CHAPTER ONE

The Writer as National Hero

In the introduction I asserted that a good definition of Eastern Europe would be the part of the world where serious literature and those who produce it have traditionally been overvalued. If my definition does indeed capture some truth about the region, it is logical to wonder how this situation came about. What cultural and historical factors thrust writers into positions of esteem and status that in other parts of the world have been reserved for statesmen, philosophers, businessmen, or entertainers? The short answer to this question is that the majority of East European countries were in substantial measure invented by writers. Literature here, far from being a reflection of reality, was very frequently a creator of new identities and new social and political realities.

In the year 1800, only one of the countries that exist today in Eastern Europe (Russia) was independent.[1] The other peoples of the region were ruled by three empires.[2] The Russian empire controlled what are now Estonia, Latvia, Lithuania, Ukraine, Belarus, and part of Poland. The Austrian Habsburgs ruled over what are today Hungary, the Czech Republic, Slovakia, Croatia, Slovenia, the northern part of Serbia, and part of Poland. And the Ottoman Empire held sway in Albania, Bulgaria, the rest of Serbia, Macedonia, and Romania. In most cases, imperial control had been a long-term fact of life for the peoples in question.[3] One result of

---

1. Montenegro was also more or less independent at this point, but it was not an independent country at the time this book was written.

2. Actually, the northwestern section of Poland was ruled by Prussia. On the partitions of Poland at the end of the eighteenth century, see Davies, 1982.

3. Most of these peoples had once been independent, but that independence had in most cases been long lost. The Balkan territories ruled by the Ottomans had been under their control since the fifteenth century at the latest. The Habsburgs had taken full political control

the domination of foreign powers was that the vernacular languages were generally not employed in political, juridical, or even urban contexts. Even in Russia, nominally a political powerhouse, cultural discourse had in the course of the eighteenth century been denationalized to such an extent that, as Lev Tolstoy pointed out at the beginning of *War and Peace*, most Russian aristocrats were more comfortable in French than in their native tongue.

When national "awakenings" occurred in this region, they invariably began with cultural and linguistic movements rather than with political ones. This was the result not only of the political weakness of the peoples of Eastern Europe but also of the source of national ideology in the area, which derived primarily from German thought (and to a lesser extent from French). In the German model the nation was defined, following Johann Gottfried von Herder, first and foremost by linguistic categories. A nation was a nation (and could, therefore, hope for an independent political existence) insofar as its putative citizens spoke a common language. Perhaps the most extreme linguistic definition of the nation can be found in the thought of the Slovak L'udovít Štúr: "Every nation is most ardently coupled with its language. The nation is reflected in it as the first product of its theoretical spirit; language is, then, the surest sign of the essence and individuality of every nation. Just like an individual human being, the nation reveals its deepest inner self through language; it, so to speak, embodies its spirit in language."[4] But in most of these lands the vernacular had become primarily a language used by peasants and in the marketplace. Before a national revival on the basis of language could begin, the language had to be recreated (or simply created) as a vehicle for the expression of cultural and political thought.[5]

One can find the first conscious stirrings of what could be called patriotic linguistics in Eastern Europe as early as the mid-eighteenth century. As

---

over the Czech lands after the Battle of the White Mountain in 1620 and had reconquered the Hungarian lands from the Ottomans by the late 1680s. Poland was the most recently independent of these lands, having been carved up between Prussia, Russia, and Austria between 1772 and 1798. It is, however, anachronistic to talk about East European nations before the nineteenth century if by "nation" we understand the word in its modern sense.

4. Quoted in Pynsent, 185.

5. Countries in Eastern Europe varied widely in terms of both the length and depth of the vernacular literary tradition. Poland and Croatia, for example, could boast extensive traditions in the vernacular, dating back to the fifteenth century. In Serbia, Slovakia, and Ukraine, however, there was essentially no written literature in the vernacular before the end of the eighteenth century, though there was an extensive oral tradition in these lands.

Russia's great eighteenth-century Renaissance man, Mikhail Lomonosov, put it in his defense of the Russian language, "The Holy Roman Emperor Carl the Fifth used to say that one should speak Spanish with God, French with one's friends, German with one's enemies, and Italian with the fair sex. But had he been skilled in Russian he would of course have added that it would be appropriate to speak with all of these in it, for he would have found in it the greatness of Spanish, the liveliness of French, the force of German, the tenderness of Italian, and, in addition, the richness and strong terse descriptiveness of Greek and Latin."[6] Lomonosov wrote the above in his introduction to a Russian grammar, and indeed, the first step in national revivals, even before the creation of literary work, was often a codification of the language through a grammar or dictionary.[7]

Although the existence of a codified language was important, it alone was not considered proof that a given people had attained a level of cultural development sufficient for its pretensions to nationhood to be taken seriously. For that, the appearance of literary work, epic and lyric poetry in particular, was crucial. The ideology underlying this worldview was again imported from Germany, in this case outlined in the work of Johann Gottlieb Fichte in his *Reden an die deutsche Nation* (*Addresses to the German Nation*, 1808).[8] On this view, the task of the writer was inherently patriotic: "The noblest privilege and holiest office of the writer is to assemble his nation and consult with her about her weightiest affairs. In particular, this has always been the exclusive office of the writer in Germany while the country was split into several states. The Germans were held together in a communal whole only through the writer's instrument, that is, language and writing. Today this is also his most essential and urgent office."[9] In the absence of political unity writers were necessary to pull a nation together, to make fellow citizens aware of their very nationhood by creating the conditions for community.

Particularly important in this regard was the appearance of a national poet capable of capturing the nation's collective spirit or essence (so, at least, claimed the nation-building intellectuals who pushed the candidacy

6. *Rossiiskaia grammatika*, in Lomonosov, vol. 2, 195 (translation mine). The work was written in 1754–1755.

7. Thus, in something of the same vein we can see the work of such dedicated linguists from the region as the Slovenian Jernej Kopitar, the Serb Vuk Karadžić, and the Czech Josef Dobrovský.

8. That theories of independent national development are in almost all cases imported is one of the inherent paradoxes of nationalist thought.

9. I am grateful to Robert Pynsent for supplying both the reference to Fichte and the translation of this quotation.

of their "national poets"). Elites in each country mobilized fellow citizens by using the person and the work of the national poet as a source of pride and a rallying point for future cultural and political development. The result was what can only be called a cult of national literature in general and of national poets in particular, a cult whose credos were originally created by a handful of nationalist-oriented intellectuals.[10] These authors were presented as codifiers of the national literary language (which eventually allowed for the political existence of the nation) and producers of literary work that is claimed to have expressed the nation's spiritual core, its soul. First canonized by nation-building intellectuals, then exploited by fledgling national states, and finally recanonized by communist regimes, they were accorded the status of national heroes. Their example bestowed an unprecedented prestige and status upon the literary profession. Nation-building writers are venerated to this day, lauded in the research and teaching of respected academics, in textbooks used in schools at all levels, and as part of public political discourse, long after the demise of many of the regimes and ideologies that helped to nurture their cults.

Curiously, although this phenomenon occurs throughout Eastern Europe, there has been little recognition among ethnicities that they shared it with their neighbors. Rather, each country's discourse insists not only that a given poet was uniquely able to express the nation's soul but simultaneously that no other country possesses any figure remotely similar. For our purposes, of course, it is worth emphasizing that the status accorded to figures like Alexander Pushkin in Russia (see figure 1), Adam Mickiewicz in Poland, Taras Shevchenko in Ukraine, Christo Botev and Ivan Vazov in Bulgaria, Mihai Eminescu in Romania, Sándor Petőfi in Hungary, France Prešeren in Slovenia, Petar Petrović Njegoš in Serbia and Montenegro, and Ivan Mažuranić in Croatia has guaranteed that generations of ambitious youngsters have wanted to become writers.

As not all readers will be familiar with the rhetoric surrounding the cults of writers canonized as nation builders in Eastern Europe, I will briefly examine the life, work, and posthumous fate of two of them here. The national poets of Slovenia, France Prešeren (1800–1849), and of Poland, Adam Mickiewicz (1798–1855), were quite different both in personality and literary output. All the more striking, then, are the analogous claims made posthumously for them in their societies.

10. On the role of intellectuals in creating national consciousness in the smaller European nations, see the seminal study of Miroslav Hroch.

FIGURE 1. Monument to Alexander Pushkin in Tsarskoe Selo. (Original photograph by
Proctor Jones, San Francisco.)

France Prešeren led no revolutions, proposed no political programs, and
died of tuberculosis, impoverished and almost alone, at the age of forty-
nine. What is more, with the exception of his rather odd romantic epic, *The
Baptism on the Savica*, he confined himself to lyrical genres, and many of
his works exhibit a strongly pessimistic tone. Nevertheless, Slovenes credit
him with enormous positive influence. He is identified as the creator of
the modern Slovenian literary language and as the nation's greatest lyric
poet.[11] In 1866, one of the central architects of the cult of Prešeren, the

11. As a rule the cults of nation-building poets are as much about forgetting as about
remembering. What is forgotten is that no one creates a language or literature in a vacuum, and
that all of the national poets in question had important predecessors. In the case of Slovenia,
the modern literary language was in fact created during the Protestant Reformation. Primož
Trubar (1508–1586) produced a Slovenian translation of the New Testament in the 1550s that

critic Josip Stritar, concluded his introductory essay to an edition of the poet's works with the following rhetorical flourish: "We dare to say with pride that our Prešeren is also one of those chosen vessels through which heavenly beauty, celestial poetry, is brought to earth. When all the nations stand before the judgment seat and are asked to explain how they used their basic talents, how each of them made their contribution to universal human culture, the small Slovenian nation will dare without fear to present a thin book with the title *Prešeren's Poems* alongside the others."[12] The most important assertion here is the comparative: Slovenes could justify their right to exist as a nation precisely because they had produced a single poet on par with Shakespeare, Goethe, Pushkin, or Dante.

Stritar's essay dates from the mid-1860s, precisely the period when the group of so-called Young Slovenes began the process of Prešeren's canonization. This work was continued on a consistent basis by nationally minded Slovenian intellectuals throughout the nineteenth and into the twentieth century. By the turn of the century, however, the Prešeren cult had outgrown narrow intellectual circles and become an element of a broader civic, and ultimately political, project. This was manifest in the campaign organized by Ivan Hribar, the longtime and powerful mayor of Ljubljana, to erect a Prešeren monument. Hribar, who was experienced at raising money for similar activities, commented: "It was easier to raise money for this than for any other monument. It is no exaggeration to say that people competed with each other to make their contribution."[13] After great expense and a number of controversies regarding the style and location of the monument, the neoclassical statue was dedicated on Ljubljana's central square on September 10, 1905.[14] It remains to this day the most prominent monument in Slovenia's capital (see figure 2).

---

served as a model for literary writing in the language. However, during the Counter-Reformation the Slovenes were brought back into the Roman Catholic fold, and thereafter most intellectual activity in the Slovenian lands took place in either German or Latin until the nineteenth century.

12. Stritar, 1969, 48.

13. As quoted in *Slovenska hronika*, 54.

14. As is typical in these cases, the only people unhappy with the bourgeoisification of what had formerly been a literary cult were leading cultural figures. Thus, Ivan Cankar, Slovenia's great modernist writer, commented acidly about this event: "Who was being celebrated: Prešeren, or his monument, or Daddy Janež Bleiweis [one of the Young Slovenes who had initiated and nurtured the cult of Prešeren], or Mayor Hribar was impossible to guess. What could be guessed was that this was the biggest and most imposing celebration the people had ever experienced. Everyone was exalted, perhaps all the more so because they did not know why." Quoted in *Slovenska hronika*, 54.

FIGURE 2. Unveiling of Ivan Zajec's monument to France Prešeren in Ljubljana, September 10, 1905.

18

To understand Prešeren's importance we must appreciate that tiny Slovenia had no history of national statehood and no possibility of achieving political independence in the mid-nineteenth century. Simultaneously, there was a real chance that the Slovenian language would disappear. All educated Slovenes spoke German, which was the language of civil and even cultural life in the urban centers, such as they were. What is more, some Slovenian intellectuals of the national revival period, most notably the poet Stanko Vraz, felt that Slovenes would do better to throw in their lot with their fellow South Slavs and give up their native language in order to amalgamate with speakers of the newly codified Illyrian (Croato-Serbian).[15] This view was eventually rejected, and the national language, and primarily creative work in it, came to be seen by many Slovenes as the sole repository of the Slovenian spirit.[16]

Through his creation, in response to the dual threat of Germanization or Croato-Serbianization, of a body of world-class poetry in his native language, Prešeren is seen to have ensured the very existence of the Slovenian nation. This naturally lends his entire oeuvre a political dimension. The quote that follows, taken from a recent journal article designed to introduce Prešeren to Anglophone readers, illustrates perfectly the rhetorical steps that encourage the recognition of a poet as the father of his nation: "Prešeren raised the Slovene language and Slovene culture to a level that made possible the expression of the highest artistic works. *As a result,* by succeeding in defending the unity of the Slovene language, the middle classes were able to integrate. Later in the 19th century, this middle class of Slovenes became the elite, who put forth the March Revolution of 1848 and created the first national and political programme for United Slovenia."[17] On this view, there is a direct causal link between the works of Prešeren and the eventual appearance of Slovenian political nationalism, for had there been no Prešeren, the Slovenian bourgeoisie would have had nothing to rally themselves around. Had this been the case, the Slovenes would have shared the fate of other peoples in the region—the upper Sorbs or the Morlachs, for example—who ultimately failed to create national states and were absorbed by their neighbors.

---

15. For a full treatment of the Illyrian movement and the role of Vraz, see Desplatović.

16. The most forceful expression of this position was the book *Kulturni problem slovenstva* [The cultural problem of Slovenia] by the critic and cultural historian Josip Vidmar. Published in 1932, it was reissued with a helpful introduction by Aleš Debeljak in 1995.

17. Kustec, 64 (emphasis mine).

As noted earlier, *The Baptism on the Savica* (1835) is the only epic Prešeren wrote. It is, however, hardly a work around which a program for national revival could easily be built. Set in the Middle Ages, it describes German victories over Slavs at the time when the Slovenes were Christianized and focuses on internecine struggles between Pagan and Christian Slovenes. The central character, Črtomir, "represents the free Slovene community. He stands for Slovene independence, but he is doomed from the very beginning."[18] The majority of the poem, however, describes not national problems but the hopeless love of the pagan Črtomir for the Christian Bogomila. This plot line clearly echoes Prešeren's personal life, which was dominated by unrequited love. As a result, many readers have preferred to interpret the poem in a personal context, although convincing political readings also exist.[19]

Other than the pessimistic *Baptism*, Prešeren's work is primarily lyrical. Among these poems, one cemented his place in the nation-building pantheon. In "A Toast" (1844), Prešeren "expresses the thought of uniting all the Austrian provinces with Slovene people into United Slovenia, which was later proclaimed by the Slovene intellectuals as their national program. He personifies Slovenianism."[20]

The vintage, friends, is over,
And here sweet wine makes, once again,
Our eyes and hearts recover,
Puts fire in every vein,
Drowns dull dare
Everywhere
And summons hope out of despair.

To whom with acclamation
And song shall we our first toast give?
God save our land and nation
And all Slovenes where'er they live,
Who own the same
Blood and name,
And who one glorious Mother claim.

Let thunder out of heaven
Strike down and smite our wanton foe!
Now, as it once had thriven,
May our dear realm in freedom grow.
Let fall the last

18. Ibid., 66.
19. See, for example, Cooper, 215–225.

20. Kustec, 68.

Chains of the past
Which bind us still and hold us fast!

Let peace, glad conciliation,
Come back to us throughout the land!
Towards their destination
Let Slavs henceforth go hand-in-hand!
Thus again
Will honour reign
To justice pledged in our domain . . . [21]

The continuing allure of the national poet can be seen in the fact that these words were adopted as the text for the national anthem of Slovenia on December 23, 1991. Along with the Prešeren monument that dominates the central downtown square in Slovenia's capital, they are a potent reminder that even the most pessimistic and melancholic of national poets eventually achieve their due in Eastern Europe. As one Slovenian scholar baldly stated, "*The Slovenes*, both as individuals and as a people, *cannot be conceived of without Prešeren.*"[22]

A worthy counterpart to Prešeren is the Polish bard Adam Mickiewicz. Unlike Prešeren, Mickiewicz actively sought a political in addition to a literary role. This was natural, for the situation in early to mid-nineteenth-century Poland was quite different from that of Slovenia. Slovenia had never been a sovereign state and had no prospects for independence in Prešeren's day, but Poland had been a European power as late as the seventeenth century. Although it had disappeared from the map of Europe in the same year Mickiewicz was born, frequent rebellions, particularly in the section of the country that had been occupied by Russia (and that was the land of Mickiewicz's birth), testified to the unwillingness of the Poles to acquiesce in their new situation. Although perhaps not an unambiguous player in attempts to regain Polish independence, Mickiewicz was aligned closely enough with revolutionary circles. In 1823, the young poet, together with a number of his friends, was arrested by the tsarist authorities. He spent the years between 1824 and 1829 in exile in Russia, and the rest of his life in Western Europe.

Like his Russian counterpart Pushkin, whom he knew and for the most part admired, Mickiewicz wrote poetry on a wide variety of topics and

21. Prešeren, 31.
22. Bratko Kreft, "Prešeren et Puškin: Fragment d'une étude," in *To Honor Roman Jakobson*, vol. 2, 1112 (emphasis mine).

worked in many genres. Some of his long poems, such as *Pan Tadeusz*, have been seen as something of an "encyclopedia of Polish gentry life." Others, like his exquisitely lyrical *Crimean Sonnets*, have little to do with either nationalist strivings or Polish reality (except insofar as an exceptional ability to control one's native language is a necessary attribute of a national bard). At the same time, Mickiewicz also produced much poetry and prose that commented directly on the condition of Poland and called for her eventual liberation from foreign domination. These works include, most famously, *Dziady* (generally translated into English as *Forefather's Eve*), a lengthy work that traces the development of its hero from Romantic individualist to freedom fighter. Mickiewicz's most direct nation-building statement, however, appears in his messianic *Books of the Polish Nation and Pilgrimage* (1832), where we find such statements as "And Poland said, 'Whosoever will come to me shall be free and equal for I am FREEDOM.' But the Kings, when they heard it, were frightened in their hearts, and they crucified the Polish nation and laid it in its grave, crying out 'We have slain and buried Freedom.' But they cried out foolishly. . . .

"For the Polish Nation did not die. Its body lieth in the grave; but its spirit has descended into the abyss, that is, into the private lives of people who suffer slavery in their own country. . . . For on the Third Day, the Soul shall return again to the Body; and the Nation shall arise and free all the peoples of Europe from Slavery."[23] The connection made here by Mickiewicz between Poland and Christ, and the messianic role assigned to Poland in the national consciousness, was to become an inalienable part of Polish national thinking. What is more, although he does not make the connection explicit, Mickiewicz's own life's journey came to be seen in the minds of many Poles as a symbol for the situation of Christ/Poland. The fact that Mickiewicz died in Istanbul while trying to raise a regiment to fight against Russia for the liberation of his homeland only further burnished his dual image as a martyr to the national cause and its spokesman.

Mickiewicz's candidacy as national bard was carefully nurtured in the years after his death until it became practically an article of faith among Poles, whether or not they knew more than a few lines of his poetry. As in Slovenia, commemorative events organized by the intelligentsia played a major role. Among the most prominent of these was the reburial of Mickiewicz, whose body was moved from France to Cracow in 1890. In

23. Quoted in Davies, 1984, 202.

the words of a scholar who has written on the rise of the author's cult, "The Cracow reception of Mickiewicz's remains proved to be the public event of the decade, if not the century: Poles arrived in record numbers to witness the procession and entombment in the crypt of the Wawel Cathedral. No larger manifestation of national unity had taken place since the January Insurrection of 1863."[24]

Furthermore, the cult of Mickiewicz has been one of the few factors capable of unifying practically all factions of Polish political and cultural life. The rhetoric marshaled to describe Mickiewicz at ceremonial anniversaries or used in school textbooks to inculcate this cult in the minds of Polish youth is hyperbolic. For example,

Mickiewicz, as a writer, is a unique phenomenon in the history of world literature. It would appear that he voiced and embodied in his work the soul of his people. By means of his work he symbolized their land, its history, its customs, and its character. At the same time., he drew forth from the national subconscious the desires which were dormant there, and brought to development latent possibilities which previously were unrecognized and unexpressed. In so doing he stepped beyond the enchanted circle of art and became one of the creators of history—one of the true fathers of his people. Such a destiny, as we know, has by no means been the lot of all the great writers of the past. Even the greatest did not necessarily identify themselves with their people as Mickiewicz did. Moreover, they did not become figures—and leading ones at that—of the national myth as he did. . . . To get a glimpse of the full measure of his influence it is probably necessary to go beyond the limits of literature and recognize Mickiewicz's spiritual significance for the Polish people, as well as the myth which he created, as being equivalent to that posthumous influence which Abraham Lincoln constantly exerts upon the American soul: one must compare with the legend of the great poet who was also a political leader, the legend of the great statesman who in the Gettysburg Address produced a literary masterpiece. Zygmunt Krasiński, who even in the fullness of an exalted moment retained the judgment of a tragic skeptic, said after Mickiewicz's death: "We all are part of him." And now, a hundred years later, every Pole who takes part in the spiritual life of his people could repeat these words, each speaking for himself. . . .

Mickiewicz made the calling of a poet in Poland a prophetic mission. Through his work as a poet, publicist, and political actor he became the leader of the

24. Dabrowski, 38. The Wawel crypt was the traditional burial place of Polish kings, so the symbolism of interring Mickiewicz there was already political.

nation. In depth and breadth of influence he exceeded great and honored leaders
and statesmen. One may confidently assert that Poland recognized only two
uncontested spiritual leaders in all of post-Partition history: Mickiewicz and
Kościuszko.[25]

Crucial here is the insistence that the national poet be seen as far more than
a poet. Indeed, his poetry is in some sense beside the point. The phrase
"We are all part of him," attributed here to the nineteenth-century writer
Krasiński and repeated with great frequency in tributes to Mickiewicz,
emphasizes the position of the national poet as a metonymic substitute for
the nation as a whole. As such, a figure like Mickiewicz can perhaps be
criticized, but he is impossible to ignore: "Every Pole who takes part in the
spiritual life of his people" must take account of Mickiewicz, according
to this orator. Furthermore, we find here the insistence on the uniqueness
of the national bard, despite the fact that practically every country in the
region possesses a figure who is described as equally unique and exceptional for the identical reasons. It is worth noting the overt comparison to
Abraham Lincoln in this speech, which was delivered at a conference in
New York to celebrate the hundredth anniversary of Mickiewicz's death.
It serves to buttress the claim that poets in Eastern Europe have played
the role ascribed to statesmen and kings in other lands.

Nor is Mickiewicz lauded only by academics. His life and work are held
up as exemplary in many documents meant for mass consumption. In
a famous nationalist work designed for young children, the *Katechizm
polskiego dziecka* (Catechism of the Polish child), written before Poland
had achieved her modern independence, we find the following quatrain
in a poem called "The Polish Tongue": "Within it is hidden a mysterious
power, / The magical power of a sorceress: / It was once expressed in the
poems of Mickiewicz, / And again in the slogans of Kościuszko" (18). The
words of Mickiewicz are raised to a level of importance equal to, if not
greater than, the words of the greatest Polish political figure.

I have not included information about each East European national
poet in this introduction, as to do so would only multiply examples without adding to the overall picture. Suffice it to say that it would be simple to uncover almost identical quotes relating to other national poets in
the region. These authors are lauded both as the codifiers of the modern
national literary language and for having expressed the essence of each

25. Jan Lechoń, "Mickiewicz in Polish Poetry," in Lednicki, 1–2, 6.

nation's spiritual core. First canonized by nation-building intellectuals and then exploited by fledgling national states, they were accorded the status of national heroes. Their example lent the literary profession a prestige and status unprecedented anywhere else in the world, for their work was seen not simply to have reflected an existing nation, but rather to have created the reality of their nation's existence.

To close this section, it is worth taking a moment to compare the status of canonized national writers in Eastern Europe with that of their counterparts in other countries. In so doing, we find striking differences, along with certain similarities. The primary difference is that the nation-building roles credited to individual writers in Eastern Europe are elsewhere generally parceled out among a number of figures, not all of whom are writers. Thus, in Italy, Dante is clearly identified as the founder of the vernacular tradition and therefore plays the role of codifier of the nation's poetic language. However, his work and his person were not suited to serve as the rallying cry for national awakening when modern ideas of the nation arrived some five hundred years later. Those roles were taken by Mazzini in literature, Verdi in music, and Garibaldi in the political realm. In England, of course, Shakespeare fills the role of national poet, and he is asserted by some to have dominated the entire British literary tradition. At the same time, even such a Shakespeare worshipper as Harold Bloom would not contend that Shakespeare played the crucial role in the creation of the modern British state, which is generally seen to center on its political history from the Magna Carta forward. Certainly, I do not believe that any serious person has made the claim that without Shakespeare there would have been no Englishmen and no Great Britain.

The figure most similar to the East European poets I consider here is unquestionably Goethe. Indeed, he was the model on which many East European nation builders drew to create their image of the national poet. In his day, Goethe was seen as the all-encompassing genius of the German soul, the new Proteus. But, in contrast to the situation we find in Eastern Europe, the cult of Goethe did not have staying power. By the twentieth century (and certainly for the Nazi regime), Goethe was of only secondary importance, having been replaced as the essence of the German soul by Nietzsche and Wagner. And today, when asked about their cultural standard-bearers, Germans are more likely to point to philosophers such as Kant or Hegel, or composers like Beethoven, than they are to Goethe. Overall, then, I agree fully with György Konrád and Iván Szelényi, who, in their study of intellectuals in Eastern Europe, note the importance of writers in particular and aver: "Nowhere in the West did literature have such prestige and such a wide echo in society; even a snob like Balzac could never have gained admittance to social circles of the sort in which Eastern European noble intellectuals were entirely at home."[26]

The prestige that had been attached to the position of national authors, and by extension to writers in general in the nineteenth and early twentieth centuries, was deepened and augmented under communist rule. What is more, communist governments in Eastern Europe pursued a number of policies which, taken together, had the effect of providing substantial financial incentives to writers. They thus created an almost utopian system for writers of imaginative literature, one that provided a significant segment of the educated elite with both high status and high incomes relative to the rest of the population. This was not only true for those who chose to become "official writers," agreeing to accept communist party dictates in exchange for a good living; it also held for a large number of dissident and quasi-dissident writers who liked to think of themselves as independent from or persecuted by the communist state. As we will see in greater detail below, these writers were able to benefit from the status that accrued to writers in general and even to reap some of the financial rewards that went along with the profession, though admittedly they suffered harassment and had to recognize that their work was unlikely to be published, at least through official channels.

It was by no means inevitable that communist states would continue to elaborate the cults of national writers that had originally been nurtured by bourgeois intellectuals and then, in many cases, co-opted by precommunist regimes. In order to understand how and why this happened, we need to sketch the development of cultural policy in the Soviet Union in the 1920s and 1930s, for these policies were to be exported to all other communist states in Eastern Europe after World War II, albeit with certain local modifications. When the USSR was established in 1917, the state did not have a well-elaborated cultural policy. Karl Marx had been primarily concerned with political and economic questions, and though Friedrich Engels had written on cultural topics from time to time, the Bolsheviks were more or less on their own to formulate a cultural policy appropriate for the new revolutionary state.

In the period after 1917 and into the 1920s, three basic routes to the creation of socialist culture were proposed and vigorously debated. The

26. Konrád and Szelényi, 112.

first, and initially best elaborated, was that of the artistic avant-garde, most of whose members embraced the new government early on. Their attitude toward the culture of bourgeois Russia had been expressed before the political revolution, most famously in the 1913 manifesto "A Slap in the Public's Taste," which had insisted on "throwing Pushkin, Tolstoy, etc. from the steamship of modernity." In the post-1917 period, the position of the avant-gardists, many of whom attained positions of power in the first years of Bolshevik rule, was that a new revolutionary state required a new culture, one that broke sharply with what had been created in the past. As professional artists, they saw themselves playing a leading role in the creation of this new culture, and indeed, many of them believed that they had been doing so even before 1917. Just as the Bolsheviks saw themselves as a vanguard group leading and educating the still unprepared masses in the political arena, so the artistic avant-garde arrogated to themselves the role of *Kulturträger* to the masses. Had their position won out, the cults of nineteenth-century romantic writers would have been suppressed, to be supplanted by those devoted to new artistic supermen.

Another school of thought held that because the Soviet state was created for the workers and peasants, the new socialist culture should be created for and perhaps even by them. Prerevolutionary culture had been created for the enjoyment of the aristocracy and the bourgeoisie and was clearly inappropriate for contemporary times. Avant-garde culture was, however, equally inappropriate because it was elitist and incomprehensible to the masses. Rather than following either the bourgeois or the avant-garde model, the theoreticians of proletarian culture felt that the state should trust the spontaneous creative instincts of the workers and peasants, who would quickly create a culture for themselves. All they needed was some rudimentary education and the leisure time they would have now that they had become the owners of the means of production.[27]

A third position, and the one that was ultimately embraced by the pragmatic state authorities, was that completely abandoning prerevolutionary culture was wasteful and silly. Just as the state was not ready to hand political power to the masses, so it did not trust them to create their own culture. Thus, this view supported the avant-garde's belief that an artistic vanguard was necessary, but it sided with the proletarian movement's

27. For an excellent discussion of the travails of working-class writers who attempted to express their independent views in literary works after the creation of the Soviet Union, see Steinberg.

contention that modernist methods were inappropriate for future socialist culture. What is more, it disagreed with both the avant-garde and the
proletarians regarding the value of prerevolutionary culture. Lenin neatly
summarized this view in a statement that would become socialist ortho-
doxy regarding precommunist culture and the state's attitude toward it:
"Proletarian culture does not appear from who knows where; it is not the
invention of people who style themselves experts in proletarian culture.
That is complete nonsense. Proletarian culture must be derived from the
logical development of those stores of knowledge that humankind built up
under the oppression of capitalist society, landowner society, and bureau-
cratic society. All these paths and trails lead to proletarian culture just as
the political economy developed by Marx showed us where human society
must go and pointed out the move toward class struggle, to the beginning
of the proletarian revolution."[28]

The artist's role, thus, was not to build socialist culture from scratch,
but rather to do so by making use of past achievements under the active
guidance of a party that held a top-down cultural view. The task of building
this culture was of utmost importance (a fact agreed upon by practically
all groups in society), because, following the nineteenth-century East European attitude discussed above, language and the literature created in it
were seen as the surest way to mold the minds and hearts of the nation's
citizens. In the famous words attributed to Stalin, writers were "engineers
of human souls" (a paradoxical formulation, given the official atheistic
policies of the state) and thus crucial to the nation- and state-building
projects of the Bolshevik and later the East European communist governments. These engineers were exhorted to mold future socialist citizens by
building on carefully chosen progressive monuments of the past.

Included among these works—indeed, foremost among them—were
the nation-building oeuvres of the national poets. This might appear paradoxical given that communist ideology is expressly nonnationalist, aiming
as it does to create a world in which solidarity is based on notions of class
rather than of nation. And indeed, when the Bolsheviks first took power,
they expected that their revolution would be followed by working-class
takeovers in other states. This led them to follow an internationalist line,
downplaying the importance of separate national cultures. When analogous communist movements failed to arise (or to succeed in taking power
when they appeared), the Soviets had to focus on "building socialism in

28. Lenin, as quoted in Rostoskii et al., 4.

one country." One way to do so was to emphasize the solidarity of the communist and the national vision. And after World War II, when the Soviets sponsored communist regimes in Eastern Europe that were not necessarily popular, communist parties at times used the nationalist card to draw at least a modicum of legitimacy.[29] As a result, whether seen as artists who had been "progressive in their time" or as national symbols, national poets and their cults became a central pillar of state cultural ideology under communism.

The full rehabilitation of the national poet for communist state- and nation-building purposes was signaled in the USSR by the pompous celebrations on the hundredth anniversary of Pushkin's death in 1937. Coming as they did at the height of the Stalinist purges, these "Pushkin days" took on a grotesque quality. "Pushkin was hailed by official decree of the Party's Central Committee as 'creator of the Russian literary language,' 'father of new Russian literature,' forerunner of communism and herald of the glorious socialist present.... It was not merely a question of holding a tremendous celebration for Pushkin's anniversary but of establishing, literally, a 'Pushkin Year.'... Every class in every school organized its own special Pushkin programs and activities; they staged school productions of his works, mounted special exhibits and created Pushkin libraries, went on pilgrimages to 'Pushkin places,' wrote poetry to him and drew illustrations to his works."[30]

In the postwar years, all socialist states assiduously attended to the cults of national writers, taking every opportunity (hundredth anniversaries of births, deaths, and so forth) to remind readers that these icons had been the forerunners of socialist art. The image of the nation's poet, the greatest master of its language, holding the entire nation in the palm of his hand as he calls for national liberation, proved to be irresistible, and not merely for poets. A speech on Sándor Petőfi by the Hungarian cultural tsar György Aczél, provides an excellent illustration of the rhetoric that was employed to recycle national writers under communist regimes:

> Petőfi, the son of the people, put reality into verse, he thought of the people's progress as a revolutionary democrat, he acted for the freedom of his country and of humanity as a people's revolutionary.

29. For a good discussion of the interplay between communism and nationalism in Eastern Europe in the postwar period, see Kemp, 94–126.

30. Levitt, 163.

That is how he could become the harbinger of our social system. . . .

The identity of nation and people was Petőfi's aim. Under changed conditions, other times forged this union, and such an identity has been created, by the Hungarian working people, the working class and their Party.

The work of Petőfi argues, from a historical distance, in favour of people's Hungary, the Communists and their allies.[31]

No figures from the nonliterary sphere were accorded this kind of treatment in socialist countries, and the fact that writers merited such celebrations surely raised the prestige attached to the profession enormously.

But it was not only long-dead writers who were needed by the state. Their living brethren were also of utmost importance to the task of engineering human souls fit to live in the perfect communist state of the future. The complex relationship between the communist regime and living writers was cemented at the 1934 First Congress of Soviet Writers. That meeting formulated the so-called doctrine of socialist realism, which would become "the sole method of writing" acceptable in the Soviet Union from 1934 until the late 1980s and in East European communist countries (with the exception of Yugoslavia) from the late 1940s until the fall of the Berlin Wall. While the definition of socialist realism would remain contentious for much of this period, the position of the writer would not. Those writers willing to accept the state's mandate and control were offered a privileged position in communist countries. Indeed, it would be no exaggeration to say that as a corporate group, after high communist authorities, writers occupied the second-most-privileged position in these societies. In the USSR in the 1930s, privilege went hand in hand with danger for communists and writers, as both groups suffered mass arrests and executions during the purges. In the post–World War II period, however, and especially after Stalin's death in 1953, the privileges that accrued to officially accepted writers were not, as a rule, accompanied by any real danger.

The phenomenon of state-sponsored writers under communism and the perquisites that went along with their position were well documented by a number of individuals familiar with the system, including Czesław Miłosz, Miklós Haraszti, Iván Szelényi, and György Konrád. They talked about why this position was so tempting and described anecdotally what authors

31. Aczél, 98. For a discussion of a similar phenomenon in Bulgaria, see Alexander Kiossev, "Heritage and Inheritors: The Literary Canon in Totalitarian Bulgaria," in Cornis-Pope and Neubauer, vol. 1, 134–139.

got from it. Miłosz was the first to portray the phenomenon in his 1951 volume *The Captive Mind*. He attributed the fascination on the part of writers and intellectuals with the communist project (the new faith, as he called it) to their fear of being alienated from society. They were attracted to the communist system under which "the intellectual has once more become *useful*. He who may once have done his thinking and writing in his free moments away from a paying job in a bank or post office, has now found his rightful place on earth. He has been restored to society, whereas the businessmen, aristocrats and trades-people who once considered him a harmless blunderer have now been dispossessed.... We must not oversimplify, however, the gratifications of personal ambition; they are merely the outward and visible signs of social usefulness, symbols of a recognition that strengthens the intellectual's feeling of *belonging*."[32]

In short, in communist societies, art was important. Every writer could imagine him- or herself as a new Mickiewicz or Petőfi, helping to strengthen the nation through literary work. While American education officials in the 1960s and 1970s were worried about matching Russian achievements in science, Soviet curricular watchdogs were far more concerned with the role of art and culture in the schools. As an orthodox volume entitled *The Soviet School Today* (published in 1977) stated, "We can say with pride that in our country today an enormous number of adults and children act as creators of culture: more than 13 million workers and 10 million children participate in collective cultural activities. With the help of books, movies, theatre, radio, and television many tens of millions of others fall under the influence of culture [note the order of importance of various media in this list, with books first and television last]. This is a key fact—art is actively forming the ideologico-political and moral vision of the people."[33]

Given this view of culture, the state's efforts to ensure that its citizens received the proper kind of culture are understandable. And the proper kind was litero-centric, highly oriented to the classics, and generally antipathetic to all that is called "popular," "pulp," or "mass" culture in the West. Through the censorship apparatus and their control over the publishing system, communist governments for the most part suppressed such Western literary genres as detective novels, thrillers, horror novels, fantasy, and romance on the grounds that literary work of this kind could not play a positive role in nurturing communist society. Similarly, they suppressed the

32. Miłosz, 9.
33. Kuzin and Kolmakova, 165.

import of such Western phenomena as rock-and-roll music, modern jazz, television soap operas, most Hollywood films, and so forth. This was true even in relatively liberal communist societies like Yugoslavia, although it was far more drastic in societies under greater control, such as Bulgaria and the USSR. Although in a few cases communist states allowed for domestic production of works that attempted to reproduce these genres in a social-ist context, for the most part they were entirely absent. Given high rates of literacy and reasonable quantities of leisure time, however, communist citizens had to read something, and in the context of such a "protected market" many of them turned to the only thing available—high culture.

Writing some thirty years after Miłosz, long after any vestiges of post-war idealistic attraction to communism had disappeared, the Hungarian sociologist Miklós Haraszti pointed out the cozy relationship that had de-veloped between official writers and the state in the post-Stalinist period under the conditions of cultural protectionism: "Never in the history of Eastern Europe have more pieces of art been exhibited. The writers' offi-cial country retreats, the studios, the theaters, and the artists' colonies are jam-packed, and should there be a need for more, we would get them. The supposedly unbearable fact of undeniable censorship has compelled not one single artist to refuse any state honor or decoration. Of course, some of the grand old men, heroes of previous censorship trials, are still around, but for the most part they are just as willing to participate in the new culture of censorship as is the younger generation of artists. The persecuted artist is, on closer inspection, just not that unhappy."[34] While Haraszti's claims are exaggerated to some extent, they do capture a general truth, particu-larly about those communist countries that had relatively weak dissident movements (e.g., Hungary, Bulgaria, and Romania).

I would like to add a few more details to the comments of Miłosz and Haraszti, to show something of the size of the official literary world in communist countries as well as to explain the material perquisites offered to official writers in communist states. Under communist regimes, the ac-tivities of writers were managed, from 1934 in the Soviet Union and from almost immediately after full communist control of the governments in East European states, by national writers' unions. These organizations pos-sessed enormous power and resources. Membership in them, which was strictly controlled, virtually guaranteed that a writer could make a good living by the pen alone. As John and Carol Garrard put it in their study

34. Haraszti, 9.

of the Writers' Union of the USSR, "The Union is the writer's full-time employer, giving him a job description and setting him tasks. But, at the same time, the Union provides its members and their families with social and medical benefits that place them instantly in the upper middle class of Soviet society. One émigré estimated that Union members enjoy the social prestige and military benefits of a colonel or lieutenant-colonel in the Soviet army."[35] What was true in the USSR was true all over Eastern Europe. The membership of writers' unions was large. According to the Garrards' statistics there were almost 10,000 members of the Soviet writers' union in 1986.[36] At this time the analogous Polish union had some 1,000 members, in Hungary there were approximately 650 members, in Bulgaria approximately 400 members, and in Romania approximately 1,200 members.[37]

Readers of this book who did not experience the daily reality of communism need to be aware that in communist countries the main problem faced by consumers was not money, but rather access to consumer goods. What writers' unions provided was not so much cash as the right to purchase goods and services at official state prices (rather than on the black market). These benefits included subsidized (in most cases practically free) vacations at writers' colonies, coupons allowing for the acquisition of big-ticket consumer goods (including apartments and automobiles) at official state prices, generous pensions, high-quality medical care, and even state-funded funerals. Some members of the union (the best of the official writers as well as the most politically loyal) also were selected to be part of delegations sent abroad, an almost unheard-of privilege in the more closed countries such as the USSR, Bulgaria, and Romania.

As early as 1948, the Bulgarian government passed a law giving members of the Union of Bulgarian Writers the right to work part-time (four hours per day) and receive full salary. The standard practice was that members of the union were on staff with newspapers, magazines, and other such institutions and received salaries from them. The staff of these institutions was larger than necessary, meaning that even in the course of their half day, few writers had any real work assigned to them. As was the case in other communist countries, substantial fees for actually publishing literary work

35. Garrard and Garrard, 107.
36. Ibid., 241.
37. Regarding the numbers of writers who were members of writers' unions, the Polish figure is rather low, mostly because after 1981 many writers left the union, pace Haraszti's claims that writers were never willing to give up their corporate privileges. Before 1981 the number of writers in the Polish union was closer to 2,500.

were added to the base salaries received as sinecures. Thus, for example, a published short story would pay between 100 and 160 leva (according to length), at a time when the average monthly salary in Bulgaria was approximately 250 leva. A novella in a journal paid between 500 and 1000 leva, and a novel could easily bring in 3,000 leva. With one book a writer could buy a car or a small apartment. Three published poems could bring in enough to spend a few weeks at the seaside at a villa subsidized by the writers' union.

Analogously, although all members of the Union of Writers of the USSR received a baseline salary that made them solidly middle class, those who published on a consistent basis fared substantially better. In the USSR, where the average monthly salary was approximately 180 rubles per month in the mid-1980s (and a very high salary might have been 300 rubles per month), the standard fee a writer received for publishing a novel was 8,000 rubles. Articles in the major cultural organs (the so-called fat journals) were compensated at between 200 and 300 rubles per signature (twenty-four pages) for an article of four to eight signatures. In Poland, the average fee for a single novel allowed a writer to buy a nice apartment in the center of Warsaw (and the writers' union gave its members the connections that provided access to such an apartment, which was even more important).

At the same time, the blandishments offered to official writers came at a price, for becoming an official writer meant accepting a moral and ethical position of dependence that some were unable or unwilling to condone. Particularly in the post-Stalinist period, there was in fact a certain opprobrium attached to official writers; seen as lackeys and opportunists, they were often perceived to be mediocre writers at best. What is not generally appreciated, however, even inside the former communist countries, is that state policies designed to support the compliant writers whom the state explicitly needed did not exclusively benefit those who "sold out." They also allowed for the financial well-being (albeit at a lower level) and self-esteem of a significant number of writers and would-be writers who did not accept state control. These policies truly made the post–World War II communist world a writer's paradise. They meant that, with the exception of the most notorious dissidents, the majority of even nonofficial writers were able to live and work as writers with the help of the state. In other words, though they would not have admitted it, in many communist states and in many periods dissident and semidissident writers functioned as the state's hired conscience.

In this sense, dissident writing can be seen as part and parcel of a larger phenomenon in East European states—the inevitability, given the construction of the system, of a parallel economy in any and every sphere of life. As Katherine Verdery notes in her discussion of socialist economies, "Since the center would not supply what people needed, they struggled to do so themselves, developing in the process a huge repertoire of strategies for obtaining consumer goods and services. These strategies, called the 'second' or 'informal' economy, spanned a wide range from the quasi-legal to the definitely illegal." Furthermore, Verdery continues, this economy, "which provisioned a large part of consumer needs, was parasitic upon the state economy *and inseparable from it.*"[38] Literary production is not identical to the production of shoes or coats, but an analogous argument can be made about the cultural "industry." Works of official literature poured out of state publishing houses in enormous editions, but they did not satisfy the cultural needs of the entire population. Dissident literature, produced on typewriters and laboriously retyped in carbon copies, came to fill the needs of that portion of the population dissatisfied with what the state provided. And, as was the case with the black market, the state agreed to tolerate this activity as long as dissident writers did not attempt to challenge state power in an overly confrontational way.

State economic policies provided both positive and negative incentives that encouraged literary production, nonofficial as well as official. Whereas a young man or woman in the West might also have found the idea of being a writer attractive, the difficulties of making a living by the pen coupled with the relative ease of entry to and the high status and pay of other professions would usually tip the scales in their favor. Even for extremely creative individuals in the West, the allure of entrepeneurship is strong, and developing one's own successful business can satisfy the creative urge. In Eastern Europe, state policy eliminated financial incentives for entering competing professions. As there was little or no private business, the possibility of earning large sums and satisfying the need to create by this means did not exist; the law was completely at the mercy of the state, so choosing the legal profession was rightfully seen as an even greater sellout than becoming an official writer; doctors were woefully underpaid and overworked. The only relatively high-paying professions were inside the state apparatus or in the military, neither of which tended to attract wouldbe writers. One result was the high demand for places in departments of

38. Verdery, 1996, 27 (emphasis mine).

languages and literature at universities in communist societies rather than in medical or law schools.

While one set of state policies eliminated incentives to take up non-literary professions, a complementary set softened the disincentives to choosing a literary career, even a nonofficial one. As described by Konrád and Szelényi, the communist state was one that under the aegis of the party organized the "rational redistribution" of the surplus created by its citizens for its own benefit and according to its own desires.[39] What this meant in practice was that salaries—all of which were paid by the state—were set artificially low, thereby giving the redistributors access to a higher percentage of the surplus (and therefore more power) than in other economic systems. In fact, state policy practically eliminated the cash economy, substituting for it a system in which connections, barter, and interpersonal networks predominated. In such a system there was little financial penalty for choosing to take a job that paid poorly, because no job paid well. As the communist era quip went, "They pretend to pay us and we pretend to work." Thus, even if nonofficial writers could not earn the large sums available to official writers, it was not difficult for them to find jobs that paid more or less the national, artificially low average and that demanded little attention. In contrast, in Western countries, the need to earn a living required most aspiring writers to get "real jobs" which took up so much time that little was left for writing. What is more, no-work or little-work jobs in communist economies were frequently available in the very industries that aspiring writers wanted to be part of—in literary and cultural journals, in humanities research institutes, in universities, and so forth. Clearly, such policies were not pursued by communist states to make life easier for nonofficial writers: they did, however, lead to this unintended consequence, just as policies that kept popular culture imports out of these same countries had the unintended consequence of creating a protected market for locally produced high culture (both official and nonofficial).

Once more, it is useful to see writing as part of the overall communist economy and to recognize the ways in which nonofficial writing was parasitic on official literary production. In discussing private farming, Verdery notes: "Although the plot itself was legal, people obtained high outputs from it not just by virtue of hard work but also by stealing from the collective farm: fertilizer and herbicide, fodder for their pigs and cows, work time for their own weeding or harvesting, tractor time for plowing their plot, and so on." In the case of writing, which does not require many material

---

39. This is the central argument of Konrád and Szelényi.

objects for production, what was stolen primarily was time. Indeed, one of the things that all Western visitors invariably noticed about socialist countries was that their citizens may not have had money and they may not have had goods but they always had time. One's friends were always ready to stay up all night talking, to take a few days off from work, to arrive late and leave early when they did go to work, and so forth. They could do so because, in the socialist economy, time was definitely not money. What this meant in practice was that when they were not drinking and talking or standing in lines, intellectuals in communist countries, even those outside the official institutions of writing, had sufficient time to produce their work, and readers had the time to appreciate it.

While black market tailors or plumbers provided necessary services, they never earned the respect of the population as a whole, but both inside and outside the communist world a real cult of dissident or nonofficial writing came into existence. Osip Mandelstam once quipped about the USSR: "Poetry is respected only in this country. People are killed for it."[40] And while his statement has, unfortunately, proven to be overly geographically restrictive, it is true that the communist state and its security apparatus spent an inordinate amount of time worrying about nonofficial literature. This concern was not lost on potential readers. A character of Alexander Solzhenitsyn's novel *The First Circle* called writers a kind of "second government" in the Soviet Union (and by extension in other communist states as well), and the view that such writers formed the conscience of the nation, the voice of truth amid oppression, was deeply held, at least among the urban intelligentsia, in all communist countries. Furthermore, unlike the status accorded official writers, the prestige of nonofficial writers, especially the best known, was international. From the 1960s on, foreign publishers vied to produce editions of the leading underground writers, major American authors such as Philip Roth could be induced to edit a series of books from Eastern Europe (Penguin's Other Europe series), such influential publications as *The New York Review of Books* devoted frequent columns to their books, and even the Nobel Committee helped out by awarding the literature prize to a number of leading dissident authors from Eastern Europe.

There was and still is a general belief that the worlds of the dissident author and the official writer were completely segregated. A typical expression of this notion is the nine-volume project entitled *Blue Lagoon Anthology of Modern Russian Poetry*. Each of these approximately

40. Mandelstam, 190.

six-hundred-page "loose and baggy monsters" presented the work of Russian "dissident, unofficial or nonconformist writers" (i.e., those writers who did not belong to the Union of Writers of the USSR), as John Bowlt put it in his introduction to the first volume. Continuing, Bowlt averred: "These terms carry an implied value judgment according to which 'unofficial work' means 'good work' and 'official work' means 'bad work.'"[41] This view was widely shared inside communist societies as well. Thus, Georgy Vladimov wrote in an open letter to the Soviet writers' union that "creative freedom... is being realized... in the activity of the so-called *samizdat*.... There are now two kinds of art in the country. One is free and uninhibited.... [Its] distribution and influence depend only it its genuinely artistic qualities. And the other one, commanded and paid for... is badly mutilated, suppressed, and oppressed."[42]

Now, more than a decade after the collapse of the system, this black-and-white view of the relationship between the official and nonofficial spheres, as well as the question of the relative quality of the art produced by them, needs to be revisited.[43] First there is the question of the relationship between nonofficial and official writing. Especially in periods of particularly harsh repression (post-1968 Czechoslovakia, post-1981 Poland, the USSR from approximately 1964 until the mid-1980s, Romania from the late 1970s until the end of communism, Albania and Bulgaria for most of the communist period, and even Yugoslavia from 1973 until the mid-1980s) there was a reasonably clear distinction between the spheres. However, it also needs to be appreciated that many writers who became famous dissidents in Eastern Europe during periods of oppression began their careers and made their initial reputations through official publication. Some of the best known include Milan Kundera and Václav Havel in Czechoslovakia, Zbigniew Herbert and Adam Zagajewski in Poland, and Alexander Solzhenitsyn and Vasily Aksenov in Russia. And such "oppositional" writers as Wisława Szymborska always published above ground. Thus, rather than seeing a stark contrast between the official and nonofficial literary worlds, it would be better to recognize a continuum between them.[44]

41. Kuzminsky and Kovalev, vol. 1, 15. To his credit, it should be noted that Bowlt recognized the pitfalls of such a characterization even as he employed it.

42. Quoted in Skilling, 7.

43. Serious scholarship on this topic, at least in individual East European countries, has already begun. See Šmejkalová, for example.

44. For a discussion of this continuum in the world of communist-era cinema, see Dina Iordanova, "East-Central European Cinema and Literary History," in Cornis-Pope and

There were, of course, high-up figures in the various national writers' unions who would simply never have anything to do with dissidents, and there were dissidents who were so committed or so far beyond the pale that they could not take part in any aspect of official culture. But for the most part the cultures crossed. Members of the writers' unions sometimes participated in nonofficial cultural activities, and, most important, non-official writers could publish (and earn significant amounts of money doing so) in official journals, albeit usually as translators. But in Eastern Europe translation was a respected and well-paid activity, and the state sponsored many translations from foreign languages, including those published in large monthly big-circulation journals such as *Inostrannaia literatura* in Russia and *Literatura na świecie* in Poland. The work published in such journals, as well as in books, was almost invariably by the hand of writers who were not members of the unions. Thus, for example, in the mid-1980s my colleague at Northwestern University, Ilya Kutik, then a nonofficial and unpublishable poet in Moscow (and definitely not a member of the writers' union), received a fee the equivalent of three years of an average Soviet salary for his translation of Alexander Pope's *An Essay on Man.* By his own admission, although the translation was difficult and took two years to complete, he nevertheless had plenty of time for his own writing projects while working on it.

The relationship of official and nonofficial literature also fluctuated depending on the internal situation in a given state. In periods of oppression, more writers produced for the underground market, and in freer periods, fewer did. The extent of the hunger to write and to be a writer in communist countries can perhaps be seen in the enormous quantities of manuscripts that were habitually submitted to Soviet literary journals and publishing houses, despite the recognition that under the conditions that obtained their chances of seeing the light of day were almost nonexistent. According to the Garrards' study of the Soviet writers' union, "Between 1981 and 1985 *Sovetskii pisatel'* [a leading Moscow publisher] received a total of about 5000 manuscripts, of which 4000 came from writers in Moscow.... It was not stated what percentage of these came from Union members, but it should be remembered that the Moscow branch only has 2000 members." According to the same authors, the journal *Novyi mir* in 1985 received 2,140 manuscripts in the prose fiction section alone, publishing

---

Neubauer, 532. For a consideration of how nonofficial and official playwrights interacted in Czechoslovakia after 1968, see McConnell.

only 22.[45] A large percentage of these manuscripts must have been by writers not affiliated with the union. The important thing to keep in mind is that whether ultimately published or not, all of those who submitted manuscripts could and did consider themselves writers with all the benefits to their self-esteem that membership in this august fraternity supplied.

In addition, official publication was not the only way for a writer's work to make it into the public sphere. By the 1960s nonofficial writings of all kinds and of all levels of quality began to appear in samizdat and *tamizdat* (publications of materials smuggled abroad and published in the West). Depending on the degree of control exerted by a given regime, these forms were of great importance. Publishing houses like 68 Publishers, founded by the Czech writer Josef Škvorecký in Toronto upon emigrating to Canada after the Soviet invasion, or journals like the Polish *Kultura*, which came out in Paris, brought out large quantities of work that had been smuggled out of Czechoslovakia and Poland, respectively. Russia was a more closed society, and hence, it was more difficult to send work abroad. Nevertheless, a surprising amount made its way over the border in the suitcases of tourists and Slavists and in the diplomatic pouches of sympathetic embassies to be published by Ardis in Michigan or in the Paris-based journal *Kontinent*. It is difficult to measure the quantity of work published as samizdat, for by definition much of it was ephemeral and has disappeared without a trace. The quip of Venichka, the narrator of Venedikt Erofeev's classic novel *Moscow Circles* (originally published in samizdat) gives a flavor of the way the medium functioned: "The first edition of *Moscow Circles* disappeared quickly—thanks to the fact that it consisted of a single copy."[46]

By no means, however, was the quality of the vast majority of samizdat texts anywhere near that of the best work. Indeed, what is striking when one examines these materials today is their enormous quantity and their generally low level of quality. From our perspective in postcommunism, for example, it would be very difficult to find much of literary value in the more than five thousand pages of the previously mentioned *Blue Lagoon* anthology. Certainly, one could find at least as much valuable work were one to leaf through five thousand pages of the leading official cultural magazines of this period such as *Novyi mir* and *Druzhba narodov*.

There are a number of reasons for the huge varietion in quality in samizdat. First of all, it was generally produced by the author him- or

45. Garrard and Garrard. The quote is on p. 279 and the figures for *Novyi mir* on p. 184.
46. Erofeev.

herself; it was by definition amateur work, something like writings found on today's Internet. That is, there was no intermediary of literary agent, editor, or publishing house to make choices based on quality. Rather, an author could say whatever he or she wanted to say, albeit to a limited audience. The variable quality is thus an indication first and foremost of a basic hunger to write (itself linked to the overall prestige that literary writing had in these countries), a hunger that led many individuals, both talented and untalented, to devote time and effort and to put themselves at a certain amount of risk in order to produce literature. What they got from this activity was rarely fame and fortune, but they were able to enjoy the benefits of being writers (at least those that accrued to one's self-esteem).

Furthermore, readers also did not pay much attention to quality when it came to samizdat. Instead, nonofficial literature was valued as a symbol of the very possibility of dissent rather than, pace Vladimov, for its literary quality. Reading samizdat was the intellectual equivalent of putting on a pair of blue jeans, which as Verdery points out were worn not so much because they were of better quality than state-produced clothing as because doing so "allowed alienated consumers to express their contempt for their governments through the kinds of things they chose to buy."[47] Analogously, the consumers of samizdat expected only the provision of forbidden words, since the point of reading it was the pleasure of encountering in a semipublic forum what all socialist citizens really wanted to say but did not. Even a semipublic enunciation of "the truth" was a kind of scandal, and audiences felt vicariously brave just by reading it. This dynamic helps explain why so few former underground writers were able to flourish after the fall of communism. They wrote against a given system, and when that system disappeared they were exposed as having had nothing to say except their protest.

In considering the relationship of samizdat writing to official literature in communist states, we must also ask why the communist states for the most part tolerated such activity (to be sure, the level of tolerance varied considerably from country to country and at various times); for unquestionably the state, with its extensive security organs, was aware of its existence and could have suppressed it almost completely. Again, the question needs to be answered in a broader context, for it is analogous to the question of why states tolerated the black market for consumer goods. In that case the answer is that had state policy been followed to the letter,

47. Verdery, 1996, 29.

the entire socialist economy would have ground to a halt. Governments were well aware of this, and black market activity was permitted, under the watchful eye of the state and with the occasional arrest and harassment of its participants, as a kind of "safety valve" in order to make up for the dysfunctions so prevalent in communist reality.[48] Samizdat literature functioned as an intellectual safety valve, but given the overall litero-centric bent of communist society, it was one that afforded its participants a high level of social prestige. As Konrád and Szelényi put it in their study of intellectuals under communist rule, "The intellectual who sets out to explore the reservation of ideological taboos is drawn to forbidden territory not so much by an indomitable hedonism which shrinks from no danger as by the prospect of an easy bag, and by the reward not only of the abstract joy of intellectual discovery but of domestic and even international acclaim for his original achievement."[49]

Undoubtedly, despite what Konrád and Szelényi say, at certain times and in certain countries writers suffered severely for their beliefs and for what they wrote. It would be insulting to such figures as Yuly Daniil, Andrei Siniavsky, and Joseph Brodsky in Russia, Václav Havel in Czechoslovakia, Drago Jančar in Slovenia, and many others to deny this. Yet, at the same time, it needs to be repeated that the vast majority of unpublishable writers did not suffer, or at least did not suffer any more than anyone else who lived in Eastern Europe in the post-Stalinist period. Generally, as long as they did not stick their necks out too far, such writers were ignored by the state. And the occasional harassment they did experience (along with the more public suffering inflicted on the major literary dissidents) served, if anything, to elevate their status and that of their avocation, for it was one more indication that literature was truly important.

The preceding should not be taken to mean that I do not think there were significant differences between official and nonofficial literature under communism. These unquestionably existed, but, all the same, writers and readers of both official and dissident literature shared a set of beliefs, all of which contributed to extending and deepening the immense prestige that had already accrued to writing in precommunist Eastern Europe. These included, first and foremost, the conviction that literature was of

---

48. These terms were developed by the Hungarian scholar Elemér Hankiss, who claimed that in communist countries the "first society" (the official power structures) tacitly permitted a "second" (nonofficial) society to exist as long as the latter did not directly attack the system as a whole. For an exposition of Hankiss's ideas, see Skilling, 160–163.

49. Konrád and Szelényi, 238.

central importance to society. There is, for example, no doubt that official and nonofficial writers, leading government figures, and much of the literate public in Eastern Europe would have agreed with the high rhetoric of Alexander Solzhenitsyn's Nobel speech: "Who will give mankind one single system for reading its instruments, both for wrongdoing and for doing good, for the tolerable and the intolerable as they are distinguished from each other today? . . . Propaganda, coercion, and scientific proofs are powerless. But, happily, in our world there is a way. It is art, and it is literature."[50] Most important here is the claim that there can be a single system of values (although there would clearly have been disagreement over what it should be), and that it should be provided by writers of imaginative literature. Secondarily, there were other shared beliefs across the official-dissident spectrum: that literature should play a serious public role, that it should be handsomely supported by the state, and that the public needed to be protected from bad (read "popular") literature. Under this belief system, writers in communist Eastern Europe had, by the late 1980s, stored up an enormous amount of what Pierre Bourdieu famously called symbolic capital. They would need all of it and more to hold onto their privileged position after 1989.

50. Solzhenitsyn, 17.

CHAPTER TWO

1989–2000
The End of the Golden Age

The fall of the Berlin wall in 1989 led with astonishing speed to the collapse of communist regimes in Albania, Bulgaria, Czechoslovakia, East Germany, Hungary, Poland, and Romania. By 1991, the Soviet monolith had also collapsed. Estonia, Lithuania, Latvia, and Russia reappeared as independent states, and Ukraine, Belarus, and Moldova achieved independence essentially for the first time. Almost all of these countries moved to create democratic governments and market economies (although in some cases words were more apparent than deeds). The collapse of Yugoslavia, which also dates from 1991, led to the creation of independent Slovenia, Croatia, Macedonia, and Bosnia-Herzegovina and a Yugoslavia consisting of Serbia and Montenegro. These events produced a series of disastrous wars but eventually also paved the way for the appearance of at least nominally pluralist democracies and semimarket economies even in Serbia where, in the former Yugoslavia, perhaps the smallest amount of progress in this regard has occurred to date.

Much has been written about the political, economic, and social restructuring of these countries since the end of communism. I do not intend to recapitulate that scholarship here. It is surprising, however, that little attention has been paid to the cultural effects of postcommunist transition in Eastern Europe as a whole. And, as far as I can ascertain, no work has attempted to survey the consequences of this transition on writers, who, as was pointed out in the previous chapter, formed one of the most consequential elite groups under communist rule.[1]

---

1. Thus, for example, no articles on the subject have appeared in such major U.S.-based journals as *East European Politics and Societies (EEPS)* or *Problems of Post-communism.*

Any survey that generalizes about postcommunism over the entire territory of Eastern Europe runs the risk of sweeping under the rug the specificities of the process in individual countries. Nevertheless, after reviewing data collected by researchers in Bulgaria, Croatia, the Czech Republic, Hungary, Moldova, Poland, Romania, Russia, Slovenia, and Ukraine, it is my contention that some important general conclusions can be reached regarding the effects of postcommunism on writers in the region as a whole. Whenever possible, I will note exceptions to the overall pattern and try to explain them by a consideration of the local situation.

The first and most obvious commonality is that the creation of fledgling civil societies, democratic governments, and market economies in East European countries ended the "objective conditions" that had placed writers on a pedestal for a century and a half. Writers were no longer needed to defend the nation's very right to exist, nor were they needed as the voice of conscience in oppressive regimes. There were, of course, exceptions to this rule, at least for a time in countries under attack (Croatia through the 1990s being an obvious example) or in countries where little or no substantive change occurred (Belarus). In the immediate aftermath of the political changes, writers, like the vast majority of their compatriots, were jubilant. In the case of former dissident writers the reasons were obvious, as they had been advocating the fall of oppressive communist regimes for years. But even most official writers had by the 1980s come to take a fairly cynical attitude toward the regimes that had supported them generously, so they joined in the general euphoria as well. In addition to their satisfaction with political and promised economic changes (the latter were, as has been recognized in studies of postcommunist societies in general, understood only in vague terms), writers looked forward to giving up what many had come to see as the heavy burden of being spokespeople for the nation, prophets, and gadflies.[2] The psychological difficulty of this role was

---

And books studying elite transformations in the region such as *Elites after State Socialism* (ed. Higley and Lengyel) or *Postcommunist Elites and Democracy in Eastern Europe* (ed. Higley, Pakulski, and Wesolowski) pay little or no attention to cultural elites. Even the authors of the excellent collection *Intellectuals and Politics in Central Europe* (ed. Bozóki) do not pay attention to writers as a particular group of intellectuals. As I noted in the introduction, the fourth volume of the *History of the Literary Cultures of East-Central Europe* promises a section on developments after 1989, but that volume had not yet appeared when I was making the final revisions to my book.

2. Chitnis focuses precisely on those Russian, Czech, and Slovak writers whose goal has been to jettison the belief that literature should have an extraliterary purpose and to turn their backs on all ideologies, missions, and services to the people. He sees this as the central tendency in recent literature in these countries.

expressed beautifully by the Russian poet Dmitry Aleksandrovich Prigov: "Here's me, an ordinary poet let's assume / But the thing is that by the whim of Russian fate / I have to be the conscience of the nation / But how to be that thing, if there is no conscience / Poems, maybe, there are, but a conscience—no / What is to be done?"[3] Prigov is a supreme ironist, and the poem is meant to poke fun at the self-importance of Russian and, by extension, East European writers. Nevertheless, the irony works only because of the more or less equal strength of the verbal reality expressed by the cliché (the demand to be the nation's conscience) and the reality of what poets can actually do in a real world that does not live by clichés.

Liberated by the fall of communism of demands to do the impossible, writers dared to dream of life in "normal societies" in which they could become "just writers," free to create whatever and however they wished. Few of them recognized the simple truths laid out in the previous chapter—that communist regimes had in many ways created a writers' utopia, and that their material well-being and/or exalted social prestige had been predicated on the overall situation of their countries in the bad old days. In exchange for a degree of censorship that varied from country to country, an extraordinary number of writers had been supported by the state (directly or indirectly), shielded from outside competition (particularly from the competition of popular culture), and insulated from market forces that had no interest in or appreciation for their work. This realization would sink in only gradually, and it has still not been fully understood or accepted.

In order to grasp what happened to writers as a corporate group in East European societies, as well as to understand some of the motivations for what they have written since 1989, it is necessary to move from general considerations to an examination of data that illustrate how the changes after 1989 affected the material and social position of writers. As I noted in the previous chapter, a generous subsidy system and a policy that limited salary differentials in socialist economies ensured that a fairly large group of writers could make a living from their profession throughout Eastern Europe. In the immediate aftermath of 1989 a number of factors conspired to compromise this system, if not destroy it outright. First, governments undergoing market reforms trimmed the subsidies formerly available to writers. Second, economic restructuring had a catastrophic impact on the cash flow of citizens in East European countries—whereas

3. Smith, 1993, 218.

under communism money was generally available but there was nothing to purchase, postcommunism saw goods of all kinds become available as cash became scarce. And, furthermore, even when cash was available, consumers now had many new products to buy in addition to books. This was accompanied by the complete collapse of the distribution networks that had guaranteed that what was published could be sent all over the country through a series of state-controlled stores and libraries. Finally, although private publishing was permitted and this increased possible outlets for literary writers, in the vast majority of cases they saw their sales fall drastically on an open market in which their work was overwhelmed by previously forbidden forms of literature, particularly translated and then native popular fiction. Taken together, these factors led to a disastrous change in the material position of most writers of high literature.

Simultaneously, the prestige of serious literature (and its producers) suffered a major blow. New heroes appeared in society—businessmen in particular. Salary differentials widened considerably, and writers, unable to make a good living in the new market-oriented world, began to seem at best quaint and at worst completely unnecessary both to ordinary citizens and to the political elites who had cultivated them.[4] In parallel, Western publishers and readers began to lose interest in East European cultural developments. During the cold war, a certain amount of energy and money was devoted to understanding the enemy and supporting dissidents within communist societies (if only by paying attention to what they said, translating it, and publishing it). But in the post-cold-war world there is no longer a political reason to pay attention to East European literary developments. What is more, as these societies have become more Westernized, they are less exotic, less "other," and hence less interesting to Western readers. In a word, just as the material base for their individual and corporate prosperity eroded at home, writers of serious literature began to seem less relevant abroad.

But writers, both as individuals and as a group, were unwilling to give up their privileged position (and in this they were no different from any other elite group whose status is threatened by new conditions). In order

4. The drastically altered situation for writing and publishing in Eastern Europe (or at least in Central Europe) has already been appreciated and described in broad outline in the book *Freedom for Publishing, Publishing for Freedom* (ed. Garton Ash, 1995). However, despite the book's optimistic conclusion that "the worst of the pains of transition are probably over" (191), our research shows that the situation for serious literature, even in the better-developed Central European countries, has yet to improve significantly.

to defend it, they needed to find ways to adapt themselves and their work to the new situation of postcommunist Eastern Europe, using their accumulated symbolic capital as a resource. The chapters that follow will trace a number of these strategies, but before we turn to them I need to show how the transformation of the political and economic structures of East European societies since 1989 affected writers on a day-to-day basis. First, I focus on the changes in income that were experienced by "official writers" (that is, members of the state-sponsored writers' unions). Then I turn to the material conditions of nonofficial writers, although these are more difficult to quantify, and examine in depth the reasons for these changes. Finally, I consider the extent to which the prestige attached to the writing of high literature has suffered since 1989. While none of these factors alone can be used to track changes in the relevance of serious literature or of individual writers to society as a whole, taken together they indicate that the position of literature in the cultural consciousness of Eastern Europe has eroded considerably since the fall of communism.

In the USSR in 1985, as was noted earlier, the average fee paid to an author by a state publisher (the only kind that existed) for a novel was 8,000 rubles. As the average salary in the USSR was at this point no more than 180 rubles per month, a published novel paid the equivalent of almost four years salary. Articles in the leading "fat journals" paid so well that a one-hundred-page critical article commanded almost a year's salary. Finally, translation, an activity in which even writers who were not members of the union could engage, was sufficiently remunerative that a translation of a single short story could bring in the equivalent of a month's salary. And because members of the writers' union could access scarce consumer goods, including such big-ticket items as apartments and cars, at official state-subsidized prices (instead of having to resort to the black market like the majority of their fellow citizens), the fees they were paid were in effect even larger than they seem.

In comparison, let us take the situation in Russia in the year 2000 (this is the most recent year for which I have statistical information—however, the situation today can be considered more or less the same). In the new market economy, the payment of fees is negotiated separately with each author—the value of an author to a publisher is in direct correlation to the success of his or her work, to popularity measured in sales. While a writer of detective fiction like Aleksandra Marinina (her work is examined in chapter 8) can sell millions of copies in this market and make enormous amounts of money, the fees paid for serious novels are modest—averaging perhaps $1,000 for a solid novel, while a major book by a famous author might reach $8,000–$10,000.

It is difficult to compare what this means in terms of quality of life with the situation in 1985 because salary differentials today are much greater. That is to say, although $8,000–$10,000 may still be a fairly large sum in comparison to an average Russian salary, it is not large at all either in comparison to the salaries earned by those urban dwellers who have taken advantage of the possibilities the market economy offers or in comparison with the income now required to sustain even a middle-class lifestyle. Thus, if the publication of a novel in 1985 provided enough money for a writer to buy a Russian-made car (the only kind then available), in today's market the fee paid for a novel would barely suffice to purchase a BMW bumper. The situation has become even worse when it comes to publishing articles or stories in the leading cultural and literary journals. If an article or novella of approximately one hundred pages in 1985 could bring in a half year's salary, in 2000 it paid approximately 4,000 rubles ($150), not enough even for one month's rent in a reasonable Moscow apartment.

The trends discussed for Russia can be discerned, to a greater or lesser extent, in all the postcommunist states. In Romania, for example, the collapse of the centralized, state-supported cultural system, the economic recession of the 1990s, changes in the book market, and the economic problems of the writers' union all led to the diminution, and even disappearance, of traditional sources of support for writers. Without financial support from the state or the writers' union and forced to find private subsidies, periodicals stopped paying fees at communist-era levels, or altogether. If, for instance, in 1985 a one-page article in *România literară* paid approximately one-third of an average monthly salary, in 2001 it could bring in only 100,000 lei (about $3.50); this represented about one-thirtieth of an average monthly salary. But at least *România literară* still paid royalties. Other journals by this point had given up the practice and attracted collaborators only by symbolic means—the prestige of the magazine and the promise of making their work and names public.

The same tendency can be seen in Romanian book publishing. In the communist period a book of poetry, for example, commanded a fee of 10,000–15,000 lei and a novel between 50,000 and 70,000 lei, rising to over 100,000 if it sold particularly well inside the protected Romanian market. Monthly salaries in Romania in this period were in the neighborhood of 4,000–5,000 lei, so a novel paid at least a year's salary, sometimes two. And, given the existence of artificially low prices and the fact that writers' union connections could ensure access to otherwise unavailable consumer goods, a successful novel brought in enough to buy a car or pay for an apartment. Fees today have diminished and are now almost symbolic: 3 million lei (just over $100) at Editura Fundaţiei Culturale Române, or at most 7%–10% of the net proceeds from a print run—that is, $200–$300. Even membership in the writers' union no longer brings the advantages of old, with the union's drastic diminution of resources after 1989. The system of supplementary retirement benefits no longer works, for example, because writers' retirement benefits have been integrated with the state retirement benefits system. Consequently, retired writers now receive small, insufficient pensions—1,500,000–1,600,000 lei, that is, under $50 a month—facing with the rest of the aging population humiliating financial problems. For such reasons many writers claim that economic censorship has replaced ideological censorship.

The situation is perhaps even more extreme in Ukraine. A survey of approximately thirty professional writers (mostly in Lviv) revealed that for two-thirds of them fees from sales of literary work constituted their main source of income before 1989. In 2000, however, not a single writer listed this as a significant source of income. Most today get by on minimal state pensions or on salaries earned in universities or editorial offices. As a final example, also from a former Soviet republic, let us examine the income of a single writer, Nicolae Rusu (born 1948), who in 2000 was president of the Moldavian Literary Fund (see table 1).

To appreciate the figures, one needs to realize that in the late 1980s 4,000 rubles was approximately double the average salary in Moldova. In 2000, 10,000 lei was also approximately double the average salary in Moldova. However, the major differences are that first of all, in 2000 the average is no longer as relevant a figure because salary differentials have increased considerably, and second, someone like Rusu has lost the privileged access to available goods that used to exist under conditions of socialist shortage. We can see the difference by keeping in mind that in the Moldovan Soviet Socialist Republic in the late 1980s, his yearly income from book sales would have allowed him to purchase a Soviet-made Fiat, whereas his $810 income in 2000 would not buy an imported refrigerator. As a result, although at first glance he appears to have retained his economic position, in reality he is far worse off than he was as a young writer in the waning years of communism.

Let us move to the situation of nonofficial writers. The changes in their material position are more difficult to determine. Under the anciens

TABLE 1 **Nicolae Rusu's Income, 1986–2000**

Year	Title of book	Fee	Awards	Average salary	Annual total (local currency)	Annual total ($)
1986	*Lia*	2,200 rubles	Ostrovsky Award, Soviet Writers' Union (1,000 rubles)	130 rubles	8,360 rubles	~ 1,400
	Grandfather's Hat (translation)	3,600 rubles				
1987	*Wild Apples*	1,700 rubles	—	190 rubles	3,980 rubles	~ 660
1988	*Everything Is the Same*	3,800 rubles	—	210 rubles	6,320 rubles	~ 1,050
1990	*Where the Rain Grows*	1,200 rubles	—	230 rubles	3,960 rubles	~ 657
1992	*Tomorrow Is Another Day*	1,800 rubles	Moldavian Writers' Union Award (700 rubles)	550 rubles	9,100 rubles	~ 1,516
1996	*Without Break*	Own money invested (3,500 lei)	—	250 lei	3,000 lei	745
1997	*The Golden Rain*	Own money invested (10,500 lei)	—	360 lei	4,320 lei	770
1998	*Rats (Sobolaniada)*	Own money invested (27,000 lei)	—	550 lei	6,600 lei	775
2000	*Long Live Nightingales*	800 lei	1,000 lei	695 lei	10,140 lei	810
	Let Others Pass the Bridge	Own money invested (15,000 lei)				

régimes, they were unable to take advantage of the majority of perquisites available to official writers. Nevertheless, they did benefit from the system in a number of ways; In terms of direct earnings from writing, many were able to earn at least an average salary from literary translations. Now, with the rates paid to translators having fallen as precipitously as all other fees for literary work, this method of earning a living has all but dried up. Nonofficial writers also benefited from the overemployment characteristic of communist economies. Given that all publishing houses, editorial offices, and the like employed much larger staffs than they needed (at least by Western standards), those nonofficial writers who were employed in the publishing sector did not have to work very hard for their paychecks. This afforded them significant free time for their writing, even if that writing was unpublishable. Now, if they have not been laid off, they have to work to earn their salaries, which leaves little time for writing. To be sure, when they do write they now have the chance to see their work in print, but the fees paid are so small as to be almost laughable.

Many reasons can be adduced for the catastrophic fall in the material rewards available to writers of literary works. These include enormous changes in the book publishing industry as a whole, increased competition for the leisure-time spending of East European citizens, and the collapse of state subsidies for cultural production. Let us focus on the first of these for the moment. It was frequently claimed, both in communist countries and in the West, that fees paid to official writers did not depend on the popularity of their books as measured in sales. This was not exactly true. Popularity with individual readers did not in most cases determine who was published and how many copies of a book would be released. The former was frequently decided on nonliterary grounds, and the latter depended in great measure on the publishing house's centrally provided plan. Still, large editions of novels and enormous quantities of journals were actually sold. Perhaps this was because of the lack of anything better on the market (given the state's ability to eliminate competition), or because they were sold to other state-funded institutions (primarily libraries) that were obliged to buy them as part of their own plan. But the fact remains that most were sold, not pulped. And at least to some extent this helped to justify the bloated staffs of publishing houses and the large fees paid to writers.

Thus, for example, the large Russian publishing house Sovremennik brought out 365 titles in 1985 with an average print run of 90,000 copies. Of these, 80% were new titles, with a large percentage in such high-prestige literary genres as poetry, fiction, and literary criticism. Books of poetry were published in editions of 10,000 or 20,000 and 50,000–100,000-copy runs for novels were normal. Similarly, in 1985 the publisher Molodaia gvardiia released around 360 titles and some 37–40 million books. They published series primarily, and the majority of their runs were purchased directly by the state and distributed to libraries (thus, of an edition of 200,000, 170,000 went to libraries). The hunger for serious literature on the part of the populace was such that even a relatively obscure book, like an edition of the poetry of Alexander Pope in Russian translation, was published in two editions (a total of almost 100,000 copies). This permitted the publisher to pay a number of translators, none of whom were members of the writers' union, fees equivalent to three years of an average Soviet salary.

By the late 1990s, the situation was completely different. In 1999 Sovremennik published only 28 titles with a total print run of 140,000 copies. Whereas in 1985 there had been 170 people on staff, this had been reduced to 30 including the janitor in 1999 (still surprisingly large, at least by American standards). The situation in the leading cultural journals was similar. According to the literary critic and publicist Sergei Chuprinin, editor in chief in 2000 of the leading cultural journal *Znamia* (a post he assumed in 1993), circulation of the journal in the late 1980s reached 1 million copies per month. In 2000, the journal was being published in a monthly edition of 8,500 copies. Of these, 1,700 were bought by the Soros fund for libraries, 700 went to the Ministry of Culture, and several went to other federal libraries in multiple copies. So subscribers accounted for very few copies. And while a romance or detective novel, translated in a couple of weeks by a team of hacks, might still provide a reasonably large fee, serious literature no longer pays. Thus, in 2001, Ilya Kutik, now an established poet, received ten free copies and no money at all for translating half of an edition of the poetry of Cyprian Norwid.

It would be incorrect to conclude from the above, however, that all sectors of the Russian publishing industry are in the same dire straights as the traditional fat journals and the old-line publishing companies. New publishers, better attuned to the vagaries of the market, have appeared and have expanded rapidly. The Eksmo publishing house, for example, was formed in 1991 and published 10 books that year. By 1999 they were releasing an average of 250 titles per month. In 1991 they employed four people; by 1999 they had expanded to 500 employees. Another new house, Vagrius began operations in the early 1990s. They publish prose fiction,

TABLE 2 **Periodical and Nonperiodical Press in the Czech Republic before and after 1989**

Type of publication	1984	1990	1999
Periodicals (titles)	759	1,870	3,894
Nonperiodicals (titles)[a]	4,115	4,136	12,551

Note: Data from before 1989 refer to the Czech portion of Czechoslovakia.
[a]In addition to books, this includes sheet music, lecture notes, folding picture books, maps, and atlases.

memoirs, biographies, collected works, science fiction, detective novels, romance fiction, and coffee-table books. In 1999 they were paying authors advances of some 10,000–15,000 rubles (approximately $500) and a percentage of sales. Their average fee amounted to 18,000 rubles. Like many leading Western houses, they publish a combination of best sellers and non- or semicommercial books. Included in the latter group are works of fiction by leading literary authors like Andrei Bitov, Vladimir Makanin, and Liudmila Petrushevskaia in editions of 5,000–7,000. Commercial series include Russian Detectives and Made in Russia, published in editions of hundreds of thousands.

To some extent, then, the collapse of the old prestigious state firms (which have now been privatized) has been balanced by the rise of new firms with more flexible publishing ideas and a better feeling for the market. But that market will not bear fees for works of serious literature that are remotely sufficient to procure its producers even an average middle-class income.

A major reason for this is that the book market has fragmented radically. In all the postcommunist countries the years immediately after 1989 saw an enormous multiplication of the number of book publishers as well as of the number of journals. Many of these publishers and journals went out of business quickly, but still, by the mid-1990s the number of publication outlets in these countries had increased enormously, and the growth has continued up until today. Thus, for example, in the Czech Republic there were no more than 30 publishers (all state run) before 1989. In 2000 there were some 450, down from an estimated 1,500 or more in the first half of the 1990s, and practically all were private.

Tables 2 and 3 provide details about the Czech and Slovak publishing industry. As can be seen clearly in the Slovak example, while the number of published titles has increased, the number of copies per title has decreased almost tenfold. And within this fragmented market, it is

TABLE 3 **Book Publication and Circulation in Slovakia in the 1990s**

	1991	1992	1993	1994	1995	1996	1997
No. of titles	2,734	2,842	3,210	3,808	3,186	3,561	3,326
No. of copies printed (millions)	31	19	18	12	8	6.5	4.5
Average no. of copies per book	11,300	6,700	5,600	3,150	2,500	1,800	1,350

extremely difficult to sell works of serious literature. The comments of Ivan Beránek, director of the Czech press Havran, are typical of attitudes toward publishing literature in today's market. When asked whether he intended to publish original Czech works, he replied: "Definitely not at present. I realize what a praiseworthy enterprise it would be, but it is far too risky. Especially in the case of a newly established publishing house which can't be expected to dispose of unlimited capital. And even more so because, to be honest, I find it highly improbable that a new Petr Šabach or another successful author is soon to be discovered."[5]

The situation of the literary publishing industry in postcommunist Eastern Europe can be seen most comprehensively in the material we have been able to collect from Hungary. There, in the communist era (actually until 1986, when a liberalization in publishing began even before the official collapse of the communist political system), 28 institutions were authorized to publish books; all but three were located in Budapest. After 1986 presses proliferated. In 1988, there were about 60 publishing houses. Not all published literature, however, and even those that did might have published only one or two literary books a year. In 1999, there were over 1,600 publishers in Hungary, but most published only one or two books per year. In reality about 30 serious houses publish literature in Hungary today. Magvető Kiadó, probably the most prestigious in literary circles, releases 70–80 titles per year. Európa publishes mostly foreign and some Hungarian titles, altogether about 220 per year, and Osiris publishes some 250, but fewer literary pieces. While in the 1980s many classic works of literature were hard to come by, the market is now saturated.

One reason for the proliferation of presses is a rule introduced in the past few years that no press can apply for grants for more than five books (in some foundations only three) from any foundation at a time. As foundation grants are one of the only ways to make serious literature pay for itself, presses found subsidiaries under different names and with leadership that

5. Petr Šabach is the author of a number of best-selling novels that treat the communist period nostalgically.

TABLE 4 **Number of Titles and Copies of Books Published in Hungary, 1985–1998**

	1985	1990	1998
Hungarian population on January 1	10,657,000	10,375,000	10,135,000
No. of titles published	8,015	7,464	10,626
No. of copies	87,956,000	113,112,000	47,046,000
No. of literary titles (book, booklet)	842	1,560	2,448
No. of copies of literary titles	17,507,000	47,009,000	14,895,000
No. of literary titles by Hungarian authors	520	832	1,210
No. of literary titles by foreign authors	322	728	1,238
No. of copies printed by Hungarian authors	8,490,000	17,741,000	2,917,000
No. of copies printed by foreign authors	9,017,000	29,268,000	11,978,000
No. of literary titles by American authors	34	275	643
No. of copies printed by American authors	2,180,000	14,794,000	8,507,000

Sources: Statisztikai évkönyv 1985 [Statistical Yearbook 1985] (Budapest: Központi Statisztikai Hivatal [Central Statistical Office], 1986), 1 (population), 305 (books and literary titles), 307 (literary titles broken down by author's nationality); *Magyar statisztikai évkönyv 1990* [Hungarian Statistical Yearbook 1990)] (Budapest: Központi Statisztikai Hivatal [Central Statistical Office], 1991), 1 (population), 282 (books and literary titles), 284 (literary titles broken down by author's nationality); *Hungarian statisztikai évkönyv 1998* [Hungarian Statistical Yearbook 1998] (Budapest: Központi Statisztikai Hivatal [Central Statistical Office], 1999), 1 (population), 240 (books and literary titles), 242 (literary titles broken down by author's nationality). The data for 1990 and 1998 are also available in Hungarian and English at http://www.ksh.hu/pls/ksh/docs/hun/xftp/gyor/pdf/kulttar.pdf.
Note: Literature here includes trashy novels, thrillers, and crime stories.

is only nominally different in order to apply for grants separately. Small presses have a hard time avoiding bankruptcy, especially if they want to keep publishing literature. They must compete with vast multinationals that flood the Hungarian market (e.g., Bertelsmann from Germany) with mostly translated popular literature and publish only a couple of original Hungarian works annually. These companies have sufficient resources to establish a vast organization with a better chance of being profitable. For example, the Hungarian Book Club (Magyar Könyvklub), owned by Bertelsmann, had a half a million members in the mid-1990s, and the fact that consumers were buying books through the club took them away from smaller presses. Table 4 reveals some trends in common with those we have seen above as well as a few surprises. First, as was the case almost everywhere in Eastern Europe, the number of literary titles published grew enormously between 1985 and 1998, but the number of copies decreased significantly. In other words, fewer copies are being sold, but a wider variety of books is available. More authors can publish, but they cannot sell their work to many readers. Even more disquieting from the perspective of this analysis is the trend related to work by Hungarian authors. Here again, the number of titles increased almost two and one-half times between 1985 and 1998, but the number of books sold dropped to one-third of what it had been. Foreign authors were also selling fewer copies per title in 1998 than they had in 1985, but the drop was less drastic. Most important, foreign authors saw their market share in Hungary rise from a bit over 50% in 1985 to over 80% in 1998. This statistic underscores the extent to which the socialist system increased the visibility (and hence both prestige and material standing) of local writers through its suppression of external competition. What is more—and this is not entirely clear from the statistics—a good percentage of the foreign books published in 1985 were undoubtedly by official authors from "brotherly socialist countries" and thus not of great interest to Hungarian readers. Now, translated books come primarily from Western Europe and the United States, with American authors in particular having gained spectacularly (going from 12% to 57% of the total Hungarian literary market). And one can be sure that these titles are not by Hemingway and Don DeLillo but rather by Danielle Steel and Stephen King.

The statistics for 1990 are also telling, for in that year the number of copies printed was extremely high—indeed, this is true in general for the period between 1989 and 1992, after which the number of copies published began to decline steeply. It is important to note, however, that the change between 1985 and 1990 is primarily in the publication record of foreign books (obviously due to the excitement caused by the liberalization of book imports), while Hungarian authors were already losing their market share (though they were still selling literary works in large quantities).

Another telling statistic relates to the number of copies sold: A typical literary book in 1999 Hungary was published in 1,000–2,000 copies. There is another, smaller peak in the percentage distribution at the 20,000 copies category: these are usually trashy novels, often by foreign authors. The literary best seller in postcommunist Hungary ((Závada Pál's *Jadviga párnája* [Jadviga's Pillow], printed ten times) sold 55,000 copies. By comparison, in the mid-1980s books were generally printed in initial runs of 30,000–60,000 copies, with reprints made when necessary. This led to a vast amount of waste, but unquestionably more books were sold (or given as gifts to factories, libraries, etc.) as well. In an article on book publishing Györgyi Pécsi quotes Mátyás Domokos, who, in a book on publishing in the 1960s, wrote that if the comrades wanted to ignore someone and push him out of the limelight, they allowed him to publish a book of poems in 500–1,000 copies.[6] This edition would be bought up almost immediately

6. Györgyi Pécsi, "A szépirodalmi könyvkiadás esélytelenségei" [The lack of prospects for publishing literature], *Magyar Napló*, 1996.

TABLE 5 **Titles Published in Hungary by Literary Genre, 1980–1995**

	1980	1990	1995
Poetry	172	219	375
Novels	427	972	1,163
Drama	64	45	23
Other prose	86	234	267
All	749	1,470	1,828

but promptly forgotten. By the late 1990s, such an edition would have counted as a decent-sized publication.

For the most part, table 5 registers no major shift in the relative importance of genres preferred by publishers (save for the almost complete disappearance of published drama). It is a commonplace, however, that only thrillers, science fiction, or romance novels make the best seller list: only these can be sold in a large number of copies (around 60,000 for successful ones) and thus have a chance of becoming profitable. Indeed, there were only three pieces of highbrow literature on a list of twenty-five Hungarian best sellers. Interestingly, many of the local writers of trashy novels are women, and they tend to publish under foreign pseudonyms (e.g., Vavyan Fable, Evelyn Marsh, Sara Garden, Hillary King, Jolante Mallow, Rose Anders, and Kate Wolf are all in fact Hungarian female authors).

Statistical information from Romania presents a picture that complements what we see in Hungary (see table 6). Because these data stretch farther back into the socialist period, we can see even more starkly the fall in demand for literary works. To be sure, because the number of copies published during the socialist period did not entirely depend on consumer demand, these statistics do not necessarily tell us much about the actual habits of Romanian readers. Still, the enormous fall in both the average size of print runs and in the raw number of books produced is an indication that the capitalist market cannot absorb as many books as did its communist predecessor.

What is more, recent data from Romania (see table 7) that focus on the kinds of material published indicate (quite ominously for authors of serious literature) that publishers may be recognizing that literature simply does not sell and, as a result, rather than lowering their print runs they may stop publishing it altogether. Note the catastrophic fall-off in literary works published in 1997 and 1998.

TABLE 6 **Indices of Editorial Production in Romania, 1965–1998**

Year	Titles published	Total copies printed (thousands)	Average print run (thousands of copies)	Copies per inhabitant
1965	5,692	69,684	12.24	3.65
1970	7,681	70,631	9.20	3.49
1980	7,350	87,223	11.87	3.93
1985	5,276	69,266	13.13	3.05
1986	4,648	60,306	12.97	2.64
1987	4,181	55,479	13.27	2.42
1988	4,097	58,987	14.40	2.54
1989	3,867	63,378	16.39	2.74
1990	2,178	52,474	24.09	2.26
1991	2,914	57,272	19.65	2.47
1992	3,662	66,598	18.19	2.92
1993	6,130	75,907	12.38	3.34
1994	4,074	50,230	12.33	2.21
1995	5,517	34,914	6.33	1.54
1996	7,199	38,374	5.33	1.70
1997	6,471	23,712	3.66	1.05
1998	6,231	14,252	2.29	.63

TABLE 7 **Editorial Production Structure in Romania since 1990, by Genre (percent)**

	1990	1991	1992	1993	1994	1995	1996	1997	1998
1. General works	2.48	2.51	1.94	1.78	2.09	1.78	2.96	11.25	22.44
2. Philosophy	1.74	1.85	2.27	2.72	2.92	4.30	3.82	3.80	2.39
3. Religion	2.02	4.02	3.63	4.16	3.63	4.19	4.18	5.97	3.74
4. Social sciences	6.15	6.93	6.94	7.99	10.58	11.78	12.68	13.69	14.48
5. Philology	4.27	5.11	5.49	5.71	4.49	5.85	5.99	5.92	5.65
6. Sciences	14.60	11.98	10.43	11.32	10.43	11.65	13.74	13.40	12.18
7. Technical	34.39	26.70	20.70	21.32	21.35	21.04	20.63	24.99	30.61
8. Arts and leisure	5.14	3.36	3.22	3.12	2.09	2.18	1.46	1.48	2.01
9. Literature	25.21	31.54	39.38	36.49	37.65	32.70	30.31	14.39	.91
10. History and geography	3.99	6.01	6.01	5.38	4.76	4.53	4.24	5.12	5.60
Total	100	100	100	100	100	100	100	100	100
N	2,178	2,914	3,662	6,130	4,074	5,517	7,199	6,471	6,471

Russian statistics tell a similar story. In 1990 (a year in which the old state publishing plan was still effectively in place), some 41,000 titles were published in Russia in editions totaling more than 1.5 billion copies. By 2000 the number of titles was 40,000, almost the same as in 1990, but the total number of books published had fallen to 400 million. Overall, the number of books published per capita has fallen from 10 to something like 2.8.

TABLE 8 **Books Published in Poland by Number of Copies and Titles, 1985–1999**

	1985	1990	1995	1998	1999
All books					
Titles	9,649	10,242	11,925	16,462	19,192
Titles (1st editions)		8378	9877	13,314	16,134
Total copies printed (thousands)	246,321	175,562	115,634	84,999	78,078
Copies printed (1st editions)		87,403	72,791	50,797	55,371
Copies printed per 1,000 people		4,606	2,997	2,198	2,019
Literature					
Titles	1,076	1,573	2,556	3,839	3,560
Total copies printed (thousands)	34,179	65,164	40,680	25,079	21,432

Source: The source for tables 2.8 and 2.9 and the following information on circulation of Polish journals is Przemysław Czapliński and Piotr Śliwiński, *Literatura Polska 1976–1998: Przewodnik po prozie i poezji* (Kraków: Wydawnictwo Literackie, 2000), 216–217, 218.

In Poland the situation is analogous. The number of titles published in 1999 was double what it had been in 1985, but the total number of copies published had dropped to approximately 30% of what it had been during the communist era (see table 8). In the field of serious literature, the change was even more drastic. The number of titles more than tripled between 1985 and 1999, but the total number of copies published was only two-thirds as high; average sales per title were thus approximately only two-ninths of what they had been.

If we examine the situation of literary journals, we can see similar trends. The most comprehensive set of data I have is for Poland, but the situation in other countries does not appear to be different. The journal market reacted directly to changes in the economy. By the middle of the nineties in Poland there were more than 200 cultural magazines; 40 had a strictly literary character, according to the data of the Central Statistical Office. In 1999, there were 71 strictly literary magazines in circulation. After a dynamic period of growth in 1989–1993, there was a period of stabilization (see table 9). Overall, since 1989, about 150 new magazines have emerged; however, only one of them, *Nowa Fantastyka* (a journal devoted to science fiction), has achieved a circulation larger than 50,000 copies per issue and become financially independent. In 1989–1997, the literary magazines with the highest circulation per issue were *Nowa Fantastyka* (75,000 copies), *Wiadomości Kulturalne* (30,000), *Literatura na Świecie* (15,000), *Scyna* (14,500), *Zeszyty Literackie* (10,000), *Nowy Nurt* (10,000), *Odra* (4,700), *Nowe Książki* (4,000), and *Czas Kultury* (2,000); by comparison, the women's magazines with the highest circulation were *Twój Styl* (430,000), *Elle* (185,000), and *Cosmopolitan* (137,000). The audience for

TABLE 9 **The Number of Emerging Literary Journals in Poland, 1989–1996**

Year	Number	Representative titles
1989	6	*Kresy, Lampa i Iskra Boża, Metafora, Pracownia, Strych Kultury, Chałtura*
1990	20	*Dekada Literacka, Ex Libris, Krzywe Koło Literatury, Nowa Fantastyka, Teksty Drugie, Borussia, Na Głos*
1991	15	*Arkusz, Fraza, Tytuł*
1992	16	*Topos, Notes Wydawniczy, Magazyn Literacki*
1993	15	*Sycyna, B1, Opcje, Głosem, Lewa Noga, Krasnogruda*
1994	11	*Wiadomości Kulturalne, Nowy Nurt, Fronda, Haiku, Kurier Czytelniczy*
1995	5	*Studium, Dykcja*
1996	9	*Tygiel Kultury, Incipit, Machina*

literary magazines in this period was 1%–2% of the population of reading Poles—that is, 250,000–500,000 (out of 25 million people who were fourteen years old and above).

It is worth recognizing that one cause of the financial problems faced by publishers is the grave situation of libraries. In the 1980s, for example, Hungarian libraries owned 41 million books, but by 1995 their stock had practically not grown, though it had doubled between 1970 and 1980. Library stock has declined overall since 1990, which indicates that libraries have had practically no money for acquisitions since the end of communism. Visits to the theater and to museums by Hungarians also declined significantly in this period. In 1985, the statistical office registered 70 million visits to the movies, 6.1 million to the theater, and 20 million to museums. In 1995, these figures were 14 million for movies, 4 million for the theater, and 9 million for museums—a vast decline in participation in every sphere of culture. Again, data from other East European countries suggest a similar trend. One suspects that this decline is directly linked to the impoverishment of the population caused by economic restructuring, coupled with a loss of state subsidies to cultural organizations (which resulted in higher prices to cultural consumers). This trend may be reversible when economies improve. However, if a full generation does not develop the taste for cultural participation when young, there is a good chance it will never do so. As a result, even if the declining interest in high culture was to some extent accidental, there is every likelihood that this accident will eventually lead to a major and permanent reordering of cultural priorities in Eastern Europe.

Another important, although theoretically more easily solvable, cause of the difficulties faced by East European publishers relates to the book distribution system. Although East European countries in the communist era had multiple publishers (all state controlled, of course), the distribution system was completely centralized. A single state-run organization saw to it that books were made available (or, as was often the case, not made available) to bookstores and libraries across the entire country. For instance in Poland, Składnica Księgarska, a wholesale distributor set up in 1953, essentially had a monopoly on the distribution of books; it was subordinated to the Minister of Culture. In 1971, Składnica Księgarska ceased being directly subordinated to the Minister of Culture, and, together with Dom Książki (the major network of bookstores), was folded into Zjednoczenie Księgarskie (the Association of Book Marketers). Składnica Księgarska had its own printing house and published *Zapowiedzi Wydawnicze* (a publication announcing new books). Bookstores received questionnaires from them, on which they put orders for specific titles; that procedure helped publishing houses to determine the volume of circulation. Certainly, under the conditions of Polish socialism, most of these "marketing activities" had small economic significance—since the decisions of editors were at least as dependent on the censorship and on governmental allowances of paper as they were on market research. Nevertheless, many activities of Składnica helped to organize the publishing market in Poland.

In 1992, however, the State Court announced the bankruptcy of Składnica Księgarska and Dom Książki. The reasons for this bankruptcy were manifold, but they included incompetent economic decisions (competing with small warehouses and inaccurately gauging market demand, buying titles that were not sold in the planned volume), the incompatibility of their infrastructure (logistics and accounting) with capitalist market conditions, and, most of all, their inability and reluctance to cooperate with their biggest creditors—Harlequin, the first private publishing house in Poland, and WsiP.

In 2000, in place of Składnica Księgarska there were some 550 book distributors in Poland, according to the Centrum Informacji o Książce. Although there were a few market leaders among them—Katalog, Holding Centrum, Współczesny Światowid—none covered the entire country. In part, the poor condition of the wholesale market was directly related to the large number of active wholesale firms. The yearly sales of the average-size wholesaler did not exceed 7 million zlotys, which barely covered the costs of rent, transport, and workers' salaries (the average commission was 12%–18% of the sales price). The major type of transaction between wholesalers and publishers is now based on consignment contracts. This system functions mainly in transactions with small publishing houses, and these publishers have to wait for money from sales longer than their bigger competitors. The major publishing houses sell books according to a system of "closed contracts"—a distributor has no right to return unsold books; he pays at the negotiated due date—usually in fourteen to forty-five days. Those wholesalers who agree to closed contracts get better discounts and more attractive titles.

And Poland is probably closer to having a functioning book distribution system than any other postcommunist country, even if Polish observers expect that in the next decade a major shakeout of the industry will eliminate the vast majority of small wholesalers. In most other countries, publishers find it exceptionally difficult to move books to stores, and many perforce act as their own distributors. This situation is particularly hard on smaller publishers. Thus, in the Czech Republic, one former owner of a small press established in 1994 told our researcher that, having found that the publishing market had stabilized to some extent, he decided to establish a poetry-oriented publishing house. It was essential to sell at least five hundred copies of a title in order to cover costs, and he was convinced he could do so, but the problem was getting the books onto bookshelves. Regular distribution was expensive and hard to control. Instead, he ended up peddling collections of poetry from a backpack directly to bookshops. Indebted and disillusioned, he terminated his publishing activity in 1997. Many Romanian bookshops specialize in the books of one publisher only, books published in the provinces may be available only in the local bookshops, and there is no equivalent of *Books in Print* to establish which publisher published which book and whether it is still available.[7]

The situation is most catastrophic in the former multinational states (the USSR and Yugoslavia). The central problem in Russia for the publishing industry is that there is no normal wholesale distribution of books in the country. As a result, the market is filled only in Moscow and a few other big cities, while there is a shortage of books in other areas. This is in sharp contrast to communist days, when, because distribution was reasonably good over the whole country and demand was far smaller outside the major cities, one was more likely to find an interesting book in the provinces than

7. The lack of any centralized informational system relating to book publishing has the further effect of making it exceptionally difficult for foreign libraries to order books from East European countries. Once all-inclusive collections have grown spotty, catch-as-catch-can, and this means that contemporary literary work may never reach the small group of academic specialists who decide such important questions as what to translate and what to recommend to their students.

in the capital. The few existing wholesale firms prefer to deal with popular literature. The Ministry of Print Media in Russia is working to create a few wholesale distributors of books in the country. One project, called Rosknigi is being made operational, but it will take a long time before it will have any real effect on the book trade in Russia. Nevertheless, one can say that by the year 2000 in Russia wholesale chains were in the process of being formed. One could name the projects Master-knigi, the network called Top-knigi in Novosibirsk, and the Petersburg firm Snark. At that point, however, none of these fitted the classic pattern of a book wholesaler, and none controlled more than twenty-five stores.

In the former Yugoslavia, the breakdown of the distribution system is compounded by barriers to trade among the former Yugoslav republics. As a result, in Croatia it is extremely difficult to find books published in Serbia and vice versa. Given that Serbian and Croatian are mutually comprehensible, the inability of publishers to sell in "foreign" markets means that they stand to lose an enormous percentage of their potential sales and readers. The absurdity of the system can perhaps best be appreciated with a story from my own experience. A book I wrote on the cultural history of Yugoslavia was published in Serbian in 2001 by the Belgrade-based Stubovi kulture publishers. In 2002, I was contacted by a Bosnian publisher who asked for the rights to produce a Bosnian edition. When I asked why he did not simply import copies from Serbia (as had been done by one book store in Sarajevo), he told me that many Bosnian readers simply would not buy the book unless the translation was Bosnianized (this despite the fact that the Belgrade publisher had set the book in Latin rather than Cyrillic letters and that any educated reader in Bosnia would have no trouble understanding the Serbian). As a result, a separate Bosnian edition may some day appear, though financial difficulties have forced postponement.

By the late 1990s and into the 2000s, however, the distribution system appeared to be improving almost everywhere in the former communist East (with the exception of the former Yugoslavia). Although smaller towns were still badly served and electronic book buying was still in its infancy in the region, bookstore chains, book clubs, and larger wholesalers were increasingly able to get books to consumers who wanted them. However, many readers were not as interested in acquiring these books as they had been, and the proliferation of titles in most countries meant that every year there were more books chasing fewer readers all over Eastern Europe.

It is more difficult to measure fluctuations in the prestige attached to writing than it is to track changes in the material base. But it is nevertheless clear from many of the comments made to our researchers that the prestige of serious literature has fallen in the region, albeit perhaps not as precipitously as the financial rewards available (an indication of the latent power of the stored-up symbolic capital of literature). One way of gauging the prestige attached to literature, at least in the public sphere, is to see how literary prizes are awarded and covered in the media.

In the Soviet Union the ceremony of awarding prizes to Soviet authors took place in the Kremlin as a solemn event. High party leaders handed out medals, prizes, diplomas, and other awards. The ceremonies were broadcast on the national channel of state television and were noted on the evening television news programs and on state radio. In newspapers like *Pravda, Izvestiia*, and *Literaturnaia gazeta* they were reported on the front page or at the top of special sections devoted to culture and art. The situation was basically the same in all other communist countries. There were relatively few prizes, and they were awarded in a public way with great fanfare. By the year 2000 prizes in Russia had multiplied. Where once there had been only three or four major prizes (including the Lenin Prize, the State Prize of the USSR in the field of literature, art, and architecture, the State Prize of the Russian Soviet Federated Soviet Republic for outstanding works of literature, and the Award of the Komsomol for a work of literature or art—most of these were awarded to more than one person, so that there may have been some thirty laureates per year), some six hundred literary prizes were offered in 2000. The numbers alone are an indication that no individual prize can capture the attention of the entire public.[8] And indeed, what appears to have happened is that each group or locality awards its own prize to its own favorites, and the general public simply does not pay much attention.

Russia is probably at the extreme end of the spectrum when it comes to changes in the prize system. In Hungary, for example, according to our researchers, "Many more prizes exist now than in 1985. In addition, many more agencies distribute these prizes; thus, exclusion is less blatant. Nevertheless, the prestige of the major prizes has increased, although getting the Kossuth Prize in 1985 did accrue prestige, even though obviously only those acceptable for the state socialist regime could receive it. The money associated with most prizes is negligible. In addition, except for

---

8. To be sure, there are prizes and prizes. The most prestigious of the new Russian awards, such as the Russian Booker Prize, do draw a fair amount of attention and provide significant financial rewards.

the recently established Hungarian Literary Prize, most of the prizes (and certainly the major ones) are still distributed and financed by central state agencies. Therefore, political considerations are not absent in the award of these prizes because even though the writers' organizations nominate the recipients, the prime minister and the minister of culture have been known to change names and modify the lists they receive. Very few significant prizes and grants are awarded by nonstate agents. For this reason what is really different is not the disappearance of politics in literary management, but rather an increased pluralism of (as well as struggle between) various political trends. Those outside these circles, or those who belong to an underrepresented group, are still at a disadvantage."

But whatever the case in terms of prizes, the overall status of writing in society has undoubtedly declined. Earlier in this book I quoted the Serbian writer and essayist Mihailo Pantić on this topic: "Artistic literature in the postsocialist cultural model has become socially unnecessary, an almost completely private affair which lacks any social importance and which is interesting only to narrow academic circles, to writers, and to rare dedicated readers who nurture their passion as other marginal groups nurture theirs. Some people belong to satanic cults, some to the Society for Lovers of Bulldogs, and others, amazingly, read Serbian poetry." A similar conviction, put a bit less colorfully, can be found in statements made in 2000 by Sergei Chuprinin, then editor in chief of the Moscow-based journal *Znamia*, to our Russian researcher Mikhail Kolesnikov: "[Under Communism] the editor in chief and the writers were widely admired. The editor might even be a member of the Supreme Soviet, his position equal to that of a minister or a field marshal. Now, the status of writers has fallen catastrophically. Thus, for example, Gorbachev would meet with the editor in chief twice a year, but Yeltsin did not do so. Putin hasn't either. Today the prestige of literature and culture has fallen in the eyes of the government and, therefore, in the eyes of the people." One finds the identical sentiment in Ukraine, where writers surveyed by Ukrainian researcher Vitaly Kutik agreed that "the social role and importance of literature has fallen considerably since 1989"—"by several times" (Viktor Romaniuk), or "immeasurably" (Valerii Shevchuk). And its "social resonance has weakened" (Mykola Ilnitsky), as has its "moral influence on society" (Paulo Movchan). And thus, to put it baldly, "it plays no role at all" (Maria Vlad) in today's Ukraine.

Simultaneously, writers from Eastern Europe have lost their cachet in the West. Whereas at the height of the cold war the appearance of

Solzhenitsyn's *Gulag Archipelago*, smuggled out of the Soviet Union and published simultaneously in multiple European languages, was a major news sensation, the appearance of new works from the region causes barely a ripple today. And it has become harder and harder for East European writers even to reach a Western audience, particularly the ever more important Anglophone readership. Book series like Penguin's Writers from the Other Europe, once edited by Philip Roth, have disappeared; the major New York houses publish fewer and fewer new authors from the region (part of a general trend by these houses to publish ever smaller amounts of serious literature). The reasons for this are undoubtedly related to the perceived political irrelevance of contemporary postcommunist Eastern Europe.

When one examines the way in which East European literature was presented before 1989, it becomes apparent that, whatever the author's style or theme, these books were marketed as political statements. In her introduction to Milan Kundera's *The Farewell Party*, for example, Elizabeth Pochoda writes: "*The Farewell Party* attests to the longevity of political oppression in Czechoslovakia by never mentioning it" (x). That either the absence or presence of a theme was seen as a guarantee of its importance was beneficial to East European writers in the cold war period, as it ensured that Western audiences could be induced to find their work worth reading. Now, however, they must pay a stiff price for previous marketing tactics, for in the absence of political relevance neither readers nor publishers find any reason to be concerned with their work.

So what do all of these facts imply for the future of literature, particularly serious fiction, drama, and poetry, in Eastern Europe? What is the balance sheet for culture after more than fifteen years of complex transition? Are writers as a group to be placed on the endangered species list, or will they find a way to weather the storms and to retain at least some of the prestige and power they accumulated over almost 150 years?

Interestingly enough, all of the material problems, fragmentation of the market, and loss of status described here do not appear to have caused writers to abandon their profession. Statistics relating to membership in writers' organizations, for example, indicate that the number of people who identify themselves as writers has not declined, and in most countries it has increased significantly. And this is despite the fact that writers' organizations are no longer able to provide financial support for their members. As is the case with other aspects of literary life, writers' organizations have proliferated, one more sign of the overall fragmentation of literary life in the postcommunist period.

Thus, in 1980 the Union of the Bulgarian Writers (Saiuz na bulgarskite pisateli) had 348 members. By 1990 the membership had grown to 422, and in 2000 it stood at 516. Simultaneously, a second organization called the Association of Bulgarian Writers (Sdruzhenie na bulgarskite pisateli), which was founded as a liberal alternative to the union in 1994 by some 29 members, had grown to 240 members by 2000. The Romanian Writers' Union had approximately 1,100–1,200 members in 1985, while in 2000 it numbered 2,147. A competing organization, the Association of Professional Writers, was founded in 1994 and had 174 members in 2000. In Hungary, the main writers' organization (Magyar Irók Szövetsége) doubled in size (from a bit over 600 to 1,200 members) between 1985 and 2000.[9] The growth in these organizations has not been fueled entirely by young writers, but rather results both from new writers and from the inclusion of those writers whose ideological or literary profiles rendered them unacceptable in communist days. Whatever the source of growth, these numbers indicate that identifying oneself as a writer is still important to many people in Eastern Europe.

If we wish to focus on positive developments for literature in the post-1989 period, we can certainly find them. Thus, our Polish researchers considered the role of the 150 new journal titles that appeared in the 1990s, usually published in editions of 2,000 copies or fewer, and concluded that these publications illustrate the scale and the range of postcommunist cultural revitalization. Although new magazines do not have a large circulation, they have decentralized literary life by creating many autonomous

9. In this, as in many of the other categories we have been examining, Slovenia stands out as an exception. Here, continuity, not radical change, is the pattern. Thus, in 1985 there were approximately 300 members of the Slovenian branch of the Yugoslav Writers' Union; the same organization had 302 members in 2001. Nor had any other organization arisen to compete with it. While the number of companies publishing literature has grown here as in other countries, the book market is still dominated by the same firms that operated during the 1980s (Mladinska knjiga, Cankarjeva založba, and Državna založba Slovenije [DZS]). From our data, it appears that the Slovenian government increased spending on culture in general and literature in particular through the 1990s. Thus, while writers and publishing houses in Slovenia face some of the same market pressures as in other East European countries, their overall situation appears to be far healthier. This tendency to stability in Slovenia is in keeping with the overall trajectory of its postcommunist transition, which has been less fraught than in other countries. The government's concern with culture and particularly linguistic culture may well have to do with the fact that for tiny Slovenia, culture is perceived to be one of the few factors that differentiates it from its larger neighbors and therefore justifies its very existence.

centers of culture (though all still supported by the centralized Ministry of Culture and Art), which animate the literary life of various regions. One of the healthy results of this decentralization and regionalization is the break-down of the formerly unified and stultifying system of criteria and stable taste that united practically all audiences in the communist period. This has allowed for a growing diversity in literature, but it also has a negative side effect: it generates a published *graphomania*. But, most important, it accel-erates the circulation of information about books, increases the number of participants in the dialogue about them, and does not sentence the author of a book published by a small publishing house to the judgment of one of the central literary magazines. It helps small literary communities to find their own language in the discussion of their own identity; in other words, it creates local systems of communication, which support local communi-ties. Furthermore, many of the newly created magazines have given birth to new foundations, publishing houses, and literary awards, multiplying, in this way, the infrastructure of the literary market.

East Europeans continue to read and to believe in the importance of serious literature, albeit not at the levels of the communist days. Thus, a survey published in Prague revealed that in the Czech republic 74% of adults reported they had read at least one book in the previous month. Only New Zealand reported a higher figure, and the United States trailed well behind, at approximately 65%. Furthermore, a book published in Prague in 2002 about the reading habits of Czechs indicates that the percentage of Czechs who read more than six books per year is above 50%, a significantly larger figure than similar surveys find in the United States or most of Western Europe.[10]

On the negative side, however, is the obvious fact that more and more books and more and more journals are chasing ever fewer consumers of local high culture. In this sense, perhaps, the writing and publishing industry of the postcommunist countries is coming to resemble that of Western countries. Although publishers, even some commercially successful ones, are willing to publish challenging works of literature for prestige reasons, they recognize that there is a very limited audience for such works. And even when they do publish literature, they cannot pay the kinds of fees that would allow writers to make a living from the pen alone.

This situation in a sense recapitulates the experience of the East Eu-ropean intelligentsia toward the end of the nineteenth century, when, in

10. Chaloupka, 120.

the words of Konrád and Szelényi, "it was easy for educated professionals to become intellectual proletarians: Their livelihood was uncertain, their market shifting and unstable. The intelligentsia could not support its own creative artists and scholars, and the stratum of the bourgeoisie that was willing to pay for culture was exceptionally small."[11] Precisely in order to escape this situation, intellectuals in general and writers in particular allied themselves with those governments that could provide the material conditions necessary for them to do their work, including of course the communist regimes. Now, however, the market-focused governments of most East European countries are no longer willing or able to support writing as they have in the past, so intellectuals in general and writers in particular again find themselves in a precarious position.

As a result, writers in Eastern Europe today are searching for solutions, starting with the accumulation of jobs and ending with various forms of conversion of already-acquired symbolic prestige into new positions, which, in turn, can bring more income and social visibility. Depending on circumstance, education, and reputation, writers employ various strategies to convert their symbolic cultural capital into positions in politics, journalism, or the private sphere—some become freelance writers, some editors, and others are attracted to the relative safety of academic positions. However, as opposed to the communist era, there is now an expectation that writers, editors, and professors will actually work for their salary, so available time for creative writing has drastically decreased. What is more, the salaries paid by academic and literary institutions are generally not high, so writers who choose this route must have one or two other jobs, and all this besides writing literature. Thus, although writing still carries sufficient prestige in Eastern Europe to attract new participants, the financial situation makes it increasingly likely that for many writing will become a hobby rather than a profession.

The strange combination of the continued prestige attached to writing with the increasing proletarianization of writers themselves can perhaps best be appreciated in an Internet advertisement that appeared in Poland in 1999 (see figure 3). It invited Poles who wished to see themselves as writers to provide a basic story line in any popular fiction genre. For approximately $750, this ghostwriting service, presumably staffed by hungry young writers, would produce a novel in the appropriate genre, publish it, and deliver the copies to the proud "author." The ad even noted that the service was capable of producing works of "so-called serious literature," but the lack

11. Konrád and Szelényi, 119.

Fabrica *Librorum*

Książka w miesiąc!

Jeśli potrzebujesz szybko, ciekawie, profesjonalnie i tanio napisaną książkę trafiłeś pod dobry adres. *Fabrica Librorum* stworzy każdego rodzaju powieść fabularną według twoich wskazówek, zgodnie z twoimi potrzebami i wymaganiami. Co więcej, uczyni to zaledwie w miesiąc, a w Twojej książce będzie się działo więcej niż na tej stronie. Serdecznie zapraszamy.

HORROR KRYMINAŁ ROMANS SENSACJA FANTASY

Oprócz powieści popularnych jak horror, kryminał czy romans, piszemy także reportaże, felietony, recenzje czy eseje. Ponadto tworzymy również literaturę tzw. ambitną. Znajdziesz tutaj teksty młodych krakowskich autorów gotowe do druku, będziesz mógł je przeczytać i kupić oraz nawiązać kontakt z ich twórcami. Zaprszamy do częstych odwiedzin.

 Tylko 3000 zł
za powieść.

Nowa powieść **000284** *Do sprzedania*

FIGURE 3. Page from the Web site of the Polish ghostwriting service Fabrica Librorum, 2000.

of prominence given to this indicates that the operators did not feel their potential clients, most likely social-climbing nouveau riche businessmen, would be much interested in being associated with works of this type.

Perhaps the most difficult and intriguing question that arises after a consideration of the radical changes that have taken place in the material conditions of writing in Eastern Europe since 1989 is how they have affected literary production. While it is intuitively obvious that they must have had some effect, one wants to avoid the kind of vulgar sociology (itself so prevalent in East European literary criticism of the communist era) that would draw a straight line between material conditions of writing and literary output. Mindful of this problem, in the rest of this book I will nevertheless attempt to identify some broad strategies writers have employed, either to convert their accumulated symbolic capital into more readily usable market-based capital or to remain relevant as writers to their societies (and thereby retain at least some of the prestige traditionally accorded to writers there).

I have attempted to avoid vulgarization by a number of means, the most important of which is the recognition that any writing strategy can and does take multiple forms. Thus, each of the following chapters considers a given strategy in a number of incarnations. I also recognize that some strategies began to evolve even before the collapse of communism, so when appropriate I point out precursors, attempting to delineate what is new about the evolution of a given strategy under the conditions of postcommunism. In addition, I should add that any strategy identified is a heuristic category. In few cases, especially when we are speaking of literary categories, would the writers themselves recognize that their work is anything other than the work they wished to create. An outside observer, however, can discern patterns of which writers may not be aware, and indeed, the initial impetus to write this book was precisely a recognition that such strategic patterns did and do exist. Finally, insofar as it is my concern to recognize similarity among disparate texts, readers may feel I have slighted the specificity of individual works in my analysis. I have attempted to avoid this problem by treating individual literary texts at some length rather than providing an encyclopedic listing of all the works I could identify that fitted within a certain strategy. Nevertheless, as a literary critic I am well aware that any classificatory scheme will always provide a limited reading of individual works by virtue of its need to focus on one or more specific elements at the expense of the whole. I simply hope that the description and analysis of the analytic categories themselves compensates for a loss of richness in the analysis of the individual works.

CHAPTER THREE

Writers and Politics: Triumph, Tragedy, and Farce

For some reason all postcommunist states like to have writers to lead them.—Dubravka Ugrešić

One of the most striking phenomena in postcommunist Eastern Europe is the high visibility of writers in political life. In addition to Václav Havel, by far the best-known writer turned politician, other heads of state include the author of literary travelogues Lennart Meri (president of Estonia between 1992 and 2001); novelist, playwright, and translator Árpád Göncz (who moved directly from the post of president of the Hungarian Writers' Union to that of first president of postcommunist Hungary); novelist Dobrica Ćosić (president of Yugoslavia in 1992–1993); and prolific author Rudolf Schuster (president of Slovakia from 1999 to 2004). We also find leaders of political parties, for some reason mostly nationalist in their leanings, including the notorious Romanian presidential finalist (in the 2000 elections) Corneliu Vadim Tudor, poet and head of the România Mare Party; István Csurka, novelist and leader of the Hungarian right-wing Magyar Igazság és Élet Pártja (MIÉP) (Hungarian Justice and Life Party); Radovan Karadžić, poet and head of the Bosnian Serb Srpska Demokratska Stranka (SDS) (Serbian Democratic Party); and the poet and prose writer Eduard Limonov, founder and head of the National Bolshevik Party (NBP) in Russia. These leaders are merely the tip of a large iceberg that is composed of a host of parliamentarians, ambassadors, and other political movers and shakers.

Almost instinctively it seemed, when it came time to elect new leaders after the collapse of the previous political system, voters placed their trust in writers. If one thinks about the political situation in postcommunist Eastern Europe, this was really not a surprise. After all, the communist political elite had been widely discredited. But because the communists had exercised an official monopoly on political power for so long, there were no well-known political figures to replace them. In the first democratic elections, the political vacuum was frequently filled by writers, traditionally among the best-known and most trusted nonpolitical actors in the various countries of the region.[1] In some cases, writers were pushed more or less reluctantly into the political spotlight. In others, they thrust themselves forward, actively seeking to move from one role to another. As the transition to a democratic order has been consolidated, the importance of intellectuals in general and writers in particular in the political life of Eastern Europe has unquestionably been waning. This is also not surprising. Given the solitary nature of the literary profession as well as the long-term, uncompromising, and sometimes irregular nature of the creative process, few writers possess an aptitude for the day-to-day political work and the horse trading that are necessary features of coalition politics. Nevertheless, a surprising number of writers can still be found in important political positions in Eastern Europe, even in those countries that are far advanced in their transition.

It is difficult to generalize about the motives that led writers into political careers. Undoubtedly, the fact that dissident writers had long been perceived as a "second government" led many to think they could successfully lead their societies when the "first government" evaporated. In the case of writers who took up hard nationalist political positions, the traditional role of the writer in Eastern Europe as inventor of the nation and defender of its interests encouraged a belief that direct political action could be successful. From a sociological perspective, we have here a clear case of the conversion by an elite group of cultural into political capital. However, as this conversion in most cases took place before the financial realities I outlined in chapter 2 had become apparent, it is unlikely that purely mercenary motives were at work. That the conversion was in many cases complete, however, can be seen in the abandonment of creative

1. The major exceptions to this rule are themselves quite telling. Most notably, in Poland, where the Solidarity trade union had emerged in 1981 as an alternative political structure, well-known writers did not achieve positions of political prominence (although various other intellectuals did). The same is true of Slovenia, but for a different reason. There, communist leaders reinvented themselves as nationalists who were credited with and rewarded by voters for having pushed for Slovenian autonomy and then independence.

writing by almost all of those who have moved into the political arena. To be sure, most of them did not actually stop writing, but their production moved into the realm of political speeches, editorials, and other nonfictional genres. It remains to be seen whether any of these former writers will resume an active literary career after their engagement with politics ends.

It is striking, however, that to my knowledge no writer who came to public attention after the fall of communism has yet attempted to enter politics. This may be because it is impossible in the postcommunist period for a writer to garner the name recognition necessary to make the switch, or it may simply be because younger writers still have too much to prove in the literary arena, seeing politics as the domain of old men (in fact men, for the percentage of women among elite literary figures and elite politicians in Eastern Europe is quite small). Thus, at least for the moment, it appears that switching from literature to politics was a strategy adopted by already established writers as a way of remaining relevant to a (somewhat) postliterary society rather than an ongoing conveyor belt from literary life into politics. It may be that only writers who came of age during the halcyon days of communism can exploit what has become a closed path. This would be consistent with a larger trend described by András Bozóki in reference to intellectuals in general: "Cultural elites always played a crucial role in Central Europe in occupying a critical stance and even in shaping politics from a moral-universal perspective.... The irony of history lies in the fact that the very success of intellectuals, i.e., to reach democracy based on popular sovereignty, undermines their formerly distinguished political role. In the new democracies of Central Europe, professionalized intellectuals might remain an important social group— among many others. Professionalization is the order of the day, which is seen by many with the melancholy of postrevolutionary times, and which creates disillusionment and provokes nostalgia among the last European intellectuals."[2]

Perhaps the most intriguing question concerning specifically writers who become politicians (as opposed to the broader phenomenon of intellectuals who turned to politics after 1989) is to what extent their political orientation and tactics in the public political sphere were determined by the trajectory of their previous literary work. Although I would not want to propose a general law on the basis of the observations to be presented

2. Bozóki, 12.

here, there does appear to be a fairly direct relationship. In his political life, each author I treat here continued to grapple with the same kinds of questions that concerned his literary heroes, and even himself to behave as if, in the real world of politics, he were a character in his fiction. Thus, we can perhaps see their political activity as a kind of translation of their literary work from one medium into another rather than as a completely new chapter in their lives.

I examine the careers of three writers who became politicians in Eastern Europe after 1989. First, as an example of a successful transformation I discuss the case of Václav Havel. The second case, that of the Serbian Dobrica Ćosić, is more ambiguous. Here we see an initial postcommunist success that was succeeded by marginalization and embitterment. Finally, I consider the pathetic situation of the talented Russian Eduard Limonov, whose National Bolshevik Party remains marginal and who has spent extensive time in Russian jails as a reward for his political ambitions.

From the outset, we can find a number of important similarities among these authors. First, all belong to roughly the same long generation. Ćosić, born in 1921, is the oldest. Havel was born in 1936 and Limonov, born in 1943, is the baby of the family. Each of them achieved initial fame as a writer of literary work in no way directly connected with politics. In the case of Ćosić, it was a novel that fully conformed to the canons of the officially accepted partisan novel (indeed, it came to be seen as an icon of the genre). Havel was a playwright rather than a novelist, and his first literary work appeared in the early 1960s. While his plays could certainly not be called examples of socialist realism, they were permitted on the stage and into print by the relatively relaxed thaw-period Czech censorship. Limonov was born too late to benefit from the Soviet thaw of the late fifties and early sixties. He began his career as a poet but was unable to publish in the USSR. His first published collection of poems, *Russkoe* (Russianness) appeared in the United States in 1979, but it contains works dating back to the late 1960s. Limonov became well known as a literary figure thanks to his scandalous pseudoautobiography *Eto ia, Edichka* (*It's Me, Eddie*) published in New York in 1979.

All three writers sooner or later fell afoul of the communist authorities. In the case of Limonov, the reasons were purely literary. His work simply did not fit the canons of Soviet literature, and his bohemian lifestyle was equally distasteful to the Soviet authorities, who encouraged him to emigrate to the United States in 1975. Ćosić's problems had little to do with literature. He remained an acclaimed literary classic throughout the communist period of Yugoslavia. However, beginning in the 1960s, he took up increasingly nationalistic political positions, and this led him into political hot water on a number of occasions. Finally, Havel, after the Soviet invasion of 1968, was excluded from literary life. He continued to write plays, but became increasingly better known as a dissident political figure.

Václav Havel: The Triumph and Tragicomedy of a Writer-Politician

In February 2003, Václav Havel stepped down as president of the Czech Republic. He had served as head of state almost continuously since the so-called Velvet Revolution he had done so much to initiate in late 1989. The event was marked by pomp and circumstance and by accolades from a host of foreign and local dignitaries. The prevailing sentiment was that Havel deserved recognition for his lifelong achievements as a playwright promoting humanistic values, an anticommunist dissident, and a postcommunist politician. A resolution honoring Havel was passed by the U.S. House of Representatives on February 11, 2003. It notes "that Havel is 'widely respected throughout the world as a proponent of democratic principles' and that the Czech Republic had become 'an important and valued member of the world community' under his stewardship. The resolution adds that Havel's 'superb skills as a playwright and essayist helped promote democracy in Eastern Europe during the Cold War...bringing international attention to the struggle for democracy in Czechoslovakia.'"[3]

At the same time, these accolades mask a certain ambivalence toward Havel's role as president, particularly in the Czech Republic, where he is a far more controversial figure than he is abroad. For while foreigners are inclined to focus on Havel's enormous moral authority, Czechs tend to be more interested in his failings as a practical politician; his unwillingness to form a political party to advance his programs and his long and public squabbles with archrival and successor Václav Klaus are held against him. So, too, is the fact that the economic situation did not improve nearly as quickly as some had hoped and expected in the early postcommunist years. Finally, even Havel's uncompromising moral stands, which play so well in the *New York Review of Books*, sometimes seemed to a people having

3. *RFE/RFL News Service*, Feb. 12, 2003, http://www.rferl.org/newsline.

difficulties making ends meet to be the hectoring affectation of a patrician out of touch with real problems. Havel himself, with his frequent public Hamlet-like self-questionings, contributed to this ambivalence inside the Czech Republic.

This is, in my view, not surprising, for I believe that Havel's career in general, as a playwright, as a dissident, and as a postcommunist politician, should be understood in terms of a dialectic between rigid moral principles and the necessary compromises of everyday life. Havel was happiest and most successful precisely when he could either assert such principles unambiguously, as when he was a leading dissident, or when he could treat this dialectic as an issue, shifting the burden of the problem to his characters in his dramatic oeuvre. He was least successful and most tormented when he himself found it necessary to live in the world of compromises; that is, as president of Czechoslovakia and then the Czech Republic. The continuum of interests and problems that follow Havel through his literary, dissident, and political career will be the focus of my analysis here.

In my insistence on thematic continuity through Havel's work and life, I differ from his most recent biographer, John Keane, who characterizes Havel's career as "a political tragedy in six acts."[4] In Keane's view, the best way to understand Havel's essential failure in political life is through the lens of figures such as Aristotle and Seneca, Shakespeare and Lessing. As he puts it, "In this book, the private anguish of a single individual—an innocent and courageous mortal with marked imperfections—is reenacted on a public stage that is cluttered with great evil and suffering caused by violent struggles for power over others. Like the classical tragic form as well, my book offers insights into how the tough-skinned victim is exposed and broken by forces that are, in the circumstances, neither fully understandable nor controllable by prudent calculation." To my mind, this overlay of tragedy, while rhetorically impressive, fails to take into account a number of important facts. Most obviously, it implies that Havel, like the great tragic figures of history, should have left the stage destroyed by his experience, an example inspiring fear and pity in his audience. This is by no means the case. While it is undoubtedly true that many ordinary Czechs do not love and admire Havel as much as do foreign intellectuals, his dignified exit from politics and the international accolades he garnered indicate that we do not have to do here with a classical tragedy of power. Even more important, however, is to recognize that tragedy has never been Havel's preferred dramatic form. His own plays certainly tend more toward comedy than

4. Keane, 15.

tragedy, although the best of them, by exploring the actions of heroes placed in hopelessly ambiguous moral situations, did indeed hint at a seriousness of purpose that elevates the work. In my view, then, both the work and the life can be seen to contain elements of many dramatic genres, from comedy, to tragedy, and even to farce. They do so because they probe issues of deep ambiguity, issues that turn out to have provisional answers onstage but cannot, perhaps, be satisfactorily addressed in the realm of politics.[5]

The best locus to begin an examination of the dialectic between moral principles and compromise is Havel's marvelous one-act play *Audience*, written in 1975. The play consists of a short dialogue between a dissident writer, Vaněk, and the brewmaster of the brewery where Vaněk has been forced to work after having run afoul of the authorities in post-1968 Czechoslovakia. The basically autobiographical nature of the play has been noted by Havel himself: "The inspiration came from personal experience—my employment in a brewery the year before."[6] As the play unfolds, we see that the working-class Brewmaster, though in a position of power over the writer, treats him deferentially, confides in him, and offers him a cushy job in the brewery. He wants only two things in exchange. First, he asks Vaněk to introduce him to a famous Czech actress (Vaněk demurs), but, more important, he asks Vaněk himself to write the weekly reports concerning his supposed seditious activity that the Brewmaster is required to provide to the Czech secret police. For the Brewmaster, everything is clear. He is a self-described little man, oblivious to the politics that have gotten his new employee into trouble. He can help Vaněk and is happy to do so as long as Vaněk is willing to help him. But the dissident turned manual laborer refuses to live by the code of mutual favor giving that was the standard modus operandi of almost everyone in communist societies. His principles, he says, prevent him from taking any "part of a way of doing things that I don't agree with" (23). This principled refusal elicits an eloquent, profanity-laced, rejoinder from the Brewmaster, a speech that could well be seen as a foretaste of many Czechs' eventual attitude toward Havel:

> You, damn it! You intellectuals. VIPs! All that stuff's just smooth bullshit, except that you can afford it, because nothin' can ever happen to you, there's always somebody interested in how you doin', you always know how to fix that, you're

5. For a completely different view of the relationship between Havel's literary writing and his moral and political thought, see Pynsent, 1–43.
6. Havel, 1990, vii.

still up there, even when you're down and out, whereas a regular guy like me is bustin' his ass and ain't got shit to show for it and nobody will stick up for him and everybody just fucks him and everybody blows him off and everybody feels free to yell at him and he ain't got no life at all and in the end, the VIPs will say, hell. He ain't got no principles! A soft job in the warehouse, you'd take that from me—but to take a piece of that shit I gotta walk knee-deep in every damn day along with it, that you don't wanna! No way! (24)

The play ends ambiguously, with an almost exact repetition of the opening scene. It is not exact, however. In the beginning, when the Brewmaster offered Vaněk a beer the latter refused, thereby signaling his separation from the world of the brewery and the Brewmaster's concerns. At the end of the play Vaněk accepts the beer and repeats the Brewmaster's own line when asked about how things are going: "Everything's all fucked up" (26). That is, despite Vaněk's apparently successful effort to stick to his principles, he seems to be slowly and almost inevitably drawn into the world of the Brewmaster, a world in which lofty principles simply cannot be the only guiding light. This subtle shift must be recognized by the audience, because there is no narrator in the dramatic form. Presumably, the implied Czech audience members of the communist period, which would have consisted primarily of intellectuals like Vaněk, were meant to ask themselves what they would have done in this situation, whether it is preferable to stick to principles and thereby hurt a real person or, instead, to choose the path of compromise. In my reading, the drama implies that Vaněk has chosen compromise, but that choice in itself does not indicate whether we are to see his act in a positive or negative light.

Havel explored the dialectic between principles and compromise further in his 1986 play *Pokoušení* (*Temptation*). This work, based loosely on the Faust legend, lacks the ironic humor of *Audience* but it presents the basic dilemma even more starkly. Here the main character is Dr. Henry Foustka, who works as a scientist in a communist-era laboratory. Foustka is tempted by Fistula, a stand-in for Mephistopheles, who offers him both the love of a woman and occult knowledge. Although Foustka struggles for a while, the temptation to accept is too great and he gives in, all the while convincing himself that he has not. In the final scene of the play, he is publicly denounced by Fistula, not for giving in to temptation, but precisely for trying to compromise when compromise is impossible. As Fistula says to him, "You weren't a victim of my line, but of your own; or rather, of your pride, which made you think that you'd be able to play both ends against the middle and still get away with it!"[7]

It is tempting to see the overt and unambiguous rejection of compromise in this play (as opposed to the more ambivalent treatment of the subject in the earlier play *Audience*) in light of the development of Havel's political ideology, which he worked out between the suppression of the Prague Spring in 1968 and the fall of the Czechoslovak communist state in 1989, for it is based precisely on a definition of the dissident as he who will not compromise. This ideology is most powerfully expressed in Havel's celebrated 1979 essay "The Power of the Powerless." Here, Havel paints a stark vision of communist society as a system built on lies. Havel focuses his attention on a fictional manager of a produce store who hangs a sign saying "Workers of the World Unite" in his shop window. Havel asks why he does so. "I think it can be safely assumed that the overwhelming majority of shopkeepers never think about the slogans they put in their windows, nor do they do so to express their real opinions."[8] Rather, they go along because it is uncomfortable not to, because they see actions like hanging the sign as an innocent compromise, their personal Faustian bargain with the system, which will leave them alone in exchange for their tacit participation. The compromise is part of the ritual of agreeing to belong to an ideology that has a life of its own and in which no one believes. In Havel's memorable phrase the grocer is "living within a lie." And, significantly, in Havel's view not only grocers were living within a lie. Ritual mendacity went all the way up to the person of the prime minister, who was similarly constrained to lie and compromise, though he was considered by Havel to bear a higher level of responsibility for his lies. In contrast to the majority, the dissident, in Havel's worldview, made the choice "to live within the truth." Essentially, what this meant was a refusal to cooperate with the system, a refusal to compromise. Even, presumably, the small opening to the system that Vaněk makes in having a beer with the Brewmaster in *Audience* is not permitted.

This idea of principled refusal to compromise underlay the famous Charter 77 movement in Czechoslovakia. Charter 77, a document whose primary author was Havel, pointed out that the Czechoslovak government had signed on to various international treaties guaranteeing human rights but had not implemented their provisions. The signatories of Charter 77 complained specifically about the absence of freedom of expression,

7. Havel, 1989, 99.
8. Havel, 1985, 27

freedom of movement, and freedom of religion in the country, as well as the communist party's efforts to force conformity on Czechoslovak citizens. The document had primarily a moral character, and its goal was to convince Czechoslovak citizens to follow its signers in an effort to live within the truth. It was for his own uncompromising stand on these moral principles that Havel landed in prison between 1979 and 1983.

This long prison stay raised Havel's status to that of dissident number 1, not merely in Czechoslovakia, but all through the communist bloc. His status was confirmed by his rearrest and brief imprisonment in 1989. As his recent biographer puts it, "His early release from prison, for the last time, on May 17, 1989, consolidated his fame. The welcome-home party held in his honour was attended by everyone who counted in the opposition.... Those who believe the conventional story say that the warm welcome proved that he was now the unrivalled symbol of oppositional integrity, the personification of a principled life lived in the open, the good-looking man who had lost his fear, who always played clean and—despite shy protestations to the contrary—was good at politics."[9]

It is perhaps the case that much of this conventional story was true, but the last statement would definitely turn out to be questionable. And it was questionable for clear reasons. For if as a dissident fighting a quixotic battle against a monolithic state one could live by conviction and principle alone, in the real world of postcommunist democratic politics compromises of all kinds were inevitable. In his earlier dramatic work Havel treated such compromises ironically. In his high dissident days, in his public posture, his essays, and his drama, he presented moral issues in black-and-white terms. His tragedy, then, if tragedy it was, was to have staked out a public position that could not be realized when, after the Velvet Revolution, the world went from black-and-white to one consisting of many shades of gray.

The story of the end of communism and Havel's role in that process is well known, so I will not repeat it here.[10] For our purposes, it is necessary only to recall that, after a great deal of behind-the-scenes maneuvering, the parliament elected Havel president of the Czechoslovak Federation on December 29, 1989. In his New Year's address to the nation on January 1, 1990, he cited the example of the first president of independent Czechoslovakia, the legendary Tomáš Masaryk. "Masaryk based his politics on morality. Let us try, in a new time and in a new way, to restore this

9. Keane, 362.
10. See, for example, Garton Ash, 1990.

concept of politics."[11] This turned out to be a difficult promise to keep. In the words of Havel's biographer, "The Republican monarch soon had his first taste of the maxim that elected political men who get mixed up in state politics are strongly pressured into playing by its rules, which means they quickly learn the arts of manipulation, keeping matters secret, pulling strings, turning others' weaknesses into sources of strength, even turning themselves into devilish creatures who stop at nothing to get their ways."[12] As a playwright, Havel could control the actions of his characters. As a dissident, he had only his own actions to control. As a politician, he had an army of admirers and enemies who simply could not be controlled, even by a man with as much charisma and political capital as Havel.

As Keane puts it, "Havel's tactic [in his relation to the lustration controversy of 1991] revealed a subtle but important change in his presidency. He had evidently bidden farewell to his old noble habit of drawing black-and-white distinctions between 'truth' and 'lies.'"[13] There would be many more such compromises over the next decade. It is important to insist that there was nothing wrong with such compromises per se. Very rarely did anyone claim that Havel was compromising for nefarious reasons. However, precisely because he had set himself up as a paragon of uncompromising morality, and because he had insisted that under his rule politics was to be based not on practicality but on morality, these compromises seemed like hypocrisy. That is, they came to look more like the compromises of Foustka than those of Vaněk. Toward the end of his political career, however, Havel appears to have made his peace with the compromises that were necessary during his presidency. Thus, in a speech given at the City University of New York on September 19, 2002, he spoke at first of what he had learned from his political odyssey. "I've discovered an astonishing thing: although it might be expected that this wealth of experience would have given me more and more self-assurance, confidence, and polish, the exact opposite is true. In that time, I have become a good deal less sure of myself, a good deal more humble. You may not believe this, but every day I suffer more and more from stage fright; every day, I am more afraid

11. Havel, 1997, 7.
12. Keane, 410
13. Ibid., 436. Lustration was the process whereby those who had benefited from the former regime were to be barred from public positions in the new. Havel attempted to avoid a radical lustration of former communists, arguing essentially that all had been guilty of collaboration with the regime to some extent and that, therefore, only the most egregious offenders should be barred from office.

that I won't be up to the job, or that I'll make a hash of it."[14] Yet after this Hamlet-like moment of self-doubt, Havel continued: "Please understand me: I'm not saying at all that I have lost my fight, or that everything has been in vain." In this same speech, Havel spoke of hearing others talk about his life as if it were that of a fairy-tale hero, but also about his recognition that humanity cannot rely any longer on the simplicity of fairy tales. Perhaps, in the end, Vaněk was correct. Havel's best work and the most difficult parts of his life teach that while principles are necessary, tactical compromise is equally important if one is to avoid living in a fairy tale. The only tragedy, in this view, was one of expectations, both on the part of Havel and on the part of some Czechs. It is my guess that in time the Czechs will get over theirs as Havel seems to have gotten over his.

Dobrica Ćosić: King Lear of Serbia

The story of Dobrica Ćosić seems to elicit literary images. According to Nebojša Popov, a former classmate of Slobodan Milošević, the relationship between Ćosić and Milošević was that of Faust and Mephistopheles.[15] To my mind, however, the appropriate literary analogue is not Goethe's poem but rather Shakespeare's *King Lear* or Mary Shelley's *Frankenstein*. Ćosić, the ideological godfather of modern Serbian nationalism, reached the office of president of Yugoslavia in 1992 at the behest of Slobodan Milošević. But by 1993, after having realized that he had created a monster, he attempted to check the worst excesses of Serbian nationalism and was deposed by the very nationalist forces he had helped to create. In so doing, he repeated the actions of the literary characters with whom he most sympathized, idealists who attempt to nurture unity among Serbs but who are doomed to failure by the tendency of Yugoslavs in general and Serbs in particular to betrayal and fragmentation.

Ćosić first became known as the author of the classic partisan novel *Daleko je sunce (Far Away Is the Sun)*.[16] By the early 1960s, however, he gradually became convinced that the Yugoslav Communist Party's policy of "brotherhood and unity" among the various peoples of Yugoslavia was leading not to the creation of a Yugoslav nation but rather to the rise of

14. Havel, 2002, 1.
15. Doder and Branson, 35.
16. For a short summary of Ćosić's literary career, see Segel, 114–116.

nationalist movements in the other Yugoslav republics. In a famous article of January 1961 he railed against the specter of "vampire nationalisms" and claimed there would always be obstacles to significant international (within Yugoslavia, that is) mixing "as long as the republics existed."[17] This statement provoked a caustic response from the Slovenian critic Dušan Pirjevec, who accused Ćosić of noticing separatist nationalisms but of ignoring tendencies toward a restoration of a form of forced unitarism that would inevitably have Serbian hegemonic overtones.[18] In Ćosić's long rejoinder, an article entitled "O savremenom nesavremenom nacionalizmu" (On modern unmodern nationalism), the author strenuously denied the charges that he was in favor of a forced unitarist culture or of great Serbian nationalism; rather, he claimed that his view was absolutely in keeping with the founding ideals of the postwar state, which saw the separate republics not as ends in themselves, but as means toward the creation of a single socialist Yugoslav culture.[19] According to one historian who has worked with the archival material relating to this polemic, Ćosić's position was supported by conservative Serbian political heavyweights Jovan Veselinov and Aleksandar Ranković, as well as by Tito himself, while Pirjevec's theses had the approval of, and even benefited from emendations made by, Boris Kraigher, the most powerful political figure in Slovenia.[20] If this is true, the Ćosić-Pirjevec debate can be seen as a kind of culturo-political proxy fight. It reopened the Pandora's box to which discussion of nationalism in Yugoslavia had been confined, and that box proved impossible to close.

By the late 1960s, having become convinced that the Yugoslav communist project was a dead letter, Ćosić's cultural politics became overtly Serbophilic. Indeed, by 1968, he broke with the Yugoslav League of Communists after his outspoken criticism of government policy regarding Kosovo. He claimed (with some truth) that Serbs and Montenegrins were being pushed by the Albanian majority to emigrate from Kosovo, and that the party had failed to take account of the "chauvinist bent and nationalist psychosis among the members of the Skipetar [Albanian] nationality."[21]

---

17. Ćosić's article appeared in *Telegram*, 39 (Jan. 10, 1961); quoted in Peković, 301.

18. Pirjevec's article appeared in the Slovenian periodical *Naša sodobnost*, 3 (1961).

19. Ćosić, "O savremenom nesavremenom nacionalizmu," in *Sabrana dela*, vol. 8, 17–46. He made an even stronger statement against Serbian nationalism in 1965, in a speech entitled "O civilizaciji, naciji, i drugom," in *Sabrana dela*, vol. 8, 186–200.

20. Gabrič, 345.

21. Quoted in Banac, 148.

By 1969, he had taken on the position of president of the Serbian Literary Guild (Srpska književna zadruga). As Nicholas Miller puts it, "Ćosić's move had important institutional connotations: he had now begun to refocus his efforts, switching from the Yugoslav context, where he had concluded that the dream of integration had failed, to the Serbian context, where the task was parallel, but narrowed. Now, under his leadership, the Serbian Literary Guild would contribute to the integration of the Serbian people, wherever it lived."[22] In particular, the Serbs whom Ćosić took on as his personal flock were those of Kosovo.

Although this new phase in Ćosić's career might lead one to believe that the critics who had lambasted his earlier Yugoslavism as nothing more than a mask for Serbian hegemony had been correct, I am not inclined to think so. To be sure, he had undoubtedly always had a soft spot in his heart for a certain populist romanticism, but there is no reason to disbelieve his strenuous denials when he had been attacked for Serbian nationalism. Instead, I believe that by the late 1960s Ćosić came to recognize that the government had indeed truly abandoned its earlier Yugoslav policy in favor of a multinational federalism. This betrayal, as Ćosić must have seen it, completely changed the political and national equation in Yugoslavia and led him to conclude that the Serbs would have to assert their national rights if they did not wish to become second-class citizens in their own country.[23]

Ćosić remained a vocal figure on the Serbian cultural and political scene through the 1970s and 1980s. In particular, he became notorious as the instigator of a draft "Memorandum" sponsored by the Serbian Academy of Arts and Sciences devoted to the crisis of Yugoslavia. Although the "Memorandum" was ostensibly written to find a way to preserve the integrity of Yugoslavia, its authors spent much of the document alleging that Tito's Yugoslavia had discriminated against Serbs in a variety of ways, supposedly permitting Serbia's economic subjugation to Croatia and Slovenia, as well as allowing the "genocide" perpetrated by the Albanians against

22. Miller, 1999, 522–523.
23. Because of the way Yugoslavia was divided, Serbs had the most to lose were the country to break up on republican lines. As opposed to other national groups, most of which lived overwhelmingly on the territory of their republics, Serbs were spread over many republics, forming sizable minorities in Croatia and Bosnia-Herzegovina. Thus, Serbs could all live in the same country only were Yugoslavia to continue to exist, unless of course they attempted to secede with their territories in the event of a breakup. The latter, of course, is precisely what happened in the early 1990s.

the Serbs of Kosovo.[24] There is some question about how direct a role Ćosić played in the composition of the "Memorandum," but its obsessive concern with the position of the Serbian nation in general and the Kosovo question in particular marks his hand, and it is probably correct to assign him the credit (or blame) for the anonymous document's overall thrust.[25]

As Slobodan Milošević rose gradually to power in Serbia, it appears that Ćosić at first did not know how to react. Even in the late 1980s, he was quoted as saying: "Milošević's intentions remain a big question. Is this present victor a democratic reformer or a new political chief who threatens to draw upon the conservative essence of the League of Communists and a deluded and desperate [Serbian] people? I'm not acquainted with him. We will see."[26] By 1991, however, any doubts had been erased. In an interview in that year he averred: "Compared to all Serbian politicians over the last five decades I am confident that Slobodan Milošević has done the most for the Serbian people. His general national policy, strategy and tactics, I consider realist and courageous."[27]

As a reward for his longtime services to the Serbian cause and his supposed loyalty to Milošević's policies, Ćosić was appointed president of what remained of Yugoslavia on June 15, 1992 by the parliament. Thus, like Havel in Czechoslovakia and Göncz in Hungary, a writer assumed what was officially the highest political office in the land. In none of these nations, however, did the president wield much power. "Under the constitution of Milošević's Yugoslavia, the federal presidency was a largely ceremonial job, but with important residual powers: the president was commander in chief of the armed forces. The office of prime minister was given greater responsibility for the conduct of foreign, fiscal, and economic policy. Milošević's built-in insurance policy was the provision that both the president and the prime minister were elected by the parliament, which was dominated by men who served Milošević."[28]

---

24. The *Memorandum* itself was not officially published at this time, but a leaked copy was published in September 1986, and it circulated broadly. For an analysis of the document, see Nenad Dimitrijević, "Words and Death: Serbian Nationalist Intellectuals," in Bozóki, 128–131.

25. Thus, Lenard Cohen says that Ćosić "only participated indirectly in the process of writing the document" (72). However, Eric Gordy notes that Ćosić "is generally assumed to be the principal author of the 1986 *Memorandum*" (126).

26. Quoted in Cohen, 73.

27. Quoted in Cohen, 164.

28. Doder and Branson, 131.

Nevertheless, Ćosić attempted to assert himself despite the weakness of his position and his own political inexperience. He allied himself with the premier, the colorful former émigré Milan Panić, in attempts to strengthen the power of the federal state vis-á-vis the Republic of Serbia. In the end, however, these efforts failed completely, and on May 31, 1993, Ćosić was removed from office by the same parliament that had acclaimed him less than a year before. Since his ignominious departure from the political scene, Ćosić has cultivated an image of dignified semisilence befitting the eminence grise of the Serbian nation. As Nicholas Miller has noticed pointedly, when Ćosić is asked about politics, as he was by a reporter in 1996, he demurs, "claiming simply, 'I am a writer!' as though the burdensome task begged the empathy of outsiders and also protected him from the sort of scrutiny reserved for political figures."[29] In 2000, however, he called directly on Yugoslav voters to support Vojislav Koštunica against Milošević, not because of the latter's crimes but rather because under his rule "our beautiful country is neglected and soiled."[30] Whether, like King Lear, Ćosić will be willing at the very end of his life to recognize in a public way his own central role in creating the monster of Serbian nationalism remains to be seen.

However, it is worth recognizing that Ćosić's own political trajectory is quite closely connected to that of the novelistic heroes with whom he appears to sympathize. According to Nicholas Miller, in Ćosić's view "his Serbian people, treacherous at heart, are plagued by a tendency to betray and kill one another. They are fratricidal."[31] At the same time, Serbs are also seen as a special people, chosen by God and marked by a love of and an ability to suffer for freedom. As the narrator of Ćosić's World War I epic *A Time of Death* avers in a Tolstoyan aside, "A long time ago the powerful Austro-Hungarian Empire resolved to crush the small nation of Serbia, a freedom-loving democratic country."[32] They are also boundless idealists, ready and willing to sacrifice themselves naively for their brothers, be they allies, Yugoslavs in general, or other Serbs: "At Valjevo we gave our lives for Paris and the French; on the Kolubara we defended the Dardenelles for the English; at Milovac we shed our blood

29. Miller, 2000, 274–275.

30. "Ex-Yugoslav President Blames Milosevic, West for Serb 'Decline,'" UPI, Sept. 11, 2000, http://web5.infotrac.galegroup.com/itw/infomark/453/635/31934772w5.

31. Miller, 2000, 268.

32. Ćosić, 1983, 99.

for the Russians and the Ukraine. And on Bačinac we've perished at the hands of our Croatian brothers, giving our lives for their freedom."[33] But this sacrifice goes for naught, because their leaders never understand that they must think of Serbs first and foremost. As one character with whom the author clearly sympathizes argues describing the probable outcome of World War I, "What I'm afraid of, my boy, is that we'll win the war as planned by Pašić and our politicians, by professors and their students. Have you read in the newspapers about us uniting with the Croats and Slovenes? I mean that declaration of the Assembly about the creation of a large state consisting of Serbs, Croats, and Slovenes? Three separate faiths, estranged by fire and sword, and divided by blood—but now they're to be combined in a single state! What louse or reptile shot this poison—this death-dealing sickness—into Serbian heads?"[34]

Ćosić, we may say, played the political role of a Serb as he had defined the breed. In his attempt to rescue his people from the "vampire nationalisms" of the other Yugoslav nations, he naively decided to trust in his own kin, his spiritual son Slobodan Milošević. Milošević, however, quickly displayed the fratricidal (or parricidal, as the case may be) tendencies that are the flip side of the Serbian coin as Ćosić has described them, and in so doing led to Ćosić's political demise and to the degradation of the nation as a whole.

Eduard Limonov: Politics as Farce

Eduard Limonov was born Eduard Veniaminovich Savenko in Dzerzhinsk in 1943. He spent his youth in Kharkov, where his father was an officer in the local KGB. A rebel all his life, he says that between the ages of fifteen and twenty-one "[I was] a real criminal, breaking into stores and apartments. I stopped only when my close friend Konstantin B. was arrested and sentenced to death."[35] In 1967, he moved to Moscow, where he rapidly made a name for himself among nonofficial poets and writers. A glance at the poetry from that period published subsequently in emigration indicates just how restrictive the Soviet postthaw censorship had become, for there is nothing in either form or content that is particularly

---

33. Ibid., 125.
34. Ćosić, 1980, 344.
35. Flyleaf of *Eto ia, Edichka* (Limonov, 1982).

dissident. Rather, most of his work is quite lyrical and, other than a youth-
ful restlessness and arrogance, lacks any hint of an oppositionist political
stance.

Having broken with the shadows of his family
Why does he run from his homeland

Why doesn't he just head to the store with a shopping bag
Strolling unhurriedly
A genius among dolts?
But then his soul would fall silent.[36]

Nevertheless, as he was not willing to let his soul fall silent in the years
of Brezhnevian stagnation, Limonov took the opportunity to leave the
USSR when it was offered in 1974. He himself, however, has said: "I was
never a dissident.... I never expressed any opposition to the politics of
the USSR or against its ideology. I simply struggled for the expansion of
artistic freedom."[37]

There is some evidence that Limonov expected to be welcomed as a
kind of savior in the West, at least if his poem "My—natsionalnyi geroi"
(We are the national hero) published only in 1977 but written earlier, can
be taken as evidence of the author's own point of view. Here, Limonov
imagines the ecstatic reception that he and his wife, the Moscow poet Elena
Shchapova, will receive in the West. By 1975, having failed to make much of
an impression in the "free world," Limonov was living in New York, where
he developed a deep revulsion to the American way of life. Unlike such
dissidents as Solzhenitsyn, however, who walled themselves off from day-
to-day life in the United States and whose distaste for American civilization
was based more on theoretical than observational grounds, Limonov lived
among the poor Russian and other émigrés of New York, and he frequently
and brilliantly wrote about that life in his pseudoautobiographical novels
and stories.

One could define Limonov's entire literary output is an exercise in
self-fashioning. A Limonov alter ego, generally called Edichka, appears
as the main character in much of his work, some of which is narrated
in the first person, and some in the third. It is impossible and unnecessary to know whether all the descriptions in the novels and stories are in

36. Limonov, 1979, 181.
37. As quoted in an interview in the newspaper *Trud,* Mar. 23, 1996. Excerpted on the
Web site http://imperium.lenin.ru/~verbit/Limonov/nns-limonov.html.

fact autobiographical, but there is no question that readers are meant to see the whole package as a portrait of the artist as the hero of an ongoing story. That is, Limonov's central topic is the creation of himself as a larger-than-life hero. His self-image is that of an iconoclast, a rebel with or without a cause, and a misunderstood genius. In the Soviet Union, that hero could be an antiestablishment bohemian. In the United States, he was an individualistic Russian who refused to succumb to the blandishments of Western-style capitalism. Until the beginning of the 1990s, readers could easily imagine that this was merely Limonov's literary persona, and that some other Limonov must be hiding behind it. However, events of the past decade would seem to indicate that, perhaps unfortunately, Limonov took this posing seriously, and that, indeed, his exceptional literary talent was, in his own view, of no importance compared to his true, political vocation.

Limonov achieved lasting notoriety among Russian readers with the publication of his pseudoautobiography *Eto ia, Edichka* in New York in 1979. The book opens with a stunning scene of a half-naked Edichka sitting on the balcony of his cheap, long-term, sixteenth-floor hotel room in Manhattan cooking cabbage soup and musing on himself and his own unrecognized genius, the venality and stupidity of Americans, and the disappointment of a Russian émigré (and through him of all Russian émigrés) with American life. The tone is raw, the language a brilliant idiolect of Americanized Russian, and the book seems precisely designed to be as scandalous as possible. Russian émigré readers were horrified by its negativity and ingratitude toward the United States, its frank portrayal of the narrator's or author's (Russian readers are traditionally not willing to separate one from the other) bisexuality, and the implication that in escaping the USSR they had merely exchanged one form of exploitation for another. As Edward J. Brown put it, "He is estranged as a down-and-outer even among the émigrés. He hasn't made it in American life. Not only has he not landed a job as poet-in-residence anywhere but the best job he could get was that of busboy, in a high-class hotel it is true. He speaks for the down-and-out but speaks with a Russian voice in Russian, and as he does so he remembers how it was to be down and out and rejected in Moscow too. One hears in that book the authentic voice of those on the bottom who very seriously hate those who have made it, whether here in our own dear land, or at home in Russia."[38] This raw hatred of those who have made it (in the Soviet, American, or post-Soviet Russian establishment)

38. Edward J. Brown, 353.

characterizes both Limonov's life and work, and helps to explain the extreme political position he would eventually espouse in post-Soviet Russia. (See figure 4.)

Limonov's literary career continued with a string of novels and stories, two set in his native Ukraine (including his masterpiece, *Podrostok Savenko* [Adolescent Savenko], from 1983), and others set in the United States and Europe. A few were translated into English, but perhaps not surprisingly, given his negative view of the United States, he never became as well known as some other émigré novelists. He did, however, make an impact in France, where he became a citizen in 1987, after which he began to spend the majority of his time in Europe. After the collapse of the USSR, however, Limonov became more and more active in the political life of postcommunist Russia.

As was the case with *Eddie*, what is most striking in the Kharkov-based autobiographical novels is the extravagant, epic, and theatrical nature of the self that Limonov projects. Limonov's persona is Mayakovskian in his grandeur and conceit. What is important, what is foregrounded is the transgressive, and this is flouted as publicly as possible. As Patricia Carden noted in an insightful essay on Limonov's Kharkov novels, "At fifteen he prides himself that 'he has fucked them all over,' that he has established his specialness and his dominance."[39]

His motivations for turning from literary work to politics are worth considering. Limonov's own public view, as expressed in interviews, is that the switch was not surprising. "Political work is the natural continuation of what I did when I was a writer. The writing of pamphlets and revolutionary articles provides just as much passionate pleasure as I once got writing poetry. Then and now I serve Russia. Don't forget, my first book of poems was called 'Russianness.'"[40] His claim, then, is that in the days of the Soviet Union the best way to serve his country was as a writer of literature, but in conditions of postcommunism direct political action is more necessary and appropriate. Less sympathetic observers agree that Limonov's post-Soviet political adventure is in a sense a natural continuation of his earlier work, but they view the work in progress in more personal and less altruistic terms. Thus, Evgeny Bunimovich, a Moscow Duma deputy and poet, said in a 1999 interview: "Limonov is connected not to the creation of a Russian national idea, but to the creation of a personal literary myth. That's correct

39. Patricia Carden, "Eduard Limonov's Kharkov Cycle," in Harris, 236–237.
40. http://imperium.lenin.ru/~verbit/Limonov/interv-limonov.html.

FIGURE 4. *Top*, Eduard Limonov in 1976, at about the time that *Edichka* was published. Despite the prominent cross in this picture, there is no evidence that Limonov has ever been religious. (Photograph by Lenka Lubianskii.) *Center*, Limonov with the notorious Serbian paramilitary leader Arkan in Vukovar, November 1991. *Bottom*, Limonov near Knin, Croatia, spring 1993. The region was held by Serbian paramilitary forces before they were driven out by the Croatian army in 1995. (All photographs from the Web site http://imperium.lenin.ru/~verbit/Limonov/foto.html.)

because [for] an artistic type like Limonov, for whom personal life is a sort of artistic research, that is natural."[41] An even more cynical observer might suspect that, given the falling visibility of literature in postcommunist times, the switch to politics was motivated first and foremost by Limonov's ongoing desire to be in the public eye, to be a hero, and to shock. This desire, one might guess, was one of the motivations for taking up the most extreme positions he could find, regardless of whether they had the support of a significant portion of the population. The uncalculating nature of Limonov's politics can be gauged by his abject failure at the ballot box, where, for example, he received exactly 1.84% of the votes case for a seat in the State Duma in the 1995 elections.

It took a while for Limonov to find his place in political life. Rather than beginning immediately, he edged into politics through journalism. As he puts it in his 2002 "political biography," the goal of his immediate post-Soviet articles was "to explain to my compatriots that they were insane and that they should stop the insanity. That European prosperity had been achieved gradually, over hundreds of years, at the cost of the pitiless exploitation of colonies. That projects like 'Five Hundred Days' were completely unrealistic."[42] At the same time he began to travel to Russia, and he renewed his Russian citizenship in 1992. From the beginning, he sided with Russian nationalist political forces, at first joining Vladimir Zhirinovsky's Liberal-Democratic Party, where for a time he was announced as a member of its shadow cabinet. Quite quickly, however, he fell out with Zhirinovsky and attempted to form his own party. He burnished his credentials as a defender of Russia's historical interests by traveling to the former Yugoslavia where he had himself photographed with Bosnian Serb forces in a variety of warlike poses.

In 1994, after returning once again to Russia, he became one of the founders of the National Bolshevik Party. The party's program, couched in highly inflammatory rhetoric, can be characterized as communitarian, conservative, authoritarian, and nationalist, a mix of fascist and communist ideologies. The preamble announces that "essence of National-bolshevism is the incinerating hatred to antihuman SYSTEM of the trinity: liberalism/democracy/capitalism," and it promises to construct a "traditionalistic, hierarchical community."[43] This will be realized in an empire that stretches

---

41. *Russia Journal*, June 14, 1999. as published on the Web at http://www.therussiajournal.com/index.htm?obj=324.

42. Limonov, 2002, 19. The "Five Hundred Days" project was touted by the early shock therapy economists as a quick fix for the economic problems of the country.

43. http://www.nbp-info.org/party/programm.htm.

"from Vladivostok up to Gibraltar" constructed "on the basis of Russian civilization." The party's economic policy is one of strict economic autarchy. Within the country the NBP promises to realize the Soviet ideals of collective ownership of all the major means of production, along with guaranteed minimum living standards.

Limonov's own heroes are a curious amalgam of Russian conservatives like Konstantin Leontiev, anarchists such as Mikhail Bakunin, and leftists such as Lenin. Describing the men and women who joined the party, Limonov writes: "You are young. You are disgusted by the Russia of priests, moneybags, and the KGB. You experience a feeling of protest, your heroes are Che, or Mussolini, or Lenin, or Baader, or even Timothy McVeigh (he got his revenge on the system!), you are a nats-bol."[44] The only trace of the irony and humor that once characterized Limonov's literary work is the National Bolshevik Party symbol, an apparently about-to-explode grenade of a type called *limonka* (little lemon) in Russian, which is simultaneously a play on the author's literary pseudonym. This symbol also gives its name to the party newspaper, which will be discussed in chapter 6 of this book.

When Limonov first entered politics, it is safe to say that many saw his engagement as a kind of stunt, the actions of a publicity-seeking writer who could no longer attract attention through his literary work. Limonov's fate since Vladimir Putin took over as President of Russia indicates that, whatever his initial motivations, he has come to take himself seriously, at least if a willingness to suffer for the cause can be understood as seriousness of purpose. Limonov and his party had already run into a certain amount of legal hot water during the later years of Boris Yeltsin's presidential term. Thus, in 1996 his newspaper was accused of fanning hatred against various nations, which is a crime in Russia. Much more serious, however, were the accusations brought against Limonov in October 2001, when he was arrested and accused of "organizing an illegal armed formation." On February 3, 2003 (the wheels of justice in Russia turn slowly), in Saratov District Court, Limonov was found guilty of most of the charges brought against him and the state prosecutor recommended a fourteen-year prison sentence for the writer turned politician.[45] According to the

44. Limonov, 2002, 240.

45. Upon his release from prison, Limonov wrote a nonfiction memoir devoted to his experiences (Limonov, 2004). Although Limonov attempts to write himself into the grand tradition of Russian prison narratives that stretches from Dostoevsky's *Notes from the House of the Dead* to Solzhenitsyn's *Gulag Archipelago*, the memoir succeeds only as an anti-Putin screed and lacks any literary value.

RFE/RL Newsline, in a subsequent interview with a Saratov television station, "Limonov said that he is being prosecuted in the same way as the nineteenth-century writer Nikolai Chernyshevskii. 'After Soviet power, after 70 years of the dictatorship of the proletariat, we see that our valiant special services have turned to the methods of 140 years ago and the time of Chernyshevskii.'"[46] Perhaps Limonov's invocation of the famous Russian radical novelist and literary critic is an indication that he will eventually return to literature. Whether or not he chooses that path, he has certainly come to understand that one difference between literature and politics is that powerful enemies in the latter sphere have far more power than those of the former. Limonov's case, then, illustrates the high risks of attempting to transpose a literary mode of being directly into a political one, and his fate indicates that farce can indeed turn into tragedy.[47]

As was the case with both Havel and Ćosić, Limonov behaved in political life precisely as if he were a character in one of his novels. Although on the surface he did what anyone who wishes to engage in democratic politics would do—organize a political party, develop a platform, attempt to attract supporters and voters—in the end the need to be an iconoclastic hero who could be appreciated only by himself led him to adopt a political platform that was unacceptable both to voters and the state in a fledgling democracy such as Russia. Patricia Carden notes that Limonov's "autobiographical hero fit easily into a European conception of the *poet maudit*, and indeed it was clear from the book [*Eddie*] that Limonov conceived himself in a romantic tradition fed by these very legends."[48] In literature, however, there is always a loophole. Although any reader can tell that Limonov's books are autobiographical in nature, they are not actually autobiographies, and they make no truth claims. The author can always hide behind the persona. In the world of political statements, rhetoric, however extravagant, adheres to the writer. Eventually, Limonov would be tried and convicted primarily on the basis of the words he wrote in his newspaper *Limonka*. In the interview he gave after his conviction, it is clear that he is outraged by this, and he compares his trial and sentencing to that of Chernyshevsky in the nineteenth century. Like Havel, what he fails to appreciate fully is that in the world of politics a distanced irony from

46. *RFE/RL Newsline*, vol. 7, no. 23, pt. 1, Feb. 5, 2003, http://www.rferl.org/newsline.
47. Limonov was released from prison in June 2003, having served almost two years of his sentence.
48. Carden, "Eduard Limonov's Kharkov Cycle," 227.

one's own words is impossible. The inflammatory statements of Limonov the politician are his statements, and he can be held responsible for them in a way that his narrators could not.

While one hesitates to draw grand conclusions on the basis of three cases, it is nevertheless tempting to speculate on why writers turned politicians tend to behave as if they were characters in their own literary works. To some extent, of course, it is natural to expect an author to identify with his heroes. In Eastern Europe, however, I suspect that this tendency is strongly supported by an unwillingness to accept the separation between life and literature that is generally acknowledged in the West. Thus, for example, in nineteenth-century Russian criticism, it was almost always assumed that literary characters should be judged as if they were real-life figures, and authors have historically been held accountable for the actions of their characters in a way that American and West European writers have not. In this environment it appears that writers also have a tendency to identify even more strongly with their characters, and to blur thereby the lines between art and life. When, as was the case in the 1990s, they have the opportunity to enter "the real world," they may well imagine it and themselves as extensions of the literary worlds they have created in the past. In any event, that appears to be the case with the writers we have considered here, for good or for ill.

CHAPTER FOUR

Writers and Nationalism

The issue of nationalism and literature in postcommunist Eastern
Europe is extremely complex, primarily because the term *nationalism*
can be used to cover an extraordinarily broad range of phenomena. Secondarily, there is the problem of how and under what circumstances nationalism was expressed in the literatures of Eastern Europe even before the end
of communism. I begin by focusing on the surprising strength of nationalist
thought in Eastern Europe under communism, surprising because according to Marxist theory nationalist sentiment was closely related to bourgeois
capitalism and should have begun to disappear after the introduction of
socialism. As Ronald Suny puts it, "Marxists long maintained that modern
nations resulted from the capitalist mode of production—that they were, in
fact, so dependent on it that with the end of capitalism, nations themselves
would begin to disappear. Marxists rejected the nationalist legitimation of
independent nations-states constituted on the basis of ethnicity, claiming
that nations were neither natural nor eternal and that priority must be given
to class as the foundation of a future nationless society."[1]

Nevertheless, from the earliest attempts to put communism in practice
it became clear that at least in the present, nationalism was not going
to be overcome easily in the Soviet Union. Nor did the tension between
nationalism and internationalism lessen when other countries joined (or
were joined to) the communist fold in the aftermath of World War II.
Although there was some discussion of Bulgaria's becoming a sixteenth
republic of the Soviet Union, as well as plans for a Balkan federation that
would have joined Albania to Yugoslavia, in the end the postwar map of
Europe featured the same patchwork of small nation states that had existed

1. Suny, 4.

in interwar Europe (albeit with many of their borders altered and with the exception of Estonia, Latvia, and Lithuania, annexed by the USSR as part of the 1939 Ribbentrop-Molotov pact).

In each of the communist countries of Eastern Europe, there was a clearly dominant national group, but all contained minority populations of varying sizes.[2] The official policy toward these minorities was one of tolerance. However, the local communist leadership was generally drawn heavily from the majority population, and they often played the nationalist card when they felt a need to garner the legitimacy that communism failed to provide. In response, minority groups tended to develop ever more strongly their own national identities, putting themselves at odds with the majority population. As a result, as Walter A. Kemp puts it, "by the time of its collapse, communism as an ideology had long since been discredited—in large part due to its inability to come to terms with nationalism. Communism as a political system had now also broken down, in large measure for the very same reason. In short, the fostering of internationalism had been a part of the communist design; ironically, communism's failure to cope with nations and nationalism contributed to the strains under which it withered away."[3]

As was the case with many other truths that could not be spoken aloud in Eastern Europe, nationalist thought under communism was rarely expressed in political discourse. Instead, it tended to appear in literary works. But because many communist governments tacitly did not oppose nationalism, writers could pursue nationalist writing.

There can be a variety of ideas about what it might mean to write a "nationalist" literary work. Most Americans tend to equate nationalism with chauvinism and therefore see it as a purely negative phenomenon. And certainly, given the damage that has been caused in Eastern Europe, particularly in the former Yugoslavia, by chauvinistic nationalism, such a view might be shared widely in the region as well. Nevertheless, given the history of East European literature, particularly its role in building national consciousness in the first place (outlined in chapter 1 of this book), it would be a mistake to limit a discussion of writing and nationalism to

2. The percentage of minority inhabitants varied widely. Hungary, for example was close to 97% Hungarian, but minorities in Bulgaria made up some 25% of the total population. The situation was more complex in avowedly multinational states such as Yugoslavia and the Soviet Union. There, minorities were relevant at the republican rather than the federal level, and percentages again varied considerably.

3. Kemp, 206.

those works that employ a discussion of a given nation in such a way
as to denigrate or vilify neighboring nations (i.e., in a chauvinistic way).
A more plausible and broader definition, one more in keeping with the
way nationalist writing has historically been understood in the region,
would encompass any literary work that attempts to define a given nation's
particularity, be that in the realm of national history, destiny, or "soul." Such
a work attempts to imbue its readers (at least those belonging to its initial
target audience) with a feeling of belonging to the nation described in the
text. It thereby simultaneously (and in varying combinations) describes
an existing phenomenon and creates it. To be sure, a work of this kind
will by implication exclude those who do not possess the same history,
destiny, or "soul." But as these peculiarities can be defined in a number of
ways, this does not automatically mean that nationalist literature is a coded
form of chauvinism. To adduce a fairly uncontroversial nineteenth-century
example, Lev Tolstoy's *War and Peace* is a nationalist work insofar as it
aims to define the essence of the Russian national character (personified
in General Kutuzov) and to show that this character allowed Russia to
defeat Napoleon. At the same time, Tolstoy provides a reasonably nuanced
picture of both the French enemy and the Russians themselves, so it would
be incorrect to assert that his novel is a chauvinistic work.

Already by the late 1960s in Russia, and in the 1970s in various Yugoslav republics, Romania, and Bulgaria, we can speak of the existence of
nationalist literature of this type in the context of communist states.[4] By the
1980s one could find a wide range of nationalist works, including overtly
chauvinistic ones, in many East European countries. Interestingly enough,
however, in the 1990s, the period of primary interest to us, chauvinistic
national discourse was not very important in literature. Instead, taking
advantage of the new possibilities afforded by democratizing states, nationalists tended to migrate from literature directly into politics and into
journalism (see chapters 3 and 6 for more on this). Nevertheless, literary works espousing chauvinistic points of view could still be found, and
discourse about the nation and its particularities, that is, nonchauvinist
nationalist discourse, turned up in some surprising places.

As an example of nonchauvinist nationalist literature in the period before the collapse of communism one could look at the oeuvre of Danilo Kiš.

---

4. The best-studied literary nationalism under communism is that of Russia. See Brudny,
for example. On literature and nationalism in communist-era Yugoslavia see Wachtel, *Making
a Nation*, 1998.

Half Hungarian and half Montenegrin, Kiš was vocally opposed to ethnic nationalism.[5] The central goal of his fictional work is to account for what in Kiš's view were the two great evils of the twentieth century—Nazism and communism. Precisely because Yugoslavia prided itself on its antifascist resistance, when Kiš's fiction focused on the former—the novel *Hourglass* being the most powerful example—Yugoslav critics and political actors welcomed it. But his *A Tomb for Boris Davidovich* (subtitled *Seven Chapters from a Single Story*) caused an enormous uproar when it was published in Yugoslavia in 1975, even though it contains not a single Yugoslav character and none of the stories is set in Yugoslavia. Kiš's critics, however, understood that this fictional work was precisely about Yugoslavia, although they did not generally say so openly (preferring to attack the work on other grounds). As the author noted, "I wrote in a country with certain manifestations of Stalinism, which I have seen and experienced myself. When I wrote *A Tomb for Boris Davidovich*, I was convinced that such a book would not be received in Yugoslavia without problems. And I was not mistaken."[6] Indeed, without presenting Yugoslav characters, it was seen, for good or for ill depending on who was reading it, to tell the true story of Yugoslavia's experience with communism and to show, despite the claims of the government, that Yugoslavia's history had not differed from that of other East European countries, marked as they all were in the twentieth century by the twin traumas of fascism and communism. In this sense, Kiš was attempting precisely to define the essence of the Yugoslav nation of which he felt himself part, and to connect the experience of that nation to that of others in the region.[7]

Elsewhere in Eastern Europe as well, painful truths about the nation's past could often be treated only by writers of literature, and not by journalists or historians. Thus, although 2002 Nobel laureate Imre Kertész emphasizes the universal message of his novels, many have asserted that at least part of his contribution was to force communist-era Hungary to

5. In his most famous attack on chauvinist nationalism Kiš said: "Nationalism lives by relativism. There are no general values—aesthetic, ethical, etc. Only relative ones. And it is principally in this sense that nationalism is reactionary. *All* that matters is to be better than my brother or half-brother, the rest is no concern of mine." Kiš, "On Nationalism," in Ali and Lifschultz, 127–128. This text was originally published in 1973 and widely commented on in Yugoslavia.

6. Quoted in Mihailovich, 172.

7. The book's direct relationship to Yugoslavia could be seen in the dedication of the first story in the collection to Karlo Štayner, a Yugoslav who had spent many years in the Siberian camps and whose autobiography, *7000 Days in Siberia*, was a major source for Kiš.

confront the reality of the Hungarian Jewish experience during World
War II, a topic that was more or less taboo until the publication of Kertész's
work. Even in his Nobel speech, Kertész insisted on the particular importance of his Hungarianness, implicitly forcing together Jewishness and
Hungarianness in a way that chauvinistic Hungarian nationalists would
certainly not accept: "It makes me especially happy to be expressing these
thoughts in my native language: Hungarian. I was born in Budapest, in a
Jewish family, whose maternal branch hailed from the Transylvanian city
of Kolozsvár (Cluj) and the paternal side from the southwestern corner
of the Lake Balaton region. My grandparents still lit the Sabbath candles
every Friday night, but they changed their name to a Hungarian one, and it
was natural for them to consider Judaism their religion and Hungary their
homeland. My maternal grandparents perished in the Holocaust; my paternal grandparents' lives were destroyed by Mátyás Rákosi's Communist
rule, when Budapest's Jewish old age home was relocated to the northern
border region of the country. I think this brief family history encapsulates
and symbolizes this country's modern-day travails."[8] In both in his public statements (explicitly) and in his novels (implicitly), Kertész is thus
a Hungarian nationalist. However, the vision of the nation he proposes,
based on the use of the Hungarian language and personal choice, is in
conflict with the ethnically based Hungarian nationalism expressed by, for
example, the former novelist István Csurka, leader of the MIÉP political
party.

Many readers might think it strange to include works and writers such
as these in a chapter about nationalism. After all, even if we can agree
that not all nationalism has to be chauvinistic, isn't it hard to accept as nationalists writers who were either dissidents, opposed to the governments
of their countries, or at the very least pilloried by the critical and political
establishments at home? In order to justify this choice, I need to return to
my original definition of nationalism, in which I insisted that a nationalist
work is one that attempts "to define a given nation's particularity, be that
in the realm of national history, destiny, or 'soul.'" Both of these authors,
and many others that could be cited, attempt to fill in gaps in the nation's
history, to tell its true story. Furthermore, although they were frequently
attacked (and sometimes still are attacked) as antipatriotic, these authors
identify themselves as patriots and see their works as necessary for the
nation's own healing from self-inflicted wounds.

8. Excerpted from Kertész's Nobel acceptance speech, translated by Ivan Sanders, on the
Web at http://www.nobel.se/literature/laureates/2002/kertesz-lecture-e.html.

By no means were all communist-era nationalist writers as antichauvinist as Kiš and Kertész, particularly in those states whose governments at least tacitly condoned a nationalist-oriented form of communism. Under the leadership of Nicolae Ceauşescu the Romanian communist state played an active role in the project of national definition. According to the Romanian literary critic Eugen Negrici, literary works celebrating the Romanian "motherland" came into vogue after 1964, when de-Stalinization finally arrived in force. It was an important theme at this time even in the work of major independent poets such as Marin Sorescu. In this period, according to Negrici, "the urge to write such poetry was genuine, and its success at that time was authentic, that is, it had not been 'cooked' in the ovens of the propaganda machine. For Sorescu's generation, the motherland was a new and exciting theme, unimaginable just a few years before. It carried something of the forbidden truth and it was worth the poets' attention. Also, it was the first theme since 1948 to fulfill public demand."[9]

Very quickly, however, the Romanian Communist Party came to realize the efficacy of the nationalist card that had first been played in independent literary works. With the active encouragement of the regime, writers, historians, and journalists contributed to an ever-increasing frenzy of Romanian nationalism. The overall theoretical direction of their work came to be called "protochronism." Katherine Verdery provides a succinct summary of the movement. "During the 1970s and 1980s increasing numbers of Romanian writers and literary critics were drawn into an argument over an idea called 'protochronism.' This idea encouraged critics and literary historians to look for developments in Romanian culture that had anticipated events in the better-publicized cultures of Western Europe (thus, 'proto-chronos': first in time). From literature, protochronism spread into other fields.... Protochronism soon attracted the attention of a Romanian party leadership that also wished to raise Romania's image in the esteem of the world."[10] It is crucial to note the direction of influence here. A major ideological gambit was first tried out in the world of literature—as we have seen, the most important public sphere in any East European communist country. Only then did it spread to other fields to be taken up by the political elite and by social scientists and historians who debated the pros and cons of this approach in scholarly and semipopular publications.

9. Negrici, 70.
10. Verdery, 1991, 167–168.

The message of the Romanian national essence was not, however, delivered to the masses through academic debates. Rather, it was presented by a poet and literary impresario named Adrian Păunescu, editor of a literary journal called *Flacăra* (The flame). Although already well known as a nationalist poet, Păunescu eventually became one of the best-known figures in Romania through his organization of the Flacăra Tour. "First it developed into a grand event and eventually into a televised tour with dozens of singers and poetry performers who followed him without hesitation, as if all mesmerized by his magic wand. In their turn, the young audience who came to his shows in meeting halls, squares or stadiums would go into some strange sort of frenzy. Coming out of the bleak daily environment they were forced to live in, they thought they were taking part in an epoch-making, magical event. The Flacăra tour soon began to resemble a ritual through its structure and gestures.... Movement within the sacred place was directed by the Great Priest's carefully studied and firm gestures, and his baritone voice which he used to pass on prophecies, ultimate and breath-taking truths.... In his capacity of Great Priest and Prophet, Adrian Păunescu never forgot to remind the aroused audience that they owed The Supreme Leader (whose message he carried) their love and submission."[11]

Without the lighting and sound effects, without the scripted maidens offering themselves up for national sacrifice, without the mellifluous rhythms and sound patterns that are lost in translation, and, most important, without the presence of Păunescu himself, it is perhaps impossible to appreciate the effect of his poetry. Still, it seems important to provide some, just to give readers a flavor of the rhymed nationalist propaganda that Păunescu provided in his heyday. Here are the first eight stanzas of his 1983 poem "Viitorul României" ("Romania's Future") translated by Constantin Roman:[12]

We now live a new life, which was dreamt of and fought for
By our forbears, our national revolutionaries Tudor, Balcescu
Horia and Iancu, who were once upon a time
The martyrs of our sufferings and of Romania's fate

Today their heir is this wise old man, brought to us in Spring time
To be a hero amongst heroes. As Communist Party Leader,
It stands to reason that he is also the country's President.
And that is why, through the very person of Ceaușescu we found our own newborn ethos.

11. Negrici, 77–78.
12. From the Web site http://www.constantinroman.com/pages/cul_trans_12.html.

We too are bearing the burden of past wars through our dead
As we paid the price of life to enjoy our earthly goods
Therefore it follows that the source of sunshine does not come from Abroad, but that we have
our very own Sun emerging from our capital city Bucharest.

It is Ceauşescu himself that introduced honour within the Communist Party and the Country
He rediscovered our history unadulterated
To make us reach for the future in our dreams, as well as
In our daily deeds, full of new meanings.

That is why we always said and are still saying and will always say
Every minute of our lives, be it good or bad
That the Communist Party is strong, as it is nurtured by the whole Nation
As the Party represents the People at atomic level.

And for this very reason as Leader who embodies the whole People
He will, of course feel their desires and all their wishes
And that is why the Communist Party opens new vistas,
A future made of enthusiasm and difficulties which are overcome.

We can't accept that our life should be broken
As we make history day in, day out, the way it was prescribed
By the 9th Congress of the Communist Party
Whose philosophy is to believe in the People as the ultimate solution.

We were disinherited of our history to forget our forbears
But he inspired us with a new sense of History
As he explained to us that our Homeland cannot be reduced
Just to red flags, but above all flies our national three-coloured flag.

A few key notions should be recognized here. First is the complete identification of the state, the nation, and their ruler. Ceauşescu is an omnipresent and omniscient deity who "embodies the whole people." Second is the claim that the communist party is the logical heir to the great (noncommunist) revolutionaries of Romanian history. Third is the sense of national pride presented as Romanocentrism: "The source of sunshine does not come from Abroad" but rather from Bucharest. And it is crucial also to see that this distaste for outside influences does not extend only to the Westerners who were standard villains of communist propaganda everywhere, but to the Soviets as well: "He explained to us that our Homeland cannot be reduced / Just to red flags, but above all to our national three-coloured flag." Finally, we should recognize an undercurrent of national self pity ("we were disinherited of our history") compensated for by an overaggressive embrace of that same history.

The deaths of a few overenthusiastic young spectators at a Flacăra concert eventually led the authorities to shut the operation down (rumor had

it also that Ceauşescu, ever alert for challenges to his power, felt Păunescu
had gotten too big for his britches), but Păunescu never stopped being an
apologist for the regime and its nationalist policies. Nor had his rhetoric
changed much at the turn of the new century: "Today, Păunescu earns a
comfortable living declaiming his verse on Tele 7 abc as well as Antena 1,
a Romanian private television channel owned by Dan Voiculescu who
before 1989 was a prominent member of Ceauşescu's intelligence service."[13] It is characteristic, however, that in addition to his literary activity,
Păunescu has been directly involved in politics, serving terms as a senator
in Romania's upper house of parliament between 1992 and 1996 and again
between 2000 and 2004. This makes him a fairly typical example of a writer
who managed to transform the symbolic capital he acquired as a cultural
figure into direct political power.

   As I noted in the previous chapter, in the period following the collapse
of communism many writers of a nationalist leaning, particularly of chauvinistic leaning, gave up literature and entered electoral politics. In the
new postcommunist world, nationalist literary writing might have seemed
passé, or at the very least less significant when the possibility of achieving real political power beckoned. At the same time, most postcommunist
states already possessed a robust sense of national identity and no longer
needed to use literature for the purposes of nation building. One intriguing exception, however, was newly independent Croatia, where the regime
of Franjo Tuđman actively encouraged the production of chauvinistic national literature and supported attacks on those who were considered not
sufficiently Croatian.[14]

   Perhaps the most notorious example of the latter was the vitriolic campaign in the Croatian press launched against the "Witches of Rio" in late
1992. The "witches" were five leading Croatian women writers whose
complaints about limitations on freedom of expression in Croatia almost
resulted in the postponement of a PEN conference scheduled to take
place in Dubrovnik.[15] In response to this news, the nationalist-oriented

   13. http://www.ce-review.org/00/35/gallagher35.html, 2.
   14. Croatia in the 1990s presents a prototypical case of what Rogers Brubaker has called
"nationalizing nationalism." "Nationalizing nationalisms involve claims made in the name of
a 'core nation' or nationality, sharply distinguished from the citizenry as a whole. The core
nation is understood as the legitimate 'owner' of the state, which is conceived as the state *of*
and *for* the core nation. Despite having 'its own' state, however, the core nation is conceived
as being in a weak cultural, economic, or demographic position within the state." Brubaker, 5.
   15. Indeed, many international PEN chapters ultimately boycotted the conference in reaction to the behavior of the Croatian political and literary authorities. The "witches" were

newspaper *Globus* published an "investigative article" under the title
"Croatian Feminists Rape Croatia" in which the "witches" were accused
of a litany of sins against their motherland. Among other failures to pass
a patriotic litmus test, the fact that three of them had married Serbian
men was dubbed "a systematic political choice rather than an accidental choice based on love."[16] The article's anonymous author provided a
table which gave readers information about each witch's date and place of
birth, parents, nationality, membership in communist organizations, family
information, home address, and whether they had been out of the country
during the ongoing war with Serbian forces. In short, the article was an in-
vitation to patriotic vigilantes to lynch the five, all of whom were summarily
drummed out of public life in Croatia for the rest of the Tuđman era.

Alongside attacks on purportedly un- or antipatriotic writers, the
Croatian media and its government sponsors made active efforts to promote writing and writers who took a "proper" attitude toward issues of
Croatian national identity. By far the most famous of these became Ivan
Aralica, frequently known as Franjo Tuđman's court poet. Born in 1930 to
a Croatian family near Knin (at that time a Serbian-majority region of the
so-called Krajina), as an adult Aralica became a teacher in a town near
Zadar. In the 1960s he began to publish fiction, but he was, in the view
of most Croatian readers and critics, a workmanlike writer of unremark-
able novels imbued with the local color of his native district.[17] His first
major success was a novelistic trilogy written in the late 1970s and set in
the sixteenth century. Its main theme was the clash between Christianity
and Islam, presented in a style that owed a great deal to Ivo Andrić and
Meša Selimović. He followed up this trilogy in the 1980s with an epic tetral-
ogy. Like the writing of his Serbian nationalist counterpart Dobrica Ćosić,
Aralica's novels can be seen as contemporary versions of the "blood and
soil" narrative, valorizing patriarchal peasant life and devoted by extension to the Croatian idea. Although the novels were published in fairly
large editions during the 1980s, Aralica remained a regional figure out
of the mainstream of Yugoslav literary life, and he was not considered a
major literary talent.

Dubravka Ugrešić, Slavenka Drakulić, Rada Iveković, Jelena Lovrić, and Vesna Kesić. For
a good survey of the polemics around this issue, see Ivica Đikić, "Zastava za metenje," *Feral
Tribune*, on the Web in English at http://www.feral.hr/old/1998/679/tema.html.

16. *Globus*, Dec. 11, 1992, 42.

17. For an overview of Aralica's career see Nemec, 268–279. For a shorter summary in
English, see Segel, 49–51.

This changed radically when Tuđman was elected president of the newly independent republic of Croatia. Aralica was plucked from his modest Dalmatian surroundings and anointed Croatia's greatest living writer. He became a member of the Croatian Academy of Sciences, a senator in the Croatian parliament, and an official member of Tuđman's "politburo." Nationalist newspapers like *Globus* published articles that went so far as to credit him with having been Tuđman's ideological mentor.[18] Unlike other writers who were drawn into political careers, however, Aralica continued to produce literary works of a highly nationalist character. Of these, *Četverored* (Four abreast, 1996) is perhaps the best illustration of the imbrication of revisionist history, nationalism, and fiction.

In Tito-era Yugoslavia a number of topics related to recent history were strictly taboo. Two of the most problematic were intra-Yugoslav violence during World War II (particularly the killings of Serbs by Croatians), and the massacres of Croatian and Slovenian supporters of or collaborators with fascism in the immediate aftermath of the war. Silence on the former was broken in Serbian literature in the 1980s, but the latter did not come up for reconsideration until the 1990s.[19] Though the whole affair was severely covered up by communist officials, the overall outline of what happened in the confusing days after the fall of the so-called Independent State of Croatia (NDH) is now relatively clear. Well over one hundred thousand anticommunist Croatians and Slovenes (they were generally but not always profascist and included the most notorious leaders of the fascist Ustaša movement that governed the NDH during the war) attempted to flee the territory of Yugoslavia. Tito's partisans followed in hot pursuit and trapped a large group of refugees near Bleiburg in southern Austria. To the surprise of the leading Yugoslav communist leaders, the British military forced the refugees to return to Yugoslavia, where tens of thousands were executed. They were regarded as collaborators who deserved nothing better than summary justice, their bodies were thrown into mineshafts, limestone caves, or mass graves, and they were apparently forgotten.

---

18. *Globus*, 15 May 1992.

19. Some Serbian novels that discussed interethnic violence during World War II include Vuk Drašković, *Nož* [The Knife] (Belgrade, 1983); Danko Popović, *Knjiga o Milutinu* [A Book about Milutin] (Belgrade, 1985); and Slobodan Selenić, *Timor mortis* (1989). The last of these not only provides graphic descriptions of Croatian atrocities against Serbs during World War II, but also presents them as part of a long-standing, illogical historical animus characteristic of Croats in general rather than as incidents which arose against the background of Serb-Croat enmity during the interwar years.

Unquestionably, many had been implicated in the horrifying behavior of the NDH regime, but in the frenzy of killing no one took the time to check for details, and one can be certain that some of those killed bore little or no guilt for wartime atrocities.[20]

Aralica's novel is an attempt at a full-scale revision of the Bleiburg story. It is narrated in the first person by Ivan Telebar, a stage manager at the Croatian National Theater in Zagreb. As the NDH is collapsing, he is convinced by his common-law wife Mirta (a makeup artist) to flee to the West to make his fame and fortune. With the assistance of Mirta's brother Baja (a convinced but apparently totally upright and moral Ustaša youth), they acquire surplus army uniforms and leave Zagreb à trois in a motorcycle with sidecar. It is of cardinal importance to Aralica's plot that his narrator and central hero is completely nonpolitical and has never had anything to do with the Ustašas. He, then, can be a neutral observer with whom any reader naturally sympathizes, a Walter Scottian mediocre hero who is immersed in events but cannot influence them. We follow Telebar and his friends on their horrifyingly confused and confusing flight north. They are frequently attacked by partisans, and during one of these attacks Mirta disappears. Along the way to Bleiburg, Ivan meets a variety of fellow travelers, each of whom turns out to be entirely sympathetic. One is a violinist in the NDH leader's orchestra, another a schoolteacher drafted into the home guards. Most important, in the course of the novel we never meet anyone who has had anything to do with the excesses of the NDH regime. The impression is that the entire column of refugees is composed of innocent babes whose only crime, if it was a crime, was to have been drafted into the Croatian army and to have followed orders. They are to a person noble, self-sacrificing, brave, and morally clean.

The partisans, on the other hand, are presented as a grotesque gang of cutthroats, ill clad, ill fed, sadistic, and bent on revenge. "As for disorder, filthiness, hostile behavior, and animus, the women were even more remarkable than the men. Women made up a good third of their group, and they were even more despairing and nasty than the men. When they looked at us, we saw doglike hatred and hyenalike greed in their eyes."[21] If conditions for the fleeing refugees were dangerous on the road to Austria,

---

20. The guilt or innocence of those murdered after the war is still hotly debated. One certain thing is that the majority of the most notorious Ustaša leaders managed to escape. For a particularly nuanced discussion of the issue of the postwar killings, see Ballinger.

21. Aralica, 111.

things change dramatically for the worse when they are forced back into Yugoslavia. After sham investigations during which they are unable to convince the partisan judges of their innocence, they are forced to march four abreast (hence the novel's title) in extreme heat with no water and are shot if they cannot keep up with the column. Their virginal women are raped and murdered by partisan leaders. Partisans and Red Army detachments rob them of any possessions they have brought with them. Finally, after having watched the sadistic murders of most of his companions, Telebar is taken to be shot at point-blank range at the edge of a huge pit. Thanks to the advice of a comrade, he manages to avoid being killed, and he rises from among the dead. Miraculously, he is later rescued from a prison hospital by Mirta, whose ability to remake herself into a partisan has allowed her to survive. Telebar is finally allowed to go home, on the condition that he never tell anyone about his experiences, a secret he keeps until the 1990s, as the novel tells us.

Although the novel presents itself as a revisionist history telling truths that had been suppressed by the communist regime, it is in effect a mirror image of the previous truths. Whereas previously, if the events had been spoken of at all, they were understood to be the legitimate revenge of the morally pure communists against fascist murderers, Aralica's novel shows us morally repugnant communists humiliating and murdering Croatians solely because they were Croatian. Naturally, not a single one of the repressed is guilty of anything other than belonging to the Croatian nation, and the uninitiated reader would be hard pressed to realize that the Ustaša regime had ever committed enormous crimes against its own citizens. Such a position dovetailed perfectly with that of Tuđman, who frequently minimized or whitewashed the horrors of the Ustaša regime. Whether the novel was written in response to the regime's desires or Aralica made the decision to present his material in this way on his own is not important, however. In either case the novel stands as a paradigmatic example of nationalist fiction designed to present the nation in a positive light and, by extension, to deflect from it criticism for past or present excesses.

While Aralica's *Četvorored* stands as an unfortunate attempt to rehabilitate the nation's past, in other countries nationalist fiction of this type played a more positive role. Thus, for example, literary works that confronted the reality of Stalinism were influential in Russia from the perestroika period on, while the end of the century saw an outpouring of Polish fiction devoted to Jewish themes and to the Holocaust. Still, by this period fictional work was already losing its prominence as a site for truth telling because the appearance of a more or less free press and the gradual opening of communist-era archives finally allowed historical material to be treated evenhandedly in nonfiction and journalism.

Be that as it may, the issue of how the nation should be defined (rather than historical facts about it) remained and remains an important literary question. In my view, the most interesting postcommunist novel to bring to the fore the essence of an East European nation is Oksana Zabuzhko's 1996 novel *Pol'ovi doslidzhennia z ukraïns'kogo seksu* (Field studies of Ukrainian sex).[22] Like many of the other novels that will be treated in this study, Zabuzhko's could have been considered in a number of other contexts. As is the case with the novels I analyze by Drago Jančar and David Albahari (see chapter 5), the narrator is the author's alter ego, an alter ego who alternates between stays in the United States and returns to her native country. In addition, because this work was the first true best seller in postcommunist Ukraine, gaining a wide audience that ranged from housewives to intellectuals, and because the narrative clearly shows the influence of such popular or semipopular writers as Erica Jong and Henry Miller, it could have been considered along with Michal Viewegh's *Bringing up Girls in Bohemia* as a popular novel (see chapter 8).[23]

In the broadest sense, Zabuzhko's novel can be considered feminist, for in its stream-of-consciousness narration it tells the story of the sexual odyssey of a thirty-something Ukrainian poet. She lives primarily in the United States at present, but the narrative flashes back frequently to her life in Ukraine and chronicles her search for the Ukrainian Mr. Right. He does not exist, however, because he, and Ukrainian culture in general, have been emasculated by centuries of oppression, which have now, in

22. Zabuzhko was born in 1960. Her education was in literary studies and philosophy, and her first extensive publication was a historico-philosophical study of the Ukrainian idea as developed in Ukrainian literature. Thus, her interest in problems of Ukrainian identity was first developed through philosophy and cultural studies and only later incorporated into her fictional work. According to her extensive Web site, http://www.zabuzhko.com, the novel has sold more than sixty-five thousand copies in Ukrainian, making it one of the best-selling literary works of its generation.

23. In an intelligent review published in *Literaturnaia gazeta* in 1997 (July 16, 13), Andrei Okara points to the work's crossover "belletristic" (rather than purely intellectual) appeal as its most lasting contribution to Ukrainian literature: "In contemporary Ukrainian literature there is an almost complete lack of original, entertaining belles lettres.... As life shows, any national cultural that lacks a full-fledged 'lower story'—a culture of mass entertainment—is fated to die. With her highbrow intellectual work, Oksana has a chance to inspire a whole trend of Ukrainian-language epigones and followers. High culture won't care about these, but for contemporary Ukrainian culture a belletrization of this sort would be a very good thing."

the narrator's view, been thoroughly internalized by most of her compatriots. Two things set the novel apart from a typical middlebrow feminist "confessions of" text. The first is the literary language, which exhibits a complex mixture of Ukrainian, Russian, and English. The second, and the more interesting from our perspective, is the presence of frequent digressions devoted to the fate of Ukrainian literature and the related fate of the Ukrainian nation.

In order to give readers a feeling for the rhythm of Zabuzhko's prose as well as the strange mixture of national definition and personal confession, I need to provide a relatively long excerpt. This one appears about a quarter of the way through the novel, during a section in which the heroine imagines (or recalls) herself giving a lecture entitled "Field Studies of Ukrainian Sex" to an audience of American colleagues:

> "You are a superb poet," [in English in the original] say the local editors (while putting off the publication of your book, however), thanks I know, so much the worse for me—but you have no choice baby, not because you couldn't switch languages—you could easily switch if you really tried—but because you are fated to be faithful to the dead, to all those who might also have written in Russian, or Polish, or even in German and lived a completely different life but who instead flung themselves, like so many pieces of firewood, onto the dying bonfire of Ukrainian, and no damn thing came of it other than maimed fates and unread books, however, today there is you, and you aren't capable of stepping over all those people, not strong enough, and then the embers of their presence will suddenly flare up amid the ashes of everyday life, and there you have your motherland, your family tree, you damned aristocrat, I beg your pardon for this ridiculously long digression, ladies and gentlemen, particularly since it has, in fact, nothing to do with our theme. Ladies and gentlemen, a tormented pity toward my own body which is being destroyed for no reason—a feeling that is known only by inmates of the GULAG: in the evenings in the bath in front of the mirror (putting on my owlish glasses, the same ones with the thick lenses, so I really look quite funny) I examine my breasts—still to this day so round and firm with their enticingly pointed nipples ("Wow, said one of my un-Ukrainianized men not long ago—they've got to be size D and look how well they hold up!")[24]

The speed with which Zabuzhko's narrator can cut from plaintive musings about the fate of a minor literature and language like Ukrainian

24. Zabuzhko, 38–39.

(not letting the reader forget that she, the narrator and implied author, is the great white hope for this literature today and tomorrow) to a consideration of the specifics of her own body (and a reminder that men still find her extremely attractive despite her thirty-something years) is breathtaking.

The connection between her feminism and her nationalism must also be considered. There is no doubt that the two are related, if only because through her assertive text Zabuzhko is attempting simultaneously to overturn a gender hierarchy in which women are subordinate to men and a literary hierarchy in which the Ukrainian language has been subordinated to Russian (and to a lesser extent to Polish). She is equally concerned, at least as far as her monologue can be assumed to reflect her concerns, with Ukrainianizing her men (one heritage of centuries of Russian control was that even after independence a large percentage of the Ukrainian population, even those who considered themselves ethnically Ukrainian, felt more comfortable speaking Russian than Ukrainian) as she is with remaking the Ukrainian language in order to allow it to do what her literary work requires. In both cases, this is not an easy task. In the former, it is not merely a question of teaching her men to speak proper Ukrainian and to acquaint them with the history of the culture (up to and including giving lectures on Ukrainian poetry while making love [33]), but also curing them of the emasculation that, in her view, centuries of foreign domination have caused. Simultaneously, like the national poets who preceded her in the nineteenth century (described in chapter 1), she must remake the national language, turning it from either a stiff and artificial literary or a peasant colloquial form into a flexible instrument capable of expressing the sentiments and ideas she wishes to present to her readers. In the course of the narrative at least, she fails to find (or create) a true Ukrainian man, so in that sense the novel can be seen as a narrative of failure. She does, however, manage to liberate her language from some of its shackles, so in this sense the narrative is one of triumph, and for this reason it would be correct to consider Zabuzhko's work one of the most literarily successful works of national-oriented literature in the postcommunist period.

The complex strategies employed in Zabuzhko's novel are not, however, the only way in which nationalist thought manifests itself in contemporary East European fiction. Perhaps the most scandalous literary work in recent Russian literature is Aleksandr Prokhanov's *Gospodin Geksogen* (Mister Hexogen, 2001). Prokhanov was born in 1938 and began publishing in the 1970s.[25] He became prominent, however, only in the 1990s, as the editor in chief of the radically nationalist and anti-Semitic weekly newpaper *Zavtra* (Tomorrow) and as an adviser to various nationalist Russian politicians. Unlike his contemporary Eduard Limonov, however, who chose a similar political path but who has not yet used his considerable literary talent to produce works of nationalist fiction, Prokhanov did not abandon literature. *Mister Hexogen*, by far the most successful of his fictional works at least in terms of sales and publicity, was the winner of the 2002 Bestseller Prize. Most of the sound-bite criticism of the novel available in both English and in Russian focuses the novel's anti-Semitic and anti-Chechen bias, and on the fact that this roman à clef asserts that the Moscow apartment bombings of 1999 that propelled Vladimir Putin to power were organized by a conspiracy headed by ex-KGB officers. What it fails to do, however, is describe in any detail how Prokhanov presents his material and why the novel has been so popular, even among educated readers.

Let us start with the first of these issues. Prokhanov does not present his nationalist views in anything like a simple fashion. This has been extremely frustrating to those who despise his journalism (in which Prokhanov's views on Jews—bloodsucking, power hungry, and always willing to exploit Russians—and on people from the Caucasus—terrorists, power hungry, and always willing to exploit Russians—are quite explicit). In the novel, however, things are more complex. The entire story is filtered through the consciousness of a retired KGB agent, Viktor Andreevich Beloseltsev. Like Prokhanov himself, Beloseltsev is a butterfly collector, and, also like Prokhanov, during the palmy days of the late Soviet empire he was posted to such hot spots as Angola, Mozambique, Nicaragua, and Afghanistan. Although we don't get detailed descriptions of everything he did in those places, there are sufficient flashbacks to give the reader the impression that he was something of a James Bond–type secret agent (in this case he is not a copy of the author, who was a journalist working for the prestigious *Literaturnaia gazeta*), convinced that his actions were for the good of humanity in general (and the Soviet Union in particular).

After the collapse of the Soviet Union, unlike many of his former colleagues, who move seamlessly into business or become powerful advisers to various oligarchs, Beloseltsev is unable to find a place for himself in the new, capitalist world of Russia. At the beginning of the novel, however, which takes place sometime in 1999, he is contacted by some old colleagues

25. For some information on Prokhanov's early career see Brudny, 155–158.

and discovers that whatever their outward appearances or jobs, they are all part of a secret society whose goal is the restoration of the Soviet empire.

The plot of the novel consists of various episodes drawn from recent Russian political history. Through them we watch a group of conspirators bring down what they see as the debauched regime of President Boris Yeltsin (called in the novel by the code name "Istukan," "the Idol"). To do so, they maneuver an unknown figure from the security forces ("Izbrannik," "the Chosen One," a thinly veiled portrait of Vladimir Putin) who is unaware of their purposes and will be their puppet. Along the way, the novel paints a picture of a Russia that has descended into complete debauchery. The president is permanently incapacitated, and affairs of state are run by a corrupt kitchen cabinet consisting of his daughter and two powerful Jewish businessmen (Astros, a portrait of television magnate Vladimir Gusinsky, and Zaretsky, a portrait of the oligarch Boris Berezovsky).

At one level, the appeal of the novel is clear; it connects to a fantasy among Russians of many classes and backgrounds according to which everything that happens in the world is the result of some sort of conspiracy. This fantasy, which initially grew up under a totalitarian state that kept its citizens in the dark on almost all matters of import, has by no means disappeared under postcommunism. Thus, the loss of the Soviet empire, for example, is not understood as the result of a series of decisions (good or ill) by Mikhail Gorbachev, but rather as some kind of shadowy agreement between him and the CIA, or perhaps aliens of some other kind, whose goal was to weaken the Russian nation. Prokhanov's novel is constructed as a Chinese box of conspiracies. The central one is organized by Beloseltsev's ex-KGB colleagues. They, however, make use of other conspiracies. Thus, Astros is portrayed as the leader of a worldwide Jewish conspiracy (Gusinsky was indeed the leader of the Russian-Jewish community). This is how one of the characters in the book describes to Beloseltev the workings of the Jewish Congress, a conspiracy to turn Russia into "Virtual Khazaria" (i.e., the center of a world order controlled by and for the Jews): "Here, for example, you can see . . . how one influential member of the Congress who holds a post in the government gives inside information to another one, a player on the stock market, regarding the impending fall of the price of some shares. The player manages to cut a great deal, make a huge profit, and transfer it into an offshore zone where it melts seamlessly into the flows of worldwide criminal money. At the same time, a host of small businessmen in the Russian provinces . . . who eke out a meager living, go bankrupt as a result. They drink the bitter pill and put a bullet in their heads. Meanwhile the government official sits down in a six-cylinder Mercedes and builds a fantastic villa on Uspensky Avenue."[26]

Passages of this sort have been taken by many liberal-minded Russian critics as proof that Prokhanov's novel is nothing more than an example of the worst nationalist propaganda. This may indeed be Prokhanov's intent, but it is worth noting that if it is, he succeeds only because he exploits Russian readers' traditional willingness to ascribe all statements made in a book to the author himself. This tendency, which in Soviet days allowed for such travesties as the show trial of Andrei Siniavsky, does not do credit to readers or to Prokhanov's text. For on careful examination it is hard to see the descriptions or statements in the novel as anything other than the views of various characters, and it is not clear which characters, if any, Prokhanov sympathizes with. What is more, this supposed Jewish conspiracy is in no way dangerous, for it is fully under the control of the KGB conspirators who cleverly manipulate it for their own ends.

That conspiracy, at the beginning of the novel, appears to have as its goal the resurrection of a Russian-led Soviet Union. This is how Grechish-nikov, one of the leading conspirators, describes it to Beloseltsev: "The recreation of the state.... In the full sense of the word.... Its territorial integrity.... From Kushka to the Pole, from Brest to Vladivostok.... The preservation of the nation and the recovery of the populace ... the relink-ing of broken-down Eurasian communications networks, industrial poten-tials, oil resources, uranium, precious metals" (33). Such a project appeals to Beloseltsev, who is also attracted by the nationalist-inflected rhetoric of the messianic monarchist and holy fool Nikolai Nikolaevich, an admirer in equal measure of Russian icons and portraits of Stalin.

Because Beloseltsev is the central character and the one through whose consciousness the narrative is presented, one is tempted to see him as the author's mouthpiece. As the novel goes on, however, we see that his per-spective is severely limited and may well not reflect the author's position. For it turns out that Beloseltsev is himself being manipulated by the con-spirators. Exploiting his nationalist leanings, they tell him that their goal is the resurrection of the Soviet Union. Later in the novel, however, we discover that their actual goal in bringing Putin to power is different. They turn out to be a clique of postnationalist figures whose ideology is closer to that of Dostoevsky's Grand Inquisitor than to that of Lenin. Their real goal

26. Prokhanov, 109.

is to move Russia away from a national to an international political agenda, and to provide its people with a reasonable material standard (though a totally deracinated one) in exchange for being allowed to control all the levers of power.

Beloseltsev is naturally disappointed by this, but simultaneously he discovers that there may exist a parallel conspiracy by retired GRU (military intelligence) officers who actually do have a nationalist agenda. As described to Beloseltsev in the hypothetical mode by another former colleague, Kadachkin, "Two ideas are struggling for Russia's future. 'The Order of the KGB' is placing Russia as a resource for world energy, fresh water, and endless transcontinental transport links, which do not require a sovereign civilization and culture. Excess population will be liquidated by soft means. The center of world development will become America, and everything that contradicts globalization will be swept away and suppressed. 'The Order of the GRU' thinks in categories of a sovereign, great Russia, based on a Russian alternative to the dying rest of the world, on the great idea of Russia that will save the world from destruction" (384). At the very end of the novel, after the Chosen One has come to power, Kadachkin convinces Beloseltsev not to get on the plane taking the KGB conspirators to Sochi, and we are led to believe that the ensuing crash of that plane is the work of the "Order of the GRU." However, their actual plans remain quite shadowy, and it is impossible to tell with any precision whether the KGB plot was in fact controlled by them (i.e., whether it, too, was part of the novel's Chinese box of conspiracies) or the two were truly at odds.

However one chooses to read *Mister Hexogen*, there can be no doubt that the work exudes a strong nostalgia for a powerful Russia, confident in its own national idea and destiny. Whether that destiny can be achieved, whether those who are trying to achieve it should be linked to the anti-Semitic and anti-Chechen attitudes of many of the novel's characters, and whether the present political leadership of the country is in its thrall, are all questions that, despite the opinions of many of Prokhanov's critics, are left open at the novel's mysterious conclusion, which depicts the Chosen One literally disappearing into thin air.

Whatever one's views on Prokhanov and his novel, it expresses a type of thinking that will remain powerful for many years to come. Indeed, as Eastern Europe's rush to integrate with European and American political and economic structures and its unavoidable concomitant willingness to accept European and American values accelerates, one can expect that the inevitable backlash will produce more such works. Most probably, they will emanate precisely from those countries that have traditionally been marked by strong strains of messianic self-understanding—Russia, Poland, and Serbia in particular. Nevertheless, the fear of dissolving without a trace in the greater European soup is strong even in countries that have not traditionally taken a messianic view of themselves, which leads, as we saw in our analysis of Oksana Zabuzhko's novel, to the need to assert a national self-definition through literature. As the reality of the compromises required to join the European Union sink in, we can expect to see a resurgence of literary work which strives to define the nation all over the region.

CHAPTER FIVE

The New Internationalism in East European Literature

In chapter 2 we saw that democratization and economic liberalization in Eastern Europe altered the conditions under which writers worked. They brought the region out of its self-imposed isolation but also led to a seemingly inexorable Europeanization and Americanization. One response to Westernization was nationalism, especially in those states that felt threatened. Building on a body of nationally oriented work that had already begun to appear in the era of de-Stalinization, nationalist writers, many of whom had begun their careers before the end of communism, sought to create works that would help readers to recover their "lost individual and collective identity," to quote Dobrica Ćosić.[1] The internationalism I will describe in this chapter can be seen as a reverse swing of the pendulum, favored by writers who would remain relevant to their societies not by turning their backs to internationalization, but rather by insisting on the possibility of globalization with a human face, one that would augment what their cultures have to offer rather than overwhelm and destroy them.

A preliminary example can be found in a poem entitled "Heart Washed like a Brain, Europe for Sale," by the Romanian poet Liliana Ursu.[2] It begins:

1. Quoted in Miller, 2000, 274.
2. The poem appears in her collection *Angel Riding a Beast*, 21. The collection was first published in Romanian in 1996. Further references to Ursu's poetry will be made in the main text by page number of the English edition. Liliana Ursu was born in 1949. In addition to the collection quoted here, she has published two other collections in English: *The Sky behind the Forest: Selected Poems* (Bloodaxe Books, 1997) and *Goldsmith Market* (Zephyr Press, 2003). For more on Ursu, see Segel, 595–596.

I am the sandwich man, caught between two worlds,
one in front and one behind, pressing, testing my muscles,
my heart, my stomach, and my sex.

Below this plane, crickets sing; above, the jazz of stars,
everything waiting, like me, to be reborn.
Behind me at the gate of my house at dawn
my mother is in her long white nightgown
almost childlike, begging for one last image of me,
the wandering daughter
already on her way to America,
the car waiting, the engine warming,
my father repairing the single headlight,
poor lighthouse of the Balkans,
all of this only an illusion now.

We can see displayed here a plethora of themes and images familiar
from the high modernist literary tradition: figures of family left behind,
the poverty of the native land (Romania in this case, but it could just
as easily be James Joyce's Ireland or Thomas Wolfe's North Carolina),
the solitary departure of the young artist heading for the metropolis. As
experienced readers of such texts, we guess that the motion in the poem will
be unidirectional, away from childhood, parents, the provinces, away from
the muck and mire of the everyday to the pure sky of art. Unexpectedly,
that turns out not to be the case, neither in this poem nor in the collection
as a whole. Instead, the poem's conclusion traces a complicated circle:

Noroc! Luck! the first word I wrote on the board
for my students who come to study Romanian,
who remake the voyage of Columbus
only in reverse, sailing
toward their ancestors.
Traveling on the arc of a Latin language
they journey, without knowing,
toward my Transylvania,
my California of the old world.

Noroc, the word itself, with its two round *o*'s marks the circle that is
staged by the poem as a whole. That circularity is underscored by the "arc
of a Latin language" and the mental journey that students take to their
and the poet's Romanian roots. The lines "Transylvania, / my California of
the old world" are particularly important. Not only does the poet discover
similarities between her native world and that of the United States that are
invisible to the American eye, but also her American perspective allows

her to return, through metaphor at least, to her previous world, now seen in a different light as a result of her American experience. In going to America Ursu has not lost her home, but has rather refound it.

The poem concludes with a nod to Ovid, the onetime exile from Rome to the shores of the Black Sea (present-day Romania):

In the end I will meet Ovid,
himself a sandwich man.
At the end of the millennium I will be his analyst
and he will be my shore of this sea I travel
which is called America.

Again, the crucial moment is one of border crossing, in this case borders of time as well as of space. Like Ovid, Ursu will end the arc of her poetic journey in Romania. She will not be there as an exile, however (just as she was not an exile in the United States, where she taught Romanian on a Fulbright Fellowship at Penn State), but rather as a new species of East European internationalist—one who has seen, lived in, and successfully described the other world, and one who was subsequently able to return to her home, enriched but not embittered.

The return, as well as the extent to which her own broadened horizons are echoed by her surroundings, is registered in a poem that appears later in the same collection:

My walk through this lost Balkan town
is a map of hazard...
I pass by a bank
and hear talk about the rate of the dollar
in Tokyo and New York.
I pass a common house
and see the old teacher, starving to death,
coming out to the street
to beg for some bread.
With the little money I have
I buy stinging nettles, bread
and a book by Baudrillard
about fatal strategies.
                    (61)

In a globalized world Transylvania (the traditional home of exotic vampires) turns out to be similar to California, and Transylvanians are as affected by the exchange rate of the dollar as Americans are. Particularly poignant here are the dual concerns of the poetic "I" back at home. That is, her need to strike a balance between such "exotic" topics as a fascination with Jean Baudrillard and the necessity of purchasing "stinging nettles," from which a spring soup can be made to ward off scurvy.[3]

By no means is Ursu unique in her internationalist outlook. Indeed, the kind of writing illustrated in Ursu's poem is becoming widespread in the postcommunist literary landscape of Eastern Europe. In the rest of this chapter, I would like to explore this newly emerging internationalism, examining, in addition to Ursu's poetry, prose works by Slovenian, Serbian, and Russo-French writers. Like the nationalists who helped destroy notions of modernist synthesis, internationalist writers deny the possibility of a single, unified cultural narrative for the world as a whole. But unlike the nationalists, these authors demonstrate that unstable but productive cultural syntheses can occur. Such work has the advantage of avoiding totalizing narratives of East or West and allowing for an independent, albeit not autochthonic, East European perspective. These works have the further advantage of permitting East European writers to cash in on the desires of readers in their own countries to get at least a vicarious feeling for existence "over there"; for although it has now become bureaucratically easier to travel abroad, financial realities make travel difficult for many. Finally, their combination of East and West European perspectives makes such works potentially marketable in English, French, and German translation. This last consideration is extremely important, both because it is increasingly impossible to consider oneself a "real" writer unless one has been published in major European languages (particularly English) and because such a perspective provides a way to overcome the lack of interest in Eastern Europe on the part of Western publishers now that the "automatic" political reasons for publishing East European literature have disappeared.

Books of this sort always teeter at the edge of danger, however, for in satisfying Western audiences they may oversimplify conditions at home and thereby alienate their potential local readership. Or the reverse may happen—in their desire to provide an exotic view of the West for home consumption, they may fail to see any nuances outside their home country and thereby write books that are unacceptable to Western audiences.

---

3. The choice of Baudrillard as a placeholder for West European cultural theory is particularly ironic since it is precisely postcommunist Romania's desire to become a consumerist society that has produced such real-life phenomena as the starving teacher mentioned in these lines.

Nevertheless, in the best of cases—and I will consider a few of them here—
these narratives avoid simplifying clichés and make valid and literarily
successful points about both types of societies.[4]

Before continuing, let me enumerate the central features of this new
internationalism:

1. The work's narrator, main character, or poetic "I" makes a journey from the
   home country to the West and back.[5]

2. The narrator interacts with European and American culture; he or she is not
   merely a passive observer reporting back what he or she sees to compatriots.

3. Western culture is seen as different, but it is neither blindly accepted as superior
   nor simply rejected as vulgar, crass, consumerist, and so forth. The implication
   of the whole is that the narrator's and implied author's culture and that of the
   West can and should be complementary rather than identical.

4. A synthesis is achieved between the cultures, but it is a personal, provisional,
   and hence inherently unstable one which does not pretend to the level of a
   (modernist) universal model of cultural synthesis.

5. Although clearly fictional, such narratives are often written in the first person,
   and, even when they are not, the central character appears so closely connected
   to the implied author that the work is inevitably taken as autobiographical.
   Furthermore, the narrative is generally highly reflexive, and the main character
   often plays the role of author of the text in question.

Of course, works by writers from Eastern Europe that stage a journey to
the West and a return home are not in themselves a new phenomenon. This
should hardly be a surprise given that Eastern Europe has, at least since
the eighteenth century, been involved in a kind of eternal "catch-up game"
with Western Europe.[6] The traditional lines of the East-West relationship as expressed from an East European point of view had already been

---

4. Books of this sort from Eastern Europe have recently been echoed by mirror-image
books written by Americans, including Gary Shteyngart's *Russian Debutante's Handbook*,
Arthur Phillips's *Prague*, and John Beckman's *Winter Zoo*. The first of these, in particular,
follows the narrative pattern enumerated here almost perfectly.

5. Although most works with which I am familiar bring the hero or heroine to the West,
other destinations are possible. Iztok Osojnik's *Melinda Podgorny*, for example, transports
Slovenians to Japan. Lacking a stable tradition to work against, however, such works remain
isolated examples, at least for the moment.

6. On the construction of the concept of Eastern Europe by West Europeans, see Wolff.
Wolff, however, is not overly concerned with how this process affected the self-conception of
the East Europeans.

laid out by the end of the eighteenth century in Russian literature in the contrast between Nikolai Karamzin's *Pis'ma russkogo puteshestvennika* (Letters of a Russian traveler, 1797–1801) and Denis Fonvizin's *Pis'ma iz Frantsii* (Letters from France, 1777). Karamzin, the quintessential Russian sentimentalist at this stage of his career, is in ecstasy at everything he sees and is fulsome in his praise of Western sights and institutions. Fonvizin, by contrast, grudgingly admits that Western Europe possesses certain technological advantages but finds Russia to be superior in almost every other way. Most important, in neither case is there much give-and-take between the two worlds. For the most part they are seen as antithetical; to appreciate one is to denigrate the other.

The famous conflict between the "Westernizers" and "Slavophiles" in Russia in the 1840s and 1850s can be seen as a continuation of this same discourse.[7] Even attempts by imperializing Russian nationalists to articulate a universal Russian idea that would incorporate the best of West European thought and achievements can be understood as a late echo of this debate.[8] In Central Europe, the conflict between West European and local culture was perhaps not drawn quite as starkly as in Russia. Adam Mickiewicz, for example, who spent much of his later life in France and who incorporated a great deal of progressive European thought into his version of Polish nationalism, functioned as a partial bridge between the two worlds. Still, in Mickiewicz's literary work, one searches in vain for a thematic treatment of East-West dialogue.[9]

In the first years of the twentieth century, the thematic parameters of this problem did not undergo significant revision, even as the fledgling post-Versailles East European states seemed on the verge of becoming an integral part of a new Europe.[10] If one had to choose a single East

7. See Walicki.

8. Although on the surface these thinkers seemed to be creating a synthesis of West European and Russian ideals, in fact their nationalism had no specific Russian component. Russianness was, rather, a capacious envelope of no determined content into which all world culture could be stuffed. See Wachtel, 1999, 49–73.

9. Such a dialogue is implicitly present formally in all of East European literature insofar as all authors use West European literary genres to express their local concerns. But it is an unusual work indeed that incorporates a thematic treatment of this issue. In the relatively rare cases when East and West European worlds are brought into contact in nineteenth-century East European literature, it is generally for the purposes of parody. One example is the scene in Petar Petrović Njegoš's epic *The Mountain Wreath* in which a Montenegrin mountaineer who has been in Venice describes the depravity of Venetian life to his compatriots.

10. The USSR, of course, had opted out of the European cultural sphere by the 1930s, and literary treatments of the West in Soviet literature migrated quickly toward the "Fonvizin pole." For a detailed study of Soviet literary responses to the West, see Avins.

European literary work from this period to juxtapose with Ursu's poem, one could do worse than examine Miroslav Krleža's 1932 novel *Povratak Filipa Latinowicza* (*The Return of Philip Latinowicz*). The novel offers a devastating critique of the possibilities for a cosmopolitan outlook in the context of interwar Croatia.[11] Philip, as his surname indicates, is a carrier of European cultural values in a generic East European shell. A successful modernist painter, he has been living in Paris for many years. Just before the action of the novel begins, Philip undergoes a midlife crisis which expresses itself in a fragmentation of his universe and a collapse of perception. His return home, figured as a search for his real father, is a Freudian-inspired attempt to overcome present psychic dysfunction by coming to terms with childhood trauma. Simultaneously, it is an escape from Western civilization and its discontents to the pastoral beauty of the Croatian countryside.

Initially, it seems that a synthesis of a West European sensitivity with the miasma of interwar Yugoslavia could be invigorating. "Everything round Philip was so natural, so real and alive, that it captivated him with its sheer genuineness: he revived in the blue open spaces, full of genuine light and unadulterated scents."[12] As time wears on, however, it becomes apparent that Philip's "European" side cannot be reconciled with the facts on the ground. In the first place, Philip recognizes that while the natural world of Pannonia might be invigorating, even a shared native language cannot disguise the fact that he and the uneducated local inhabitants have nothing in common. He comes to this conclusion while chatting with the local cabman: "Two men were seated there on that box-seat: one of them an eccentric neurasthenic, a sectarian in painting, a relativist, a fauvist, a colourist, and they spoke the same language, and yet actually they were two languages and two continents!"[13] As incomprehensible as the man on the street may be, his society is nevertheless preferable to that of the local European-educated elite. These men and women (all friends of his mother, including the man who turns out to be his father) have absorbed the buzzwords of advanced European culture but are nothing more than vulgar caricatures of Europeans.

11. This is despite the fact that Krleža himself was a most cosmopolitan man. Equally at home in Croatian, Hungarian, and German, Krleža early on became a convinced Marxist and dreamed of an internationalist socialist culture. But he himself was far too much of an individualist to accept any unified globalizing cultural schemes, including those proposed by the USSR. For more on Krleža, see Bogert.

12. Krleža, 68.

13. Ibid., 58.

Eventually, Philip finds a kindred soul in Bobočka Raday, an equally displaced person in the Croatian wilderness. It appears that their union might provide a fulfilling basis for some kind of Europeanized local culture (or that it will at least allow them both to escape), but this final hope is dashed at the end of the novel with the bloody murder of Bobočka by her former lover Baločanski. In the novel's final pages, which are in fact a reprise of the last scene of *The Idiot*, we see Philip as a latter-day Prince Myshkin who, far from being rejuvenated, has been utterly destroyed by the realities of interwar Yugoslav life.[14] Thus, although Krleža himself was a typical cosmopolitan of the twilight years of the Austro-Hungarian empire, his main character discovers that in the world of Yugoslavia between the wars, there is no place for an internationalist outlook. There can be no successful mediation between the primitiveness and savagery of the "real" local culture and the affectations of those who have chosen Western culture, which they accept uncritically.

During the communist era one would not have expected to see many works attempting to bridge the gap between East and West emanating from Eastern Europe. In official discourse, the West became associated with all evil, and the phrase "rootless cosmopolitan" was a term of anti-Semitic invective used with dismaying frequency in much of the former east bloc. Travel abroad became difficult or impossible, and so, unlike their older contemporaries, most postwar East European writers had no direct experience of Western life to incorporate in their work. Works that did stage journeys to the West tended to be purely descriptive travelogues at best and blatant anti-Western propaganda at worst. Still, it would be a mistake to think that the reasons for the absence of internationally oriented work should be ascribed solely to state policy. For some writers did have the chance to travel to the West and to write (and, more rarely, to publish) what they wanted about it. This was particularly true in the case of Central Europe from the 1960s on. Authors from the region (official, semiofficial, and dissidents alike) chose not to produce works of this kind.

The reason, I would argue, is that for the most part East European writers of all stripes agreed ideologically with the broad internationalist universality that was typically taught by communist states. The overwhelming majority of East European writers were joined by a belief in the

---

14. The novel that describes the catastrophe caused by an attempt to return to the past is not a uniquely East European phenomenon. Perhaps the best-known staging of this problematic topic to an American audience is Thomas Wolfe's *You Can't Go Home Again*.

possibility of a single unifying discourse, a "grand narrative," to use the phrase of Jean-François Lyotard, which identifies them all as participants in the overall project of modernity.[15] In its insistence on the possibility and desirability of a single narrative for world culture, such a worldview was inherently internationalist, for it envisioned the ultimate replacement of the local and particular with the universal and eternal. As an example of the characteristics of this internationalism (which differs from the post-modern internationalism of the works I focus on in this chapter precisely in its desire to erase all trace of difference and particularity in its pursuit of universal synthesis), let us examine excerpts from the Nobel Prize acceptance speeches given by Mikhail Sholokhov (in 1965) and Alexander Solzhenitsyn (in 1970). It would be natural to expect stark differences in the attitude and rhetoric of a leading icon of socialist realism and the Soviet Union's most famous dissident. However, regarding the possibility and desirability of a grand and universal cultural synthesis the two men sound remarkably similar.

Sholokhov couches his comments in the typical false modesty of the vanguard communist party: "Mankind is not broken up into a host of individuals moving in a state of weightlessness, like cosmonauts when they have gone beyond the limit of terrestrial gravitation. We live on earth, we obey terrestrial laws. Huge strata of the earth's population have common interests and aspire for the same goals, and the pursuit of these goals unites rather than disunites them.

"These strata are working people who create everything with their hands and their brain. I belong to those writers who regard it as the highest privilege and the highest freedom to be able to serve unreservedly the working people."[16]

Five years later, Solzhenitsyn, prevented by the Soviet State from traveling to Stockholm to receive his prize, sent a speech that asserted in equally powerful terms the belief that there could and should be a single system of values for humankind. He proclaimed, albeit less modestly than Sholokhov: "Who will give mankind one single system for reading its instruments, both for wrongdoing and for doing good, for the intolerable and the tolerable as they are distinguished from each other today? Who will make clear for mankind what is really oppressive and unbearable and what, for being so near, rubs us raw—and thus direct our anger

15. Lyotard, xxiv.
16. "The Vital Strength of Realism," in Sholokhov, 205.

against what is in fact terrible and not merely near at hand? Who is capable of extending such an understanding across the boundaries of his own personal experience? ... Propaganda, coercion, and scientific proofs are all powerless. But, happily, in our world there is a way. It is art, and it is literature."[17]

Perhaps not surprisingly, then, when artists from Eastern Europe had the opportunity to travel to the West, to see how their counterparts lived and to write about Western life, they were generally unimpressed by the messy pluralism they found. As an example, let us turn to Milan Kundera's *Nesnesitelná lehkost bytí* (*The Unbearable Lightness of Being*, 1984). It was written in France by an East European writer who, presumably, was aware that contemporary Western culture and society are not completely barren. And yet it would be hard to recognize this from the novel, despite the fact that Western Europe provided a haven for Kundera and for thousands of Czechs of his generation who felt they could not remain at home. All of Kundera's Czech protagonists migrate to the West in the aftermath of 1968, but none of them finds anything to admire. Indeed, the novel's two heroes, Tomas and Tereza, return relatively quickly to Czechoslovakia, despite the post–Prague Spring repression. It is Tereza who precipitates the return. "They had been in Zurich for six or seven months when he [Tomas] came home late one evening to find a letter on the table telling him she had left for Prague. She had left because she lacked the strength to live abroad.... She had been silly enough to think that going abroad would change her. She thought that after what she had been through during the invasion she would stop being petty and grow up, grow wise and strong, but she had overestimated herself. She was weighing him down and would do so no longer."[18] The letter, while sincere, is not meant to be taken by the reader at face value. All the things of which Tereza accuses herself are either positive characteristics in the novel's system of values (the inability to adapt to the West, to grow up, etc.) or they are untrue. Tereza does not by any means weigh Tomas down (weight being generally a negative concept in the novel); rather, her decision allows him to do what he should have done all along—return to his native country.

Both return, for all intents untouched by anything the West can offer, willing to suffer a diminished professional and material life for the sake of feeling at home. And for the Czech character who remains, the artist

17. Solzhenitsyn, 17.
18. Kundera, 1984, 28.

Sabina, the West is a site of permanent frustration because of the complete inability of her interlocutors to understand the essence of things. This is brought out most clearly in the "dictionaries of misunderstood words" that Kundera sprinkles through his novel. Each misunderstanding arises because the same word has a completely different meaning in the two societies. One might imagine that Kundera is doing nothing more here than registering difference. But, although this is never stated in so many words, the reader understands that the Czech understanding, as provided by Sabina, is the more appropriate one, while the Western definition (usually provided by her hapless lover Franz) is naive and incorrect.

Late in the novel, Sabina is riding in a car with an American senator. The senator stops his car and points out some happy children playing in a stadium. The narrator comments: "Behind his words there was more than joy at seeing children run and grass grow; there was a deep understanding of the plight of a refugee from a Communist country where, the senator was convinced, no grass grew or children ran. At that moment an image of the senator standing on a reviewing stand in a Prague square flashed through Sabina's mind. The smile on his face was the smile Communist statesmen beamed from the height of their reviewing stand."[19] We are undoubtedly meant to recognize that the senator is a fool to think that there are no happy children in communist Eastern Europe. The confidence with which he asserts the superiority of his own value system is on the surface identical to the modus operandi of communist politicians. In fact, it is even worse, because he takes himself seriously, while they are at least hypocrites. In the end, the surplus of knowledge—unquestionably a source of power in this case—belongs unmistakably to the wise East European. Americans and West Europeans are mere babes, the author implies, unable to see the deeper and more important truths available to East Europeans.

Throughout the communist period, the possibility of open and continuous dialogue between East European writers and their Western counterparts was impossible. Even émigrés, who generally wrote with a double audience in mind, ultimately had to make the choice of one world or another. Since 1989, however, East European writers are much more mobile, and the internationalist outlook of some of them reflects that mobility. The poetic work of Ursu provides an example of how a new thematic internationalism could be achieved in verse. At the same time, in Romania Ursu is not considered a major poet; that is, her synthesis is apparently overly

19. Ibid., 250.

oriented toward providing outsiders with a poeticized view of her own country rather than toward providing a convincing view of the United States for Romanians.

We can find a more spectacular version of this problem, this time in prose, if we consider the phenomenal success in France of the Russian-born Andreï Makine.[20] His novel *Le Testament français* (published in English as *Dreams of My Russian Summers*) appeared in 1995 and was awarded both the Medicis and Goncourt prizes. Makine's novel was seen by French critics as balancing perfectly between French and Russian culture. Just how delicate and important this perception of balance is can perhaps be appreciated if one considers that Makine's two previous novels were, like this one, written in French but were rejected by publishers until it occurred to him to claim that the French text was a translation from a Russian original. As French novels Makine's early efforts did not succeed in achieving a balance because, presumably, the "French" author was perceived as inauthentic. When the author was perceived to be Russian and his work a translation, its authenticity was no longer in question and the same text could be read entirely differently—a real-life case of Jorge Luis Borges's famous story about Pierre Menard's translation of *Don Quixote*.

It is also noteworthy that for all its popularity in France, the Russian translation did not have much resonance when it was published in Moscow in 1996. This could be seen as a testimony to the difficulty of creating a work that would be of equal interest to audiences in the East and West, or to the insularity and isolationism of Russian culture, or (and I would be more inclined to this third possibility) to the fact that there really is no balancing act here. Rather, I believe that Makine's book was successful in the West precisely because it serves up, in an elegant package, a perfect dose of clichés, most of them derived from literary works, about Russia and Russians. Such clichés, however, could be accepted in France only if they came from a "real Russian." What Russian readers thought when confronted with these clichés can perhaps best be seen from a review of the novel published in *Novyi mir* in 1996. "The author's 'Russian period' begins: 'Russia, like a bear after a long winter's nap, awoke in me.' It would have been better had it never awakened! It is as if Makine's Russia is stamped 'Made Abroad.'... What we have here is typical kitsch,

20. Andreï Makine was born in Russia in 1958 and emigrated to France in 1987. Since the publication of *Dreams of My Russian Summers,* an international bestseller that sold more than two million copies, he has published half a dozen novels, though none has been as successful.

presented without a shadow of irony, with meaningful grimaces and pathetic sighs. This unimaginative combination of typical stereotypes (like
the trademark bear), exotic local color, vulgar commonplaces, and pseu-
dodiscoveries could be taken as the real thing only by foreigners."[21]

Makine's novel is written as a pseudoautobiography, a genre that, for
150 years, has been the preferred form for accounts of childhood in Russian
literature. The pseudoautobiography is an autobiographically based work
that imitates the autobiography in all respects but one: its author and
narrator are not the same person. Although the formal distinction might
seem trivial (after all, if one overlooks the title page it can be impossible
to tell a "real" autobiography from a pseudoautobiography), it is not. For
both author and reader the lack of identity between author and narrator
means that the work is to be treated as fiction, read and judged by a
set of criteria different from those applied to nonfiction. Although the
pseudoautobiography often sticks quite closely to the facts of its author's
life (and must include substantial amounts of autobiographical material),
it cannot simply be considered a subset of the autobiography proper. The
pseudoautobiography affords the novelist an unusual opportunity. He can
use material from his own life in a form that has traditionally engendered
an illusion of truth in readers, yet he is not bound by truth and is able
to create the kind of fictional world characteristic for the novel. He can
describe something general, representative, within his own experiences,
the deeper logic within his character. Simultaneously, however, he need
never lose the protection of a fictional mask.[22]

Although Tolstoy initiated the genre in Russia in his *Childhood* (1852),
Makine's immediate inspiration was almost certainly Ivan Bunin's *The
Life of Arseniev*. Written in French emigration in the late 1920s and 1930s,
Bunin's work is a lyrical evocation of the twilight of tsarist Russia. Equally
important for Makine was the work of Vladimir Nabokov, whose *Speak,
Memory* shares much with the traditional Russian pseudoautobiographical
account of childhood although it is written as a true autobiography. For
both Bunin and Nabokov, their childhood and the Russia of that childhood
was a kind of utopia, and they recall it in their literary works with the
literary equivalent of a soft-focus camera lens. Though Makine's narrator
recalls a much less poetic Soviet reality for his childhood in the 1960s
and 1970s, he imbues it with the same soft focus, through his highly lyrical

21. Zlobina, 243.
22. For a full treatment of this genre in Russia, see Wachtel, 1991.

language and because his narrator's most important experiences take place in the aura of his supposed maternal grandmother, a prerevolutionary relic within Soviet reality.

Makine allows the attentive reader see the Nabokovian influence on the third page of the novel when he and his grandmother follow the flight of a "crepuscular hawkmoth" with an attention to lepidopteral detail and its inherent eroticism that the master would certainly have appreciated. Like the narrators of Bunin and Nabokov, Makine's is highly attuned to synesthetic detail, able, while looking at a photograph to "enter into that day, to taste its climate, its time, its color."[23] In addition, Makine's novel shares something of the elegant structure of the narratives of both Nabokov and Bunin, which is also, in a way, quite similar to the structure of all the narratives discussed in this chapter. That is, both Nabokov and Bunin begin in Russia, leave it as émigrés, and then return through memory. Makine manages to complexify this structure while basically retaining it. His novel contains two separate lines, the life of his grandmother, which begins in Russia, returns to France, and ends in Russia, and his own life, which begins in Russia and ends up in France, where he apparently spends his time conjuring the memories of his Russian existence.

The pictures of Russia Makine provides appear to have been chosen specifically to give a picturesque and orientalized vision of Russia, one that accords with the long-term fascination the French have had with Russia and its culture. Describing a Russian peasant house occupied by "the most picturesque of babushkas," Makine notes that it exuded "a kind of oppressive climate, but filled with a strange vitality...the breath of Russia" (19). His grandmother's trip across Russia in 1921 as part of a Red Cross mission is described in scenes reminiscent not of history but of the film version of *Dr. Zhivago*. Most important, however, and very like the position of Bunin's Arseniev, is the love-hate relationship the narrator expresses for his native land from the safety (and boredom) of his exile. Describing his mood when as a young man he heard tales of the horrors of Siberian concentration camps, the narrator says: "What caused me most pain during the course of their nocturnal confessions was the indestructible love for Russia that these revelations inspired in me. My intellect, struggling with the bite of the vodka, rebelled: 'This country is monstrous! Evil, torture, suffering, self-mutilation, are the favorite pastimes of its inhabitants. And still I love it? I love it for its absurdity. For its monstrosities. I see in it a

23. Makine, 10.

higher meaning that no logical reasoning can penetrate'" (144). Echoing
as it does Tiutchev's famous formulation "Reason cannot understand Russia," Makine's description, written in French for a French audience, also
serves to confirm the most clichéd orientalist vision of Russia, a view that,
for example, Diaghilev and the Ballets Russes purveyed with equal success
to the French in the second and third decades of the twentieth century.

Like the narrators of the novels of Vladimir Makanin and Jáchym Topol
(to be discussed in chapter 7) and Oksana Zabuzhko's *Field Studies of
Ukrainian Sex* (considered in chapter 4), Makine's narrator also finds it
necessary to discuss the role that literature and the writer played in the
Soviet Union and to note its passing in postcommunism. In an imaginary
conversation that takes place in Paris sometime in the 1990s, he tells his
grandmother that the kind of literature he and she appreciate no longer
exists in France. She responds: "'Do you remember those tiny apartments
in Russia that groaned under the weight of books? You know, books under
the bed, in the kitchen, in the hall, piled right up to the ceiling? And those
unobtainable books that you were lent for one night and which you had to
give back at six o'clock in the morning? . . . You see, it's difficult to compare.
In Russia the writer was a god. The Last Judgment and Kingdom of Heaven
were expected from him at the same time. Did you ever hear anyone there
talk about the price of a book? No, because books had no price! You
could go without buying a pair of shoes and freeze your feet in winter,
but you bought a book . . . ' Charlotte's voice broke off, as if to give me to
understand that this cult of the book in Russia was only a memory now"
(229).

It would seem that the narrator's view accords with Makine's own, for,
as he told an interviewer in 1998, "the new Russia, of mafias and business
deals and forgetting everything; no, I can live without it.... It used to
mean something to be a writer there; you had a real function, a meaning.
Now . . . it is better to write from the outside."[24] The cynical reader might
note that Makine has figured out how to sell narratives set in an exoticized
Russia to French audiences, but were he to return to Russia he would have
to find a completely different modus operandi.

One author who has been successful at attracting audiences both abroad
and in his own country is Drago Jančar, Slovenia's leading prose writer.
Although he writes on an astonishing range of topics in fiction, drama,
and essays, he managed to create a fully successful internationalist novel

24. As quoted in Masson, 63.

with his *Posmehljivo poželenje* (*Mocking Desire*).[25] Jančar's hero and alter ego is Gregor Gradnik, a Slovenian writer who has been hired to fill that most mystifying of roles, visiting professor of creative writing at a college in New Orleans. "At the thought of having to lecture American students about literature and, worse still, analyze their writing, his hands began to sweat, just as though he were facing a difficult test himself. Even at home he disliked talking about literature—literature was to be written and read, read and written. But if the Americans had invented courses and whole schools of creative writing, then they probably knew what for. The twentieth century had proved that they knew everything" (11–12). In fact, however, Gradnik's slightly alienated view allows the reader to recognize that the Americans (both the characters in the book and the potential American reader) do not know everything, particularly about themselves. In part, this is because, as the Russian formalists might have put it, everything that surrounds them is just too familiar. It takes Gregor's cigarette-smoking, nonjogging Slovenian perspective to let them see the world again as if new.

> When some future historian tries to establish what drove millions of Americans to start running at the end of the twentieth century, it won't be an easy task. It won't be easy to find an explanation for that sudden racing through parks and over beaches, through the streets of big cities, under the hot, southern sun or in the stinging cold of the north. Morning, noon, evening, and night, young and old, sick and healthy, all of them forsook their previous habits and set out at a sprint.... Some biologists attempted, as they always do, to find an analogy among other species of mammal.... But a historian will know that the human race of Western civilization had been known to do all sorts of things: multitudes had risen up all over Europe and set forth to liberate God's tomb, though few of them knew where the country was they were lurching toward.... At the end of the twentieth century they ran in jogging shoes. More than anything else they resembled the maniacal residents of a certain Alpine valley on the Slovenian border who once each year raced to the top of four mountains: men and women, children and old folks wheezed with rabid eyes from valley floor to mountaintop,

---

25. Jančar, born in 1948, has published novels, short stories, plays, and essays. In addition to *Mocking Desire*, his work in English includes the novel *Northern Lights* (Northwestern University Press, 2001). *Mocking Desire* was originally published in Slovenian in 1993 by Založba Wieser (Celovec). The English edition was translated by Michael Biggins and published by Northwestern University Press in 1998. Quotations will be noted in the text by page number from this edition. For more on Jančar, see Segel, 239–241.

breaking legs on the descent back to the valley, allowing the weakest to lag and, eventually, to collapse. (96–97)

What kind of implied reader is this description for? In the beginning of the section, it would be easy to suspect that we have here yet another Kundera-like example of European bemusement at American foibles, meant to allow a European reader (in this case the Slovenian original audience) to have a laugh at the expense of the crazy Americans. As the section continues, however, we recognize that this is not Jančar's goal. The specifically American activity is quickly linked to universal patterns (or at least to pan-European ones), and the narrator now seems not so much to be holding American practices up for ridicule as contextualizing them in a way that Americans themselves might well not recognize. The passage can now be seen as designed to allow a potential American reader to view her own culture in a different light and to show Slovenians that Americans are not that different after all. Finally, the last sentence, which brings the action back from America to Slovenia, traces the movement of the book as a whole, which begins with Gradnik's arrival in the United States and ends with his return to his native land. As was the case with Ursu's poetry, the novel, in its narrative ideology as well as in its plot, stages a give-and-take between West European/American and East European culture.

The willingness to enter into the other's culture is staged comically in this novel when Gregor takes up jogging in an attempt to win a bet and to seduce the "typical American girl," Irene Anderson. Realizing fully the absurdity of his situation, Gregor nevertheless sticks to it, and on a beautiful Sunday morning, he and Irene set out to run. Although convinced he is about to die, Gregor finishes the run, but the irony of the scene is reserved for the end: "Gregor takes a crumpled cigarette out of his T-shirt pocket, intentionally put there for this purpose. She stops massaging herself and looks horror-struck at him. He lights up and exhales smoke up toward the dark, heavenly travelers. Her horror transforms her expression.... Suddenly Irene Anderson laughs out loud" (105). The seduction, it turns out, works precisely because of the incongruous combination of chain-smoking East European and temporarily adopted American customs, neither of which by themselves would have succeeded in breaking down Irene's resistance. The crowning irony of the situation, however, comes a bit later in the novel, for it is in the aftermath of her affair with Gregor that Irene decides to marry her longtime partner, Peter Diamond, author of books on bicycle touring. This is something the reader recognizes she should have done long before, but it turns out that she can fully appreciate what is truly hers only after her exposure to the East European other.

Similarly, when Gregor returns to Slovenia at the end of the novel, he, too, is now able to see his own world in a clearer light. "He sat down on the wet leaves and leaned his back against a tree. He had arrived at the graves he had known since childhood. All around him there was rot.... This was the smell that whole country exuded, that was in the barns and peasant beds, the smell that people brought with them into pubs and buses, the smell that inhabited city streets and hovered placidly over the landscape.... From the bell tower of St. Anton's a bell tolled through the silence. Now he could hear it distinctly.... And now he knew of himself that, just like this sound, his echo and image would also find their way toward that inexorable laughter" (166–167). In Jančar's novel, then, representatives of both cultures are shown to be changed by and to benefit from exposure to another culture that is seen as different but not better than their own. In the circle traced by the narrative, they can inscribe themselves as masters of a newly globalized world, beacons for those who will follow.

Perhaps the most complex and the most aesthetically successful oeuvre of this kind belongs to the Serbian Jewish writer David Albahari.[26] Since the mid-1990s, Albahari has been living in Calgary, Canada, but he had already begun to experiment with an internationalist approach in his prose narrative *Tsing*.[27] In this work, Albahari weaves an exceptionally complex and multilayered narrative that is at one and the same time a search for self-understanding by the narrator, a hymn of praise to his Holocaust survivor father, a metaliterary search for the story being told, and a travelogue that moves back and forth from Yugoslavia to Israel to the United States. As opposed to Ursu and Jančar, who trace relatively straightforward circular journeys, Albahari cuts with dizzying speed through time and space.

26. Albahari was born in Yugoslavia in 1948. He started his career as a translator of contemporary American fiction and as a short story writer. His book *Opis smrti* [Description of death] won the Ivo Andrić Award for the best collection of short stories in Yugoslavia in 1982, and his novel *Mamac* [Bait] won the *NIN* Award for the best novel in Yugoslavia in 1996. For more on Albahari, see Segel, 41–42.

27. Originally published in Serbian as *Cink* (Belgrade: Dereta, 1995). It was published in English as *Tsing* in the author's own translation by Northwestern University Press in 1997. The title is a neologism in both Serbian and English, meant to evoke a sound that plays an important role in the work. References to the work will be made in the main text by page numbers from the English edition.

In the end, however, his virtuosic narrative technique brings all the circles together, and his cosmopolitanism is curative. A long passage taken from near the end of the work illustrates Albahari's associative narrative method:

> Somewhere in the land of the Navajo I drove off the road, stopped the car, and stepped out onto dried up grass. An eagle hovered high in the sky. A similar dark spot in the sky above Jerusalem could only signify an angel. On the bank of a creek, I took my sneakers and socks off, and immersed both feet in water. It was so cold, my legs jerked back. It is written in the Talmud that a man's father is his king, but nobody cares for that kind of teaching nowadays. In Ćuprija, in Serbia, we went together to a big merry-go-round: I screamed with delight while he pulled my chair and threw it away, but no matter how distant we would get, in the end we were always together; every attempt to go away into darkness would finish with a return into light. In Premantura, in Istria, I looked toward the pines once, and I saw my father among their shadows. The carpet of pine needles made the steps soundless. A small shiny object on the night table belonged to nobody. Near the Grand Canyon I had to stop. (95)

Ultimately, as we unravel the intricacies of this narrative, we realize that only his stay at the University of Iowa Writers' Workshop and his travels around the United States gave the narrator the distance and perspective to connect with the father who had died and to pay him the tribute that this book represents. For Albahari's narrator, the world is truly one, and connections can be made at any point across its fabric: "I followed the advice of a student tourist guidebook and in Tuba City, at a restaurant called The Truck Stop, I had 'the best *taco* in the world.' While I was eating, a drunk Navajo vomited in the toilet. He reminded me of my father. He threw up the same way" (37).

Albahari has continued to explore the complex relationship between here and there (by now, it is not entirely clear which is which for him) in a series of novels written in Canada since 1995 including *Snežni čovek* (The snowman, 1995), *Mamac* (Bait, 1996), and *Svetski putnik* (World traveler, 2001). The last of these is set in the Canadian resort of Banff and revolves around the conversations and actions of a Canadian artist, a Serbian writer, and the Canadian-Croatian grandson of a Croatian travelogue writer. The narrative is presented in the first person by the Canadian, and it is telling that this is Albahari's first novel in which the first-person narrator is not a Serbian. That is to say, Albahari now appears to be sufficiently comfortable with his new land to write from the "as if" position of a Canadian, and thereby to view "his own," that is, the Serbian, position as if it were foreign. The novel, not surprisingly, is sprinkled with considerations of the difference between Canadian and Serbian culture; perhaps one of the most comprehensive comes from the lips of the Serbian writer, Daniel Atijas, as reported by the anonymous Canadian narrator: "He couldn't think about anything except how everything here is different from the world he lives in. He said that he felt as if he had come from some other planet, rather than from southeastern Europe. In his world, he said, nothing exists except the immediate present, and in this present moment people live for the past, which each of them wants to change, while here, if he is not mistaken, the present moment is only the threshold of the future and the past is, as it should be, as unchangeable as the surrounding mountains."[28]

Such a viewpoint is, of course, a standard cliché, but the developing plot of the novel works against an easy acceptance of this position, for it concerns the ultimately unsuccessful efforts of the third-generation Canadian to atone for, or at least to come to grips with, the fact that his travelogue-writing grandfather had been a member of the Ustaša during World War II. At the end of the novel, after the accidental death of the Canadian-Croatian protagonist, Atijas returns home (a typical move in novels of this type, as we have seen), presumably with a changed view of the role of history in the West. The narrator expresses the belief that, having experienced the passions of his Serbian and Croatian acquaintances, he will be able to return happily to the Canadian prairies, but the reader recognizes that something of their past-inflected world has rubbed off on him as well, if only because he is apparently able in the aftermath to produce a novel, a genre he had always failed at before, as he told us at the beginning of the book.

All the literary works considered in this chapter can be seen as attempts to find a compromise between traditionally East and West European (or North American) ways of seeing the world. Rather than expressing the belief that one or the other of these views is superior or that one is destined to triumph over the other, they present stories that emphasize the possibility of interpenetration between the worlds, at least within the consciousness of the main, usually first-person, narrator. It would be easy to call such narratives postcommunist internationalist utopias. Perhaps, as many in Eastern Europe feel, the region will not be able to withstand

28. Albahari, 2001, 25.

the onslaught of the West. Perhaps they will ultimately be folded into a single globalized culture that recognizes no regional specificity. Perhaps a strident and isolationist nationalism is the only solution. Still, there are many writers who are convinced that it will be possible, in an ever more globalized world, to assert in a nonchauvinistic way a feeling of one's own, and through that to make the world as a whole a richer place. They would agree with Aleš Debeljak's internationalist description of his home city in the poem "Pismo domov" (A letter home):

I give in to the inescapable command
that weighs on all my muscles and eventually forces
me to flower like a thousand sweet shots
and to begin to sing from the city
that is at once Rome, Medina, and Jerusalem, and
that consoles me as only one's homeland can.[29]

29. Debeljak, 31(translation mine).

CHAPTER SIX

Writers and Journalism

Under communist regimes writers of nonfiction garnered neither the prestige nor the respect accorded to writers of fiction, poetry, and drama. The lack of prestige was particularly acute in the field of journalism. In part, the reasons were historical. In these litero-centric societies fiction writers and most of all poets were the founders of the nation, not journalists.[1] And the traditions of investigative and/or muckraking journalism were not as strong in precommunist Eastern Europe as they were in the West. In the communist period, journalists were state employees, and everything they wrote was carefully censored by authorities who worked zealously to ensure that the public was not made privy to any unnecessary information. There was, nevertheless, a wide variation in the freedom available to journalists in Eastern Europe. In Yugoslavia, for example, a number of magazines (less so newspapers) were able to lead a relatively independent and respected existence over long periods of time. To a lesser extent, the same was true of Poland.[2] The press in the Soviet Union was the most tightly controlled, although for most of the communist period the situation in Bulgaria, Czechoslovakia (with the exception of the period just before 1968), Hungary, and Romania was closer to the Soviet model than it was to the Polish or the Yugoslav. To be sure, even in the more tightly controlled countries, many people became expert at reading

1. This does not mean that these same national poets did not engage in journalism from time to time. Mihai Eminescu, for example, Romania's national poet, published many journalistic pieces, but he is not revered for these. Indeed, it is indicative of the lack of prestige accorded to journalism in Eastern Europe that Eminescu's collected newspaper articles were not published until the 1980s, while his poetry had gone through hundreds of editions by that time.

2. Poland was also home to possibly the best-known nonfiction writer in Eastern Europe, the peripatetic Ryszard Kapuściński.

between the lines to glean bits of important news that slipped into news-papers by accident, but they never appear to have credited journalists with placing this encoded information before them. The overall public attitude toward the press can perhaps best be appreciated through a joke, known to all Russians, that played on the names of the two ubiquitous Soviet-era newspapers *Pravda* (Truth) and *Izvestiia* (News)—"There's no truth in *Izvestiia* and no news in *Pravda*."

In his study of the press under Soviet rule, Jeffrey Brooks describes the role of this institution in more academic terms, but they would have resonated with citizens of most East European countries: "The press was not coterminous with all public expression, but it contextualized the Soviet experience and imposed a structure on thinking even among nonbelievers, much as censorship imposed a structure on belles lettres. It was the deep-est reservoir of the 'dark and magical night' to which Andrei Siniavsky paid sad tribute in his essay *On Socialist Realism*. It set the standard for purposive lying about one's convictions and for historical amnesia, which Czesław Miłosz has described. The press largely retained its monopoly of information after Stalin's death as the font of falsehood with which Alexan-der Solzhenitsyn and Andrei Sakharov long contended. The press and the official public culture retained much of their distinctive character until Mikhail Gorbachev introduced glasnost—'openness' or 'transparency'—after 1985."[3] One would want to add to Brooks's analysis only that while writers of belles lettres made use of samizdat and tamizdat from the 1960s on, dissident journalists were relatively rare, perhaps because publishing a newspaper in an edition of ten copies seemed an even more quixotic endeavor than publishing a novel in this format.[4]

One of the characteristic features of the postcommunist period was the explosion of new periodicals. In Romania, for example, it is estimated that some 2,000 new periodicals appeared within two years after 1989 (whereas before 1989 the total number of periodicals in the country could have been counted in the hundreds). In Czechoslovakia 759 periodical titles appeared in 1984. By 1990 that number had increased to 1,870, and

3. Brooks, xiv.
4. There was, however, a famous samizdat newspaper in the Soviet Union called *Khronika tekushchikh sobytii* [The digest of current events]. Published between 1968 and 1983, the paper devoted itself to defending human rights in the USSR, focusing on their systemic abuse by the government in a terse, dispassionate, and objective style. For a description of the paper's activities and an online version of many of its issues (all in Russian), see the Web site http://www.memo.ru/history/diss/chr/index.htm.

by 1999 there were almost 4,000 periodicals being published in the Czech Republic alone. Not surprisingly, these new periodicals required writers, and for the most part they were not recruited from the communist-era journalists, who were tainted by their overclose affiliation with the ancien regime. In many cases, writers of literature stepped into the breach. As qualified writers and respected citizens, they could produce the texts that were needed by these new periodicals and desired by readers. There was an enormous hunger for information on the part of postcommunist citizens, and many writers felt that it was their duty to use their talents to provide not more fictions but rather the facts that their fellow citizens needed and wanted.

We can appreciate what many writers came to feel at the time from the preface written by Vitaly Shentalinsky to his book of nonfiction essays (many of which were originally published as long magazine articles) about the fate of Russian writers during the Soviet period. He begins by discussing the traditional role of Russian writers in terms similar to those I presented at the beginning of this book. "Writers have always occupied a special position in Russia. For lack of democratic institutions, the Russian writer has never been just an artist, but a spokesman for the truth and a public conscience as well."[5] The implication, borne out almost immediately, is that with the appearance of democratic institutions, writers (and as his reference to "art" indicates, Shentalinsky has in mind writers of literary texts) will no longer need to play this role. And indeed, Shentalinsky proceeds to tell the story of how he, who considered himself primarily a poet, came to produce this book of nonfiction beginning in the late 1980s. "What did we need now, more than anything else? I asked myself as I walked home through the gusts of fine snowy dust. Our history had been stolen from us, and what we knew was grotesquely distorted. Yet without the past there could be no future. Now we must shake off this amnesia" (6). It has long been characteristic of Russia that writers of literature arrogated to themselves the right and duty to write or rewrite the nation's history.[6] What is new in Shentalinsky's formulation (and at least to some extent this same attitude can be found in most East European countries) is that in the name of truth the writer is supposed to give up writing fiction or poetry

5. Shentalinsky, 1996, 5. This text comes from the preface that appeared in the English-language editions of Shentalinsky's work. It does not appear in the Russian. Presumably, Shentalinsky felt that such a characterization of the role of Russian writers was so obvious as to be unnecessary for his compatriots.

6. For a study of this phenomenon, see Wachtel, 1994.

completely and to provide readers with the truth, whole and unvarnished, in journalistic form.[7]

But an altruistic desire to provide fellow citizens with the truth was not the only stimulus that encouraged literary writers to take up journalism in postcommunist Eastern Europe. For the rise in the number of periodicals coincided with the ever-increasing difficulty of making a living from fiction and poetry, a phenomenon that was discussed in chapter 2. Today writing for newspapers and magazines is among the few sources of regular income for writers, and it is thus a very rare littérateur in Eastern Europe who never contributes nonfictional journalistic pieces either to daily newspapers or to weekly or monthly magazines. As this is so, it is impossible to provide an overall picture of journalistic activity on the part of writers of literature. Therefore, rather than discussing the general phenomenon of writers and journalism here, I focus on three categories of journalistic activity that have allowed writers to remain particularly relevant in postcommunist Eastern Europe. Specifically, I examine the cases of writers who have managed to set themselves up as journalistic liaisons between Eastern Europe and the West, writers who have made a name for themselves by issuing books of nonfictional essays that originated as newspaper or magazine columns, and, finally, writers who have founded and edited their own newspapers.

In the majority of cases, the work I consider consists not of journalism per se (at least not in the sense in which most Americans would understand it), but rather of essays devoted to social or cultural commentary. There is no single word for such work in English, and it goes by a variety of names in various East European languages (in Russian it is *publitsistika*; in other East European languages it is one or another variant of the word reportage).[8] Still, in its overall thrust, the work is journalistic if by that we understand work that is identifiable as nonfiction, aimed at a broad public, and disseminated through periodicals. Some of the writers I consider, like Shentalinsky, have completely abandoned belles lettres for journalism; others use the visibility and income they derive from journalistic work to publicize and/or subsidize their literary work. As has been true of the

7. For another example of the same trajectory, consider the career of Henryk Grynberg in Poland. Grynberg first made a name for himself as a writer of fictional works devoted to Holocaust themes. In recent years, however, he has turned primarily to nonfictional essays, usually on the same topics. These books have become far better known than his fiction.

8. For a study of the history of this genre in Eastern Europe (with a primary emphasis on Poland), see Diana Kuprel, "Literary Reportage: Between and Beyond Art and Fact," in Cornis-Pope and Neubauer, 375–385.

other strategies described in this book, the turn to journalism cannot be seen in itself as either a positive or negative phenomenon. Sometimes the move from fiction to journalistic nonfiction can be evaluated positively— that is, the journalistic work of some writers is, I believe, far superior aesthetically and has unquestionably had greater impact than their earlier literary output. Other cases are more ambiguous, including those of some of the best-known writers turned journalists. In my view, many of these writers, talented as they are as producers of fiction or poetry, simply do not have the temperament to create successful nonliterary work.

Multidirectional Stereotyping: The Nonfictional Worlds of Tatyana Tolstaya, Slavenka Drakulić, and Dubravka Ugrešić

A number of the best-known postcommunist writer-journalists have taken it as their job to explain East European culture to Americans and/or West Europeans or to explain Western culture to East Europeans. In a sense, they can be seen as the nonfiction equivalents of the internationalist writers discussed in the previous chapter. Rather than using the adventures and observations of a fictional character to record the differences and similarities between East and West, they foreground themselves, and, when they succeed, they do so precisely by convincing readers that they are uniquely positioned at the interface between these still somewhat antithetical worlds. Of course, there has always been a need for such interpreters, and in the preceding period there were journalists whose function it was to do this type of bridge building. Thus, American readers devoured Hedrick Smith's volume *The Russians* in the 1970s. Russians, on the other hand, waited eagerly for the dispatches of such foreign correspondents as Valentin Zorin while Poles looked to Wiesław Górnicki. What is new in the postcommunist period is that now a single individual can go in both directions, because it has become possible to travel frequently back and forth between the former East and West and to publish in both simultaneously. And those writers who have managed to occupy this in-between position are in high demand.

Tatyana Tolstaya is a talented writer. She is, in my view and in that of most Russian critics, neither more nor less talented than a score of other contemporary Russian writers. Unlike the vast majority of her colleagues, however, she has been able to secure translations of her fiction by major publishing houses all over the world. That is to say, the work is considered by them either sufficiently relevant or sufficiently marketable to justify its publication for non-Russian audiences. How has Tolstaya managed to succeed where so many of her equally or more talented fellow writers have failed? A few extraliterary factors have helped. First, there is the name. Anyone from the Tolstoy family who takes up the pen will automatically garner attention. Second, there was, both in the West and in Russia itself, a vogue for Russian women writers that began in the early 1980s. Tolstaya, whose stories began to appear in the mid-1980s, was able to take advantage of that trend. Furthermore, it did not hurt that her stories were comparatively accessible, for the most part free both of difficult postmodernist tropes and linguistic hypercomplexity. In my view, however, more important than any qualities of her fictional prose has been Tolstaya's ability to capture public attention through her production of relatively short journalistic and nonfictional pieces both for Russian mass-circulation magazines (she had, for example, a regular column in the Russian edition of *Vogue*) and in the United States, where her texts appear regularly in translation in the *New York Review of Books*. It is on the basis of these texts, at least in the United States, that the major New York publishing houses decided to select her from among the many potentially talented and marketable contemporary Russian writers for publication. As Helena Goscilo, an admirer of Tolstaya's prose, puts it, "Tolstaya became a luxury product suitable for export and elaborate foreign marketing.... Made accessible through translation to an Anglophone readership, Tolstaya exudes panache and self-confidence, has an excellent command of English, and relishes speaking her mind—all factors that partly account for continued American and British interest in her observations about Russian and American life, academia, the literary scene, glasnost, and, above all, women and feminism."[9]

Journalistic work made up a relatively minor portion of Tolstaya's activities in the 1980s. By the 1990s, with the rise in the apparent relevance to society of journalism and the obvious financial rewards that could be garnered by a writer who could produce the kinds of texts that the Russian glossy journals and the *New York Review of Books* would publish, Tolstaya turned increasingly to nonfiction.[10] The position of a journalist whose job it is to clarify the mysteries of the other to which she belongs has its rewards, but it is a perilous one as well. This is particularly true when that position

9. Goscilo, 3.

10. According to the editorial characterization on the inside cover of a recent book presenting the stories of Tolstaya's sister Natalya and the journalistic articles of Tatyana, "In this period [the 1990s], Tatyana worked primarily in the genre of publitsistika." Tolstaya, from the title page (translation mine).

is exploited not to present an honest examination of the various "others" considered, but rather to package for each audience the kinds of clichés about the other that they wish to hear. Goscilo, writing about Tolstaya's journalism, notes her tendency to provide relatively crude depictions of America to an American audience. To my mind, there is nothing wrong with this. An outsider's glance, even a biased and uninformed outsider's glance, can still be useful if only to understand how others think of us. What I find objectionable in Tolstaya's journalism is not this, but rather the way she describes Russia to Anglophone readers and the West to Russians. In this case, she cannot be excused on the grounds that she is presenting what Goscilo calls views "typical of the middle-aged Russian intelligentsia."[11] Particularly when describing Russian reality to Americans, she is unquestionably well aware of the clichés she employs, and she has lived long enough in the United States to recognize that the reverse is true as well.

To illustrate how Tolstaya exploits the position of liaison between cultures, I propose to examine two of her articles, both devoted to the novel *Dreams of My Russian Summers* by Andreï Makine (the novel itself was discussed in the previous chapter). Tolstaya first published a review entitled "Love Story" on November 20, 1997, in the *New York Review of Books*. This short piece, approximately two thousand words, provides a generally positive assessment of Makine's work. She begins: "Russian literature may take pride in a strange success: Andrei Makine, a Russian of indeterminate French origin, was awarded two of the most prestigious literary prizes for a book written in French, in France, and about France—a book which is nonetheless quintessentially Russian. In our time, it seems, you have to be born Russian, spend thirty years of your life in Russia, a country where cruelty and reverie form a paradoxical unity (this, of course, is a cliché, but like all clichés, it's true) in order to hallucinate with such power and passion, in order to create a fabulous country—a nonexistent France—from words and dreams."

These few sentences deserve to be unpacked. First, Tolstaya situates Makine's novel in the context of Russian, rather than French literature. She does so because Makine's book, while seemingly French in every way, is actually "quintessentially Russian." What she means by this, apparently, is that a work of this hallucinatory power could have been written only by a person who had experiences of a type that occur exclusively in Russia. That is to say, Russians (and by extension Tolstaya herself) are unique by

11. Goscilo, 3.

virtue of what they have seen, and the books they write to express this are therefore inherently interesting. The particular experience they have had is of a country where "cruelty and reverie form a paradoxical unity." Tolstaya here provides precisely the kind of cliché about Russia that any Westerner would be embarrassed to utter. She gets away with it because she admits that it is a ridiculous statement even as she uses it and asserts that it is true. She thus knowingly plays on the desire she imagines American readers have to see Russia as a kind of exotic land while simultaneously extending and feeding that desire.

Nor is this the only example of cliché-ridden stereotyping of Russia and Russians in the article. A bit later in the same review, Tolstaya continues: "The Russian, locked up for decades behind the iron curtain (in a country constructed from dozens of other countries and yet unified), in a country where not even all its cities are open to its own citizens, and sometimes are not even marked on the map, a country of secrets and taboos, locked doors and underground secret railways, a country of fences and suspicious glances—the Russian has developed a capacity for reverie unlike anyone else's. The climate, regime and the huge distances facilitate lethargy and dreams." Of course, "the Russian's" capacity for reverie was already a cliché in the nineteenth century, the figure of Oblomov being perhaps its most celebrated instantiation. There was, apparently, no need for the special Soviet-era features of Russian life that Tolstaya cites to create it. The recital of these clichés is, in my view, far less crucial for Tolstaya's reading of Makine's novel (which later she characterizes as "deeply, densely symbolic, even allegorical," a love story "stranger and more profound than an ordinary love for a woman: it is the inexplicable, unshared, torturous love for Russia") than it is for her own need to situate herself as an expert on the strange attitudes and behaviors of those exotic Russians who need to be explicated for the Anglophone readers of the *New York Review of Books*. Tolstaya sets herself up as one who simultaneously lives inside and criticizes the clichéd vision of Russia, the perfect intermediary between the United States and a land that is, at a basic level, presented here as somehow completely untouched by postcommunist change.

When Tolstaya presented a review of Makine's book to Russian readers some seven months later, however, things looked rather different.[12] Of course, to some extent these differences are inevitable given the varied needs of the target audiences as well as the capabilities of the reviewer.

12. Tatyana Tolstaya, 'Russkii chelovek na randevu," *Znamia* 6 (1998): 200–209.

Thus, for example, Tolstaya said nothing about the quality of the English translation, although it is apparent from the review that she read the book in English, not in French. Still, she cannot claim to be an expert on English prose style, so she quite reasonably avoided the question of the adequacy of the English translation to the original. She does speak of it fairly extensively in her Russian review, and she is fairly negative about the work of the translators.[13] But Tolstaya's interest in the quality of the translation is somewhat beside the point. More important is her overall assessment of the novel. An American reader of Tolstaya's review could not help but put it down with the feeling that she liked the book. While never directly stating an opinion, she does nothing to undercut the sense that the prizes and awards it received were properly bestowed. Russian readers, however, would have gotten a distinct negative impression from the final paragraphs of her review: "Well, be honest: do you like the novel or not? Basically, I don't like it.... Well, be honest: is it a good novel or a bad one?—I guess that it's good. It is well conceived and thought out, it has a solid structure, all the loose ends are tied up ... but at the same time it is ponderous, slow, overly dependent on Proust (without Proust's fullness), overly serious, lacking in any unexpected events, without humor, overly calculated, overly aesthetic, stuffed with banalities, clichés, and worn-out metaphors." Are these the same banalities and clichés Tolstaya insisted were nevertheless true for the American reading public, but that had to be disowned now because Russian readers would see through them immediately?

We can guess that this is precisely the case, because if providing suitable Russian-accented clichés for American readers was a goal of the American review, the Russian review does the reverse: that is, it uses the excuse of Makine's novel to present similar clichés about the West to Russians. Thus, in the first paragraph, in place of the clichés about Russia we found in the *New York Review* article, we read the following: "The French are extremely fastidious when it comes to their own culture, literature, style, and language, more fastidious even than other nations. This often evokes

---

13. She takes the translators to task for being overly literal at one point in translating French culinary terms that appear on a dusty French menu the narrator reads in his grandmother's Siberian house. She tells us the translators were too quick to "decode the mysterious 'bartavels,' rendering them as 'red quails.' The magic is ruined, the enchantment broken, this is only food." It does not appear to have occurred to Tolstaya that the only reason the menu seemed so magical to her was that, when she read the book in English, she did not know what bartavels were. To the French reader, at least to one who knows anything about food, bartavels are a known quantity, just as red quails might be to a Russian reader. So the translators are taken to task for having deprived Tolstaya of the magic caused by her own ignorance.

laughter and protests from politically correct nations, such as, for example, the Americans, whose idea of basic equality makes them rather indifferent to the purity of their language." Russians, Tolstaya realizes, do not need to be told that theirs is the land of cruelty and reverie. Rather, they want to know that Americans (which ones? perhaps those who eagerly swallow Russian-accented clichés in the *New York Review*) are willing to allow their language to be butchered because of their beliefs about equal rights.

Some of Tolstaya's favorite tropes appear in both articles. In the American one she served up clichés about Russia while simultaneously making it clear she knew they were clichés. Here she does the same with received ideas about what journalists like or should like. After providing the details of how Makine lived in poverty in France, how he even slept in a cemetery crypt, she adds in parentheses, "Journalists really love these details." She had provided these same details to her American readers but did not feel it necessary to add the jibe about journalists, perhaps because she felt that American readers do not traditionally look down on journalists. To preserve her image among Russians, however, it is crucial to be seen not as a journalist but rather as a literary writer masquerading as a journalist.

Tolstaya has figured out how to give her readers in each country exactly what they want. And what they seem to want, if her success can be seen as confirmation, is the assurance that the clichés traditionally used to describe the other are indeed correct. That providing clichés in two directions causes Tolstaya to contradict herself is a problem only for those who take the trouble to read what she has to say for both audiences. But such readers are few and far between. And the cognitive dissonance that results in Tolstaya herself is, perhaps, assuaged by the excellent income her columns earn in both countries and from the name recognition that helps keep major publishing houses willing to make the financial commitment to publishing her fiction.

Tolstaya is perhaps the most successful writer to play this double game, but she is by no means the only one. Her Russian compatriot Viktor Erofeev occupies a similar position, as do two writers from Croatia, Slavenka Drakulić and Dubravka Ugrešić. The marketing materials for Drakulić's *Café Europa* provide a telling portrait of how Western publishers, Penguin Books in this case, exploit the body and position of the "intercultural subject" to sell books (see figure 5). The red star that separates the title and subtitle at the top of the card is a visual reminder that precisely the communist legacy keeps the concepts "Europa" (joining which has been the goal of most postcommunist societies including Drakulić's native

FIGURE 5. Marketing piece for Slavenka Drakulić's *Café Europa*.

Croatia) and "Life after Communism" apart. Centered in the picture is Drakulić herself, whose position, at a café table whose stark décor does not provide any clue to its location, both hints that she herself may be the missing link between the two and emphasizes that the speaking subject is at least as important as the subject matter. That is, the book is to be bought because of the authority of the writer, already known to readers from her previous collections. Drakulić herself is presented as glamorous, alluring, and exotic. The bright red lipstick and her direct, but somewhat melancholy gaze, however, do not seem to fit the verbal characterization (attributed to the *Washington Post*) that speaks of her humor.

It is, in fact, Drakulić's ability to present the humorous or ironic side of East European existence, particularly the existence of East European women, to Western readers that has been the key to her success. Thus, one of the blurbs on the back of her first collection, *How We Survived Communism and Even Laughed*, is by Carolyn Heilbrun, who says: "We have been bombarded with the evils of Communism, but have so far been spared the details of what if meant to be a woman enduring that regime. That neither sanitary napkins nor tampons were available is a clue. The author knows how to amuse and horrify. Her touch is light, her probe deep."[14] To readers in her native Croatia, however, Drakulić's work may well not seem particularly amusing or deep.

While Drakulić has succeeded in exporting clichés about East European women to the West, she has not tried to go in the other direction, as has, for example, Tatyana Tolstaya. Her countrywoman, Dubravka Ugrešić, has done so, and in ways so similar to Tolstaya's that one is tempted to believe that the position of journalistic liaison unavoidably leads to the presentation of simplistic portraits of the other. In the case of Ugrešić this is particularly curious and unfortunate, because she is one of the most talented prose fiction writers of Eastern Europe. That is, insofar as she gave up writing fiction to produce journalism (she published no fiction at all between the late 1980s and the late 1990s), her choice was a real loss to literature. She made this choice quite consciously, however. As a self-exiled writer, she felt that it was her duty to tell the truth about her own and other countries.[15]

Ugrešić speaks directly to this issue in an essay called "The Tale of the Bomb and the Book": "When he crosses the border, the ex-Yugo-writer arrives in territory which he does not recognize. All the traps he had succeeded in avoiding in his own cultural milieu—guarding his sacred right to literary autonomy as his most precious possession—now lie in wait for him. . . . Like it or not, he becomes the representative of his country, whether the old one or the new one. . . . Like it or not he becomes a reporter

---

14. Drakulić, 1992, from the back cover.

15. While I comment negatively here about the quality of the journalistic work of Drakulić and Ugrešić, I need to emphasize that I am not questioning the courage of their convictions. As noted in chapter 4, they were among the notorious "witches of Rio," and while not exactly exiled, they found it impossible to stay in Croatia after this branding.

of reality (which he had never been, because he was not a journalist, but a writer).... All in all, he becomes a kind of interpreter, psychologist, anthropologist, sociologist, political scientist, ethnologist—in other words a translator of his own reality and the reality of his own country into a language comprehensible to West European readers."[16] What Ugrešič does not mention is the temptation to succumb to this desire, a temptation that derives in part from the need to earn a living, but also from the writer's deeply held desire to be relevant. For the real problem is that while comparatively few readers in the West want his or her fiction, during a time of war (almost the entire decade of the 1990s in the former Yugoslavia) major newspapers are eager to publish the thoughts of "experts." Cut off from readers at home, who in any case are weighed down by day-to-day problems and no longer have the time and interest to read postmodern fiction, the writer ends up becoming precisely what he or she is not.

Here I will briefly consider two nonfictional works of Ugrešić. One, *The Culture of Lies*, deals with post-Yugoslav Croatia, while the other, *Have a Nice Day: From the Balkan War to the American Dream*, concerns primarily her observations about the United States. Of the two, the former is unquestionably the more successful. Ugrešić comes out strongly against the hypocrisy and kitsch that characterized Croatia under the rule of Franjo Tuđman. This was an important and courageous thing to do at a time when few Croatians were willing to admit what was happening in their homeland (the essays in the collection appeared originally between 1991 and 1994 in a wide variety of mostly European journals including the *Times* of London, *Die Zeit*, and *Les Temps Modernes*).

Nevertheless, being correct and courageous is not the same thing as writing a successful book. And the problem with this collection is precisely that Ugrešić is not comfortable with the genre. As Gordana Crnković put it in a generally sympathetic review of the collection, "Ugrešić is best when literary aspects of her prose overshadow analysis and interpretation resembling social science or cultural studies discourse.... These essays are characterized by excessive generalizations about the people Ugrešić describes, an attitude that can appear arrogant. All men inhabiting former Yugoslavia and its successor states come across as male chauvinists who call a woman by the name of her genitals and brag tastelessly about their sexual exploits. Millions of individuals among 'the Yugoslav peoples' are conflated (frenzied nationalists), and Westerners who have in any way dealt with Balkan

16. Ugrešić, 1998.

violence (journalists, intellectuals, scholars, and the like) are primarily
self-serving careerists or else jaded observers.... One might speculate
that some excessive generalizations of *The Culture of Lies* proceed not
only from the material, but also from uncritical transference of the main
traits of Ugrešić's literary writing."[17]

Indeed, Crnković has captured the problem perfectly. It is all very well
for writers of literature to decide that what the world needs from them are
facts, not fictions. But the production of journalistic prose is not as easy as
it sometimes looks, and even well-intentioned attempts may go astray. In
the context of a novella, such as Ugrešić's brilliant "In the Jaws of Life,"
clichés and exaggerations about characters and their society are woven
into a complex fictional text in which questions of truth to life do not arise.
When they appear baldly, as they frequently do in *Culture of Lies*, they
seem heavy handed and untrue.

It is harder to be sympathetic to Ugrešić's attempt to extend her journalistic purview to cover the United States. With characteristic self-
deprecation, Ugresić tells the reader at the beginning of *Have a Nice Day*
that "this book has been written against my personal and literary convictions."[18] But written and published it was nevertheless. And it is filled
with lines like "No American with an iota of self-respect knows who he
or she is: that's why every American has a shrink" (51) and "America is
an organized country. Organizers permeate American everyday life like
a fine-meshed net" (35). As Crnković has said, "A reader of this volume
might find it hard to avoid being increasingly uneasy about this book's
own perpetuation of stereotypes about the United States. While pointing out conventional and problematic American constructions of both
Eastern Europe and itself, *Have a Nice Day* nevertheless replicates the
same mechanisms of simplification and 'falsity' in its own presentation of
the American 'other.'"[19]

Crnković explains these lapses by noting that they grow directly from
Ugrešić's tendency to export into her nonfiction the very techniques that
make her a successful novelist. Other explanations could be adduced, rang-
ing from the indulgent (she simply doesn't know the United States well
enough to make fine-grained distinctions) to the cynical (as an émigré

17. Crnković, 545.
18. Ugrešić, 1994, 12.
19. Crnković, "Have a Nice Day: From the Balkan War to the American Dream and the
Things That Shape the Way We See Each Other." In Ramet and Crnković, 166.

Croatian author living mostly in Western Europe she needed to make a living, and such soft anti-Americanism sells well to European audiences). I will refrain from choosing among them, but simply note that, at least in my view, Ugrešić's return to fiction with her novel *Muzej bezuslovne predaje* (The museum of unconditional surrender, 1996) after almost a decade-long literary silence was a welcome step.

Recapturing History: Vitaly Shentalinsky and the KGB Files

By no means is the switch from writing fiction or poetry to journalism always a negative one. The opposite can be true as well. Such is the case with Vitaly Shentalinsky. In the 1980s Shentalinsky managed to publish a number of collections of his poetry in Russia. None of them made an impression, and it is safe to say that while he may have been a sincere poet, Shentalinsky was never a particularly talented one. His verse is filled with uplifting sentiments of the type that were called "humanistic" in Soviet parlance, as well as exhortations to fellow artists and writers to work for the good and the beautiful, all wrapped in nineteenth-century verse forms. For once, the Soviet editor's blurb on the title page of a book (a required résumé that often sounded absurd when read together with book itself) did not lie: "The book consists of poems about the distant and severe parts of our country—beyond the Arctic Circle, Kolyma, Chukhotka; about love and childhood, about civic responsibility in our day."[20]

Still, in Soviet days, Shentalinsky was a poet, and to him appertained all the rights and privileges that accrued to a member of the writing fraternity. Most important, he could and probably did sincerely believe that his poems about "civic responsibility in our day" were needed and wanted by society as a whole. He must, however, have been aware, even when his book was published, that few Soviet citizens would actually be uplifted and improved by his sententious verse. And he knew for certain that no one outside Russia would ever hear of him or it. Unlike many other officially published poets, however, Shentalinsky had a hidden talent, one he was never able to exercise in a socially useful way. For although he had worked as a journalist in the Soviet Far East and North, in that period, as we noted earlier, journalists were even less free than poets to express their mind. This all began to change by the mid-1980s. And at least in one area, it was

20. Shentalinsky, 1983.

Shentalinsky who both heroically and courageously forced that change
to go much further than its original architects wished, and who was able
successfully to present the fruits of that change to a broad public. His first
collection of articles devoted to the KGB files on repressed Russian writers
was printed as a book in 1995 in an edition of fifty thousand copies.[21]
It had been preceded by the serial publication of most of the separate
pieces in mass-circulation journals like *Ogonek* and *Novyi mir* (which still
had hundreds of thousands of subscribers in the early to mid-1990s). The
book caught the attention of foreign publishers as well, and it appeared
in French, Spanish, English, and Farsi, among other languages. Thus, by
switching genres, Shentalinsky transformed himself from a more or less
irrelevant poet into a highly relevant journalist.

Perhaps not surprisingly, when I spoke with him about his transformation, he did not acknowledge the fact that at least one stimulus to it was
that in the market conditions of post-Soviet Russia he simply would have
been unable to publish his verse and therefore to continue to consider
himself a writer. Rather, when I asked whether he was still writing poetry
he responded: "No, that is not what we need now." That is, it appears that
Shentalinsky continues to think of the writer in communist-era terms as a
person who has a primary responsibility to society as a whole. Unlike many
other such communist-era writers, however, rather than griping about a
changed society that no longer appreciates the writer's gift, he was able to
evolve together with his society, and to provide something that is indeed
considered relevant both at home and abroad.

It is characteristic as well that the best way Shentalinsky could think of
to serve society was by forcing open the KGB archives devoted specifically
to writers of literature and not, say, to those of agronomists or geneticists
or any of a number of other professions whose ranks were decimated by
Stalinist persecution. This choice presumably reflects his personal conviction, as a writer, that writers are the most important group to be resurrected

21. The first book-length edition of Shentalinsky's work appeared in France under the title
La parole ressuscitée. The Russian edition is entitled *Raby svobody: V literaturnykh arkhivakh
KGB* (1995). It appeared that same year in Britain under the title *The KGB's Literary Archive*,
and in the United States the same translation appeared as *Arrested Voices: Resurrecting the
Disappeared Writers of the Soviet Union*, trans. John Crowfoot (1996). The translator (with
the author's permission?) significantly edited the book in English. When passages that I cite
appear in the American edition, I quote from it. When they have been removed, I quote
from the Russian edition. Shentalinsky has published two subsequent collections based on
his research in the KGB archives, *Za chto? Proza, poeziia, dokumenty* (1999) and *Donos na
Sokrata* (2001).

in the search for truth. At the same time, the impact the book made illustrates the fact that in the highly litero-centric societies of Eastern Europe,
writers and their fate were generally recognized to be of central symbolic
value, for it is unlikely that all fifty thousand copies of Shentalinsky's book
were bought by fellow writers.

In its book form the material is presented in a highly effective manner
by combining excerpts culled directly from archival documents with imagined scenes based on those materials. Thus, the chapter devoted to Isaac
Babel, the first in the book, begins: "16 May 1939. It is early morning and
Moscow is still fast asleep. The only sounds are the peaceful chirruping of
the birds and the caretaker's broom sweeping the courtyard."[22] After a few
short dramatic paragraphs describing Babel's arrest, Shentalinsky writes:
"Perhaps that is how Isaac Babel would have described such an episode,
had he been allowed to finish the book he was writing about the Cheka.
Instead, that May morning he himself became a helpless prisoner of the
NKVD, arrested on the orders of Lavrenty Beria." This fictional scene is
later amplified by materials quoted directly from Babel's dossier, including
the last photograph of the condemned, excerpts from the records of his
cross-examination, as well as the handwritten testimony that he provided
under torture.

Although most of this information merely fills in a picture that had
been outlined earlier in other books devoted to the machinery of Stalin's
terror (most notably in Shentalinsky's best-known semijournalistic predecessor, Solzhenitsyn's monumental *Gulag Archipelago*), Shentalinsky is
sufficiently attuned to the specific literary aspects of the material to make
some shrewd comments about the specifics of Babel's situation. Thus, at
one point he quotes a long passage from Babel's confession in which he
discusses comments he made at a meeting with Soviet writers and film-
makers who had solicited his advice. After the quotation, Shentalinsky
comments: "We hardly find any theoretical reflections about art and the
role of the writer in Babel's books. He thought in images, like a poet. How
much more important then, is this enforced exposition of his artistic credo
for which the interrogators could find no use at all. Perhaps he committed
it to paper because he sensed there would be no other chance. Perhaps
there was even a secret calculation that one day, suddenly, his notes might
be read by another reader, and not just his interrogators" (51). Shentalinsky, in effect, becomes the posthumous amanuensis of his subjects, the
whole panoply of writers repressed by Stalin's terror.

22. Shentalinsky, 1996, 22.

With investigative journalistic finality, Shentalinsky also provides the details of the execution in all cases in which a given writer was killed: "Today we know the exact date and even the hour when Babel died: 1:30 am on 27 January 1940. Babel's name was first in a list of 16 to be executed. His remains were cremated the same day" (70). Shentalinsky's text, for all its obvious (and unconcealed) use of fictional recreations and devices, is meant to stand as the last word on the fate of each writer, at least insofar as the materials in the KGB archives can provide such a word. Each essay is a cenotaph, solid in its fact-based foundations, and replacing the previously unmarked graves in which the victims were buried.[23]

But Shentalinsky does not consider only those writers who were actually murdered by the Stalinist regime. Thus, in addition to Babel, Pavel Florensky (the only nonliterary writer considered in Shentalinsky's first volume), Boris Pilniak, Osip Mandelstam, and Nikolai Kliuev, he also considers the fates of writers who died in their beds and were never arrested, such as Mikhail Bulgakov, Andrei Platonov, and Maxim Gorky. Each case is presented in a literary format appropriate to the subject matter. Thus, the section on Bulgakov, who despite his fame as the author of the novel *The Master and Margarita* was also a prolific playwright, is entitled: "Under the Heel: The File on Mikhail Bulgakov: A Story in Six Acts with an Epilogue." It includes, in addition to the fictional recreations and documentary evidence provided in other sections, a number of scenes presented in dramatic form.

When writers were arrested or even investigated by the NKVD, their manuscripts were frequently arrested as well. Quoting Woland's famous line in *The Master and Margarita*, "Manuscripts don't burn," many Russians expected that with the opening of the KGB files a number of lost masterpieces would reappear. Unfortunately, for the most part it turned out that manuscripts did indeed burn, precisely because as opposed to depositions they were not generally considered crucial to the cases against writers (that is, in the Stalin era writers were not as a rule arrested for any specific thing they had written; and even when they were, they ended up actually being charged with belonging to fantastic Trotskyite conspiracies rather than producing seditious literature). Nevertheless, Shentalinsky did succeed in making literary discoveries in the KGB archives, and he interpolates excerpts from these into his texts as well, most notably in

---

23. In previous generations of East European writing, literary texts generally provided "the real truth." Thus, Danilo Kiš's fictional *A Tomb for Boris Davidovich* is precisely denominated a cenotaph for the victims of communism.

the chapters devoted to Nikolai Kliuev and Andrei Platonov. Shentalinsky
compares the fate of Kliuev's 4,000-line epic *The Song of the Great Mother*
to "the second birth of another one of our literary monuments—*The Lay
of Prince Igor* (twelfth century). *The Song* also rises up majestically from
the depths of time, from oblivion, and just as *The Lay* was rescued from the
Tatar yoke, so now *The Song* has been rescued from inhuman and blas-
phemous powers."[24]

Framing the stories devoted to Soviet writers in Shentalinsky's book is
the story of the volume's composition. It begins with an invocation of the
author's dacha in the waning days of the Soviet Union: "Night. A tranquil
dacha outside Moscow."[25] This opening would be echoed at the beginning
of the first chapter in the description of Babel's Peredelkino dacha. But
the first chapter is devoted to Shentalinsky's fight to get access to the documents that would make up the meat of the book, as well as the organization
of the committee that eventually forced the KGB to hand them over. The
final chapter, by contrast, takes place after the demise of the Soviet Union
and that of the Soviet writers' union (which outlasted it), a demise, it is
implied, that Shentalinsky's truth-telling exercise helped to bring about.
In the end then, Shentalinsky's book is as much the story of a mediocre
poet who had once implicitly supported the Soviet Union by writing verses
extolling the natural beauty of Kolyma and later transformed himself into
a crusading journalist who helped to destroy the Soviet Union by writing
about some of those who lost their lives in the Kolyma camps as it is the
story of those writers themselves. It illustrates that in the postcommunist
period journalism (in the broadest sense of the word) could become relevant to societies for which literature, at least the kind of literature that writers had traditionally produced, was less important than it had once been.

Feminism in Fiction and Journalism: The Work of Kinga Dunin

The type of journalistic work that Shentalinsky publishes is not the fare of
daily or even weekly newspapers. If we turn to Poland, and to a writer by
the name of Kinga Dunin, we can find an example of a fiction writer who

24. This passage was removed from the English-language text. It can be found in the
Russian version, p. 276. The entire text of Kliuev's poem was published in Shentalinsky, 1999,
285–379. In addition to Kliuev's monumental work, this volume contains fiction and poetry
by seventeen other Soviet-era writers rescued from the KGB archives.

25. This is how the Russian edition begins, at least. The English one has been changed.

has forged a second career as a successful newspaper journalist. Dunin is a well-respected author of feminist-inflected novels. In fact, her novel *Karoca z dyni* (Pumpkin carriage) was one of the finalists for the most prestigious literary prize in Poland, the Nike Prize.[26] In another era in Poland, recognition as a leading novelist might well have been sufficient. Dunin, however, wishes to be relevant for a larger audience than will buy and read complicated feminist prose fiction. So, like Shentalinsky, rather than merely complaining that no one reads literature any more, Dunin has taken matters into her own hands and become the chief columnist for Wysokie Obcasy (High heels), the weekly women's section of the newspaper *Gazeta Wyborcza*.

The newspaper itself deserves a mention in any consideration of postcommunist journalism. Having gotten its start as a samizdat publication in the days of Solidarity, it has, under the editorship of Adam Michnik (the leading Polish intellectual of our times), become a phenomenally successful business enterprise. It dominates the Polish newspaper market by combining hard-nosed journalism and political editorials with the kinds of American-style fluffy sections devoted to home, gardens, and women that are still almost unknown even in Western Europe.

Even within a single one of these "fluff" sections, however, one can discover an unusual variety of material, and the woman's section is no exception. Here we find much that would not be out of place in any broad-circulation American newspaper, including sections on fashion, cooking, and makeup. Alongside, however, there are a few surprises. The extensive book review section, for example, for the week that happens to be open on the Web version I have in front of me presents a wide variety of books chosen to interest women readers in particular.[27] They range from middlebrow fiction and pop-feminist psychology to such rarified subjects as novels by Jeanette Winterson and Margaret Atwood, a biography of Hildegard of Bingen, and a book of essays on Virginia Woolf.

Dunin's columns appear more or less biweekly in Wysokie Obcasy (she has published more than fifty of them by now), and they, too, range widely. These columns have the character of a typical feuilleton. There are frequent reviews of books, movies, and television shows, which are in fact pretexts for a more general consideration of current social and cultural issues.

---

26. Earlier novels by Dunin included *Tabu* (Warsaw: Wydawn, 1998) and *Obciach* (Warsaw: W.A.B., 1999).

27. *Gazeta Wyborcza*, Mar. 10, 2003, http://www2.gazeta.pl/obcasy/0,0.html?str=1.

Thus, for example, in her review of *Woman: An Intimate Geography*, by Natalie Angier, Dunin contests one of the stereotypes of feminism, juxtaposing it with scientific discourse.[28] In the monthly journal *Res Publica Nowa*, her review of David Lynch's *Mulholland Drive*, entitled "Lynch, a Bishop, and One Hundred Women," turned into an attack on the Polish government's policy toward abortion.[29] Another group of her texts is devoted entirely to a critique of public discourse and policy from the perspective of feminism. One of her feuilletons, for example, taking as a point of departure the holiday that in the former east bloc was called International Woman's Day (March 8) and that has now become a day of feminist street demonstrations, encourages readers to fight actively for women's rights in Poland: "I write this feuilleton, first of all, to those women who say: 'I agree with the postulates of women's movements... but to find myself in the group on the street... and besides personally I do not suffer from anything.'"[30]

In "Holiday of the Vagina"—a feuilleton centered around a review of the Polish premiere of Eve Ensler's *Vagina Monologues*—Dunin characterizes her vision of an engaged feminist journalism which would intervene into the everyday aspects of the situation of women in contemporary Poland: "I do not have the heart for creating grandiose projects—I rather prefer to act ad hoc, intervening in matters which for many people would seem to be insignificant, or even funny. Being a woman, however, I know that life for the most part consists of trifles."[31]

In her texts, Dunin frequently plays on stereotypes created by Polish "male-centered culture." She recognizes that, so far, women have rarely figured in any serious debate in Poland, including the debates regarding the question of their role in society. The major problem for Dunin, as a sociologist and publicist, follows the one formulated once by Meaghan Morris: under what conditions could women figure in such a debate?[32] The solution she promotes in her feuilletons, consistent with those of many Western theorists of feminism, demands a reframing of the public discourse in Poland away from a master narrative which legitimizes patriarchal models.

28. "Pokaż mi swoją baijkę" [Show me your fairy tale], Wysockie Obcasy, *Gazeta Wyborcza*, Aug. 18, 2001, 2.
29. "Lynch, biskup i sto kobiet," *Res Publica Nowa*, May 2002.
30. "Trzy razy tak" [Three times: yes], Wysokie Obcasy, *Gazeta Wyborcza*, Mar. 2, 2002, 40.
31. "Święto waginy," Wysokie Obcasy, *Gazeta Wyborcza*, Aug. 3, 2002, 33.
32. Morris, 11.

Avoiding essentialist, functional categories and dichotomies such as moth-
ering versus fathering functions, reproduction, fixed gender identities,
biology versus culture, she tries to show her readers how the master narrative of patriarchy is multiplied by Polish literature, journalism, or political
debates. In her feminist quest she does not even spare her boss, Adam
Michnik—a part owner of *Gazeta Wyborcza* as well as its general editor. "When Adam Michnik ... introduces himself to us: 'I am a playboy—
vodka, chicks, and that kind of stuff,' I want him to imagine that he is such
a chick, something between vodka and an appetizer—an object of play.
And so, how does it feel, okay?"[33] Dunin is undoubtedly conscious of the
fact that her vocabulary and rhetoric repeat those that have been used
by American feminists for the past twenty or thirty years, but reiterating
them is for her a necessary educational strategy for reframing the position
of Polish women. These repetitions form a kind of shock therapy for Polish
"patriarchal" society.

In sum, Dunin's strategy is to write openly about feminism, an approach
that is still rare in Poland. As a rule, women writers, even those inclined
to feminism, leave at least one layer of irony to distance themselves from
feminism in the form of an active and organized movement. Dunin, in her
feuilletons, right from the start, leaves no doubt in her belief that for a
woman's voice to be heard in Poland it must not be veiled by the comfort
of self-distancing and irony. "No one asks us our opinion, so this is why
the street is [the only forum] that is left for us."[34]

The Writer as Newspaper Publisher: Eduard Limonov
and Corneliu Vadim Tudor

While most East European writers have limited themselves to contributing
individual pieces or regular feature columns to newspapers and magazines,
a few have taken on the task of editing their own newspapers. Two of the
most notorious instances of this kind of journalistic activity are the radical right-wing papers *România Mare* (which bills itself as "an absolutely
independent weekly") and *Limonka* (subtitled *A Newspaper of Direct Action*). Constructed on a European model whereby a newspaper is often the

---

33. "Dwa osły i żona" [Two asses and a wife], Wysokie Obcasy, *Gazeta Wyborcza*, Nov.
20, 1999, 39.
34. "Trzy razy tak," 40.

mouthpiece of a particular political party or ideological orientation, these papers are the organs of the rabidly nationalistic and anti-Semitic România Mare and National Bolshevik parties, respectively. Their respective editors in chief are the writers Corneliu Vadim Tudor and Eduard Limonov.

I spoke about the literary and political career of Eduard Limonov in chapter 3. Here I would merely like to point out a few of the most striking rhetorical figures he employs in his newspaper. Perhaps the most obvious initial impression is that of an enormous level of aggression. There is practically not a single article in a given issue that does not in some way call for or glorify authoritarian rule, mass murder, or individual violence in either the past or present. Equally important is that the style and rhetoric borrow primarily from Lenin and the underground prerevolutionary Bolshevik press. Finally, one is struck by the monomaniacal presence of Limonov himself, whose voice and byline dominate the issues. Examining issue 13, for example (the issue is undated, but it appeared in May 1995), we find featured in the center of the front page a photograph of a socialist realist statue of a shock worker wielding a sledgehammer with the caption "A Man of Direct Action."[35] Just to the left of the photo is an editorial signed by Limonov that rails against the internal politics of the Russian Federation under Yeltsin. It concludes with the lines "Nevertheless, everything honest and heroic that remains in Russia will not give up without a fight. Hail to death!" Just below the photograph is an interview conducted by Limonov with the right-wing party leader Viktor Anpilov, which is accompanied by a grainy photograph of a screaming Anpilov seemingly leading a group of demonstrators into battle. Below this article is a sympathetic account of Hitler's Beer Hall Putsch. Across the top of the first page, in enormous type, is the newspaper's title, and down the right side of the page, in almost equally large letters, is the phrase "Socialism + Nationalism = Bliss."

The second page features an article by Limonov entitled "Limonka among the Croatians." This piece was one of those cited by Russian prosecutors as "fanning national hatred," and it is easy to see why. In response to the beginning of the Croatian offensive that drove the Serbs from Krajina, Limonov describes the Croatians as a malicious nation. "The double influence of the Turks and the Germans lent this nation a particular malevolence." Limonov ends his article as follows: "The Croatians are friends of the Germans. They are not our friends. The Croatians are excellent soldiers, but they can be killed and the Serbs are braver than they are. There are evil nations. One of them is the Croats. Let their children be born without fingers." Just below this article is a photograph of a young Serbian woman in combat fatigues carrying a submachine gun. Presumably she is one of those brave Serbs who will kill the attacking Croatians.

The fourth and final page of the newspaper features an article entitled "Students Learn How to Fight," describing student demonstrations against the government in April 1995, as well as a document entitled "A Short Course in the NBP." In its title, of course, it imitates Stalin's famous *Short Course in the History of the USSR* while in its uncompromising rhetoric it is closer to the manifestos produced by the Russian futurists just before World War I. After Limonov's most recent arrest, however, the newspaper moderated its tone somewhat, as can be judged by the issues that appear on the Web site http://www.limonka-online.narod.ru/. Whether this change was the result of the editor and publisher's absence or illustrates a moderation of Limonov's views is an open question.

In the waning days of the Ceauşescu regime, Corneliu Vadim Tudor (born 1949) was known as the dictator's "court poet." He was, simultaneously, closely associated with a nationalist weekly newspaper, *Săptămîa*. He became notorious in Romanian society for an openly anti-Semitic editorial he published there in September 1980. Interestingly, what triggered the editorial was the controversy surrounding the publication of the collected journalistic works of Mihai Eminescu. As was noted in chapter 1, Eminescu plays the role of the Romanian national poet and founder of the nation. Although his verse is primarily lyrical and his patriotism as expressed there remains within the bounds of acceptable national feeling, his contemporary journalism and unpublished manuscripts "were morbidly anti-Semitic, for Eminescu's xenophobia extended to any and all 'non-ethnics.'"[36]

Though his newspaper was lightly reprimanded for the tone of the editorial, Tudor was more or less untouched. Then, in 1983, in the words of Michael Shafir, a leading student of Romanian politics, "in a volume of verse entitled *Saturnali* published in December 1983, Tudor resurrected the Eminescu controversy and went well beyond any previously encountered expression of anti-Semitic instigation. A poem entitled 'Eminescu at Thirty-Three' displayed a battery of stereotypical religious and secular associations drawn from the lexicon of local and international

36. Michael Shafir, "Anti-Semitism in the Postcommunist Era," in Braham, 337.

anti-Semitism.... Though history can never be turned back, he warned his interlocutors, they would be well advised to 'return to where you take your rotten pieces of silver from,' as they were known to be nothing but 'lazy' bums renowned for blackmail.... For these and other ancient sins, 'On your head and that of your offspring, / May forever fall our ancestors' blood. / For these crimes cursed be your name / And may I live to revenge them.'"[37]

One might have expected that after Ceaușescu's fall from power in December 1989, his court poet would have fared badly. But by June 1990 a new weekly publication entitled *România Mare* (Greater Romania) began appearing under the editorship of Tudor. Until quite recently, this newspaper, along with a number of other sympathetic publications, served up a virulent anti-Semitic, anticapitalist, and antiforeign message with a glorification of the dictatorship of Tudor's former protector, Ceaușescu. Again, to quote Shafir, "In the view of the contributors to these publications, it is not communism as such that is to be blamed for Romania's misfortunes, but its 'Jewish-Soviet' version. Hence, Ceaușescu, who had Romanian-ized the RCP [Romanian Communist Party], is one in a long row of great national leaders who struggled for independence."[38]

Although the newspaper *România Mare* was founded first, since May 1991 it has served as the organ of a political party of the same name, a party whose leader is Corneliu Vadim Tudor. Thus, as in the case of Eduard Limonov, the editor in chief of the party newspaper is also the party president. Unlike, Limonov, however, Tudor has been relatively successful politically. In the elections of September 1992, the Greater Romania Party (PRM) managed to pick up almost 4% of the votes cast, and it held seats in both the lower and upper houses of parliament. Their share of public support then grew. At first this growth was gradual. Thus, in the 1996 elections the PRM garnered less than 5% of the votes. After the elections in 2000, however, its share of seats in both houses of parliament grew to more than 20%, and Tudor himself finished second in the presidential balloting, forcing the eventual winner Ion Iliescu into a runoff.

Surprisingly, it does not appear that anyone has undertaken a serious analysis of the rhetorical strategies that Tudor's newspaper has pursued in recent years. As it turns out, Tudor has significantly changed his tone and is, at least in his public persona, no longer the person whom Shafir

37. Ibid., 338.
38. Ibid., 347.

described.[39] To this day the newspaper remains highly nationalist, even irredentist (insisting that Romanians living in Moldova, Bukovina, and Vojvodina should all be incorporated into a greater Romanian state), and continues to employ extravagant, essentially libelous attacks on opponents as well as racial stereotyping and slurs of many kinds. However, its primary focus is no longer on the cult of Ceauşescu and the Jewish or communist conspiracy.[40] Rather, the vast majority of the paper is devoted to slashing attacks on Romania's current political elite, with the primary focus being on corruption. To be sure, Tudor does not hesitate to call Romania's political leaders Jews, Gypsies, lackeys of the West, and so forth. But the primary message is a nationalist and populist one.

It would appear, therefore, that in preparation for the 2004 elections (in which he ultimately fared poorly), Tudor was attempting to position himself as the voice not of wild extremism but rather as a shrill but nevertheless acceptable populist alternative to a government he portrayed as corrupt, overly pandering to outsiders, and therefore out of touch with the needs and desires of average Romanians. In addition to attacks, the paper now serves up a good dose of the wit and wisdom of Tudor himself (it serialized a collection of his aphorisms, for example), combined with some folk poetry and religious imagery. But the days of uncontrolled aggression are over. Whether this is because Tudor mellowed or was merely a tactic to attract voter support in the run-up to an election campaign is unclear.

East European writers have, as we have seen, chosen a wide variety of journalistic approaches to allow themselves to continue to attract audiences at home and abroad. Journalism, with its promise to tell "the truth" in an unproblematic way, is attractive in countries where previously nonfiction genres had been more fictional than literature, and prose and poetry filled the gap. It is also one of the few ways to earn a living by the pen in postcommunist societies. As a result, we can expect to see even more journalistic work in the portfolios of East European writers.

39. Tudor's career has also been considered in the context of other radical right-wing movements in postcommunist Eastern Europe in the study of Tismaneanu.
40. Indeed, one can even find the occasional article praising something Jewish, although not Romanian Jewish.

CHAPTER SEVEN

Dealing with Transition Head-On

What would happen if, in our days, people were really to learn to live without literature?—
Vladimir Makanin

Considering the trauma postcommunist transition has inflicted upon writers, it is curious how few literary works have appeared that confront head-on the essence of the new realities of East European society and culture. After all, given that all local readers and writers have experienced the transition "on their own skins" (as the Russians say), one would think there would be great interest among the reading public in literary works that could interpret and synthesize the recent past. And yet, writers struggling to retain their influence have for the most part shied away from this subject.

Any number of reasons can be adduced for this. The first is that the "social demand" to be politically relevant and to produce descriptions of everyday reality was the stock-in-trade of official literature in communist countries. Freed of such strictures, many writers have chosen to avoid the everyday in favor of other subjects. Second, new social conditions have been particularly problematic for writers, knocking them off their unquestioned pedestal as society's leading men and women and reducing them to at best second-class status. It is perhaps not surprising that most writers would find this a disagreeable topic. And finally, one might legitimately ask whether, in this exceptionally unstable period, the novel is an appropriate medium. After all, at the very least novels require that the implied author have some kind of Archimedean distance from the subject matter, even if this distance is itself always a fiction. In a time of flux for both writers and society not many authors dare to assert that they have found such a point.

Nevertheless, a few have tried and succeeded, and their works will be the focus of this chapter.

It is quite possible that the Russian Vladimir Makanin and the Czech Jáchym Topol do not know of each other's existence.[1] It is almost certain that they did not when they were writing the two works to be discussed here—Topol's novel *Sister* was published as early as 1994, while Makanin's *Underground, or A Hero of Our Time* appeared in 1998.[2] Nevertheless, their novels have much in common. Both are long (more than five-hundred-page) first-person narratives presented by a character who had been an author of literary work (with all that entailed) during the communist era but who claims to have renounced his profession in the postcommunist period. At the same time, such a claim clearly needs to be taken with a grain of salt, as the existence of the first-person narrative in the reader's hands demonstrates. Both narrators spend a large percentage

1. Vladimir Makanin was born in 1937 in the Urals, and he was trained as a mathematician and later as a filmmaker. His first passion was chess and then the cinema, but he made his name with his highly individual stories, which won him instant fame among the Russian intelligentsia during the years of the thaw. Unlike the hero of the novel to be discussed here, Makanin succeeded in publishing in official journals in Russia in the 1970s and 1980s, although not all of his work saw the light at that time. Also unlike his hero, Makanin continued to write prolifically after the collapse of communism and is now one of Russia's best-known serious writers. Many of his novels have appeared in translation in Germany, France, Spain, and Eastern Europe. Among his works available in English are the novel *Manhole* (which was short-listed for the Booker Russian Novel Prize in 1992), published by Ardis, *Baize-Covered Table with Decanter* (which won the Russian Booker Prize in 1993), published by Readers International in 1995, and the collection entitled *The Loss*, published by Northwestern University Press in 1998. Jáchym Topol was born in Prague in 1962. His father, Josef Topol, is a renowned Czech playwright, poet, and Shakespeare translator, who was active in dissident activities. Topol's writing began with lyrics for a rock band called Psí vojáci (Dog soldiers), led by his younger brother, Filip, in the late seventies and early eighties. In 1982 he cofounded the samizdat magazine *Violit*, and in 1985 Topol cofounded *Revolver Revue*, a samizdat journal that specialized in new Czech writing. Topol played an active part in the 1989 Velvet Revolution in Czechoslovakia, taking part in initial meetings of Civic Forum, as well as writing, editing, and publishing the independent newsletter *Informační servis* [Information service], which became, after the revolution, the investigative weekly *Respekt*. Topol remained at *Respekt* as a reporter while continuing as editor in chief of *Revolver Revue*. His first collection of poetry, *I Love You Madly*, published in samizdat in 1988, received the Tom Stoppard Prize for Unofficial Literature. Topol's first work of fiction, *Sister* [Sestra], was published by Atlantis in 1994; his novella *Andel* [Angel] (the name of a Prague metro stop) was published in 1995. An English edition of *Sestra* appeared in 2000 under the title *City Sister Silver*, trans. Alex Zucker (New Haven, CT: Catbird Press). For more on Topol, see Segel, 571–572.

2. These are by no means the only novels that discuss the issue of transition directly. One other Russian work that does so is Viktor Pelevin's *Generation P* (1999; translated into English as *Homo Zapiens*). Having as its hero a former poet, who in post-Soviet times becomes a writer of advertising copy, the novel has strong connections with the works discussed here. For a cinematic treatment of these issues, see the film *Filantropica* by the Romanian director Nae Caranfil.

of the novels in drug-induced hazes, alcohol being the primary intoxicant. Both works are structured as kaleidoscopic picaresques rather than as conventionally plotted novels. The most striking difference between them is stylistic. Makanin's narrator writes in a fairly traditional realist style (though his lexicon displays a large number of colloquialisms), building his narrative quite consciously on the nineteenth-century Russian tradition (particularly the works of Dostoevsky). Although he sometimes employs complex flashbacks, the overall narrative line is easy to follow. Topol's narrator employs an extremely loose stream-of-consciousness style reminiscent of Jack Kerouac's, and his narrative weaves reality with dreams, flashbacks, and flash-forwards. As Ivan Klíma puts it, "The plot lines are so complex and intertwined that it is pointless to try to summarize them" (back jacket). What is more, Topol's text is filled with neologisms and attempts to break down the time-honored distinction between spoken and written Czech. A final major difference concerns their spatiotemporal focus—Makanin's novel concentrates on space, in particular on the new perceptions of space created by the privatization of apartments, which coincides with the breakup of Soviet attitudes toward the collective. Topol, by contrast, is primarily interested in time, particularly in the notion that in the postcommunist period time has accelerated beyond the control of those who came of age during the stagnation of the late communist years.

Makanin's attempt (or Makanin's narrator's attempt) to find a space for his work in the grand narrative of classic Russian literature begins squarely with the jarring title—*Andergraund, ili Geroi nashego vremeni*.[3] The second half of the title is lifted directly from Mikhail Lermontov's only novel, a work often considered to mark the inception of the Russian psychological novel. The title's first half is a colloquial expression that was used by nonofficial Russian artists and writers of the Brezhnev period to identify their status. It is not a Russian word, of course, but rather an English expression transliterated phonetically in Cyrillic characters. Their choice of the English word was a conscious attempt to disassociate themselves from official Soviet anti-Western (particularly anti-American) policies and to emphasize their outsider status. At the same time, when used in a title, the word is a tip-off to the Russian reader that there will likely be some connection not only to the realities of the literary nonconformist movement of the Brezhnev era, but also to the Russian calque of this

---

3. Makanin, 1999. Further references to this novel will be made by page number in the main text. Translations are mine.

borrowing—that is to say, to the word *podpol'e*, used most famously in Dostoevsky's *Notes from Underground* (in Russian, *Zapiski iz podpol'ia*). Finally, the *or* in the title points to the most famous nonrealist work of Russian literature, Gogol's so-called poem *Dead Souls, or The Adventures of Chichikov*. Each of those potential subtexts turns out to be relevant for a reading of the novel. Thus, from the beginning, we can guess that Makanin (or his narrator, depending on who we think provided the title) is aiming very high, demanding that his work be read in the context of three of the most important classics of the Russian tradition.

The connection with the subtexts evoked by the title continues with the work's epigraph, taken from the controversial author's preface to the second edition of *Hero of Our Time*: "The hero...is a portrait, but not of a single individual: it is a portrait composed of the vices of our entire generation in their full development." The claim to typicality as well as the claim that a literary work could indeed encapsulate the experience of an entire generation was characteristic of both the Russian and the Soviet literary traditions.[4] What is more, it hints that this narrator will be linked with Pechorin, the central character of Lermontov's novel and one of the early representatives of the so-called superfluous man in the Russian literary tradition. These superfluous men, whose genealogy can be traced from Pushkin's Eugene Onegin through Lermontov's hero to the protagonists of Turgenev's novels and many of Chekhov's stories, are traditionally extremely intelligent and highly articulate but incapable of taking concrete and positive actions in the real world.

Makanin's narrative itself begins in medias res, with the narrator sitting down to read Heidegger (in Russian translation) but being interrupted by a slightly drunken visitor. The cocktail mixed from high culture and alcohol will turn out to be characteristic for the novel as a whole.[5] By the second page we discover that the narrator is a writer: "When they need me to have someone to chat with, then I'm a writer. I'm used to it. When I'm not needed, then I'm a schizo, a watchman, a failure, a parasite, whatever, just an old graphomaniac" (8). He is, however, rather a strange sort of writer, as he has never published anything, neither before the fall of the Soviet regime, when his work was apparently not acceptable for official

---

4. I treat this topic extensively in my article "Psychology and Society in the Classic Russian Novel," in Jones and Miller, 130–149.

5. In his excellent article devoted to this novel, G. S. Smith (2001) notes, "Drink is omnipresent in the novel. This is the most thoroughly alcohol-soaked Russian narrative since Erofeev's *Moskva-Petushki*" (6).

publication, nor after. Still, the fact that he is known to be a writer, that he plays the role of "the writer," is crucial, as he is well aware: "So I was needed. Needed just precisely in the role of a failure, in the role of *sort of a writer*, because the prestige of a writer in the first years of the post-Soviet epoch was still extremely high" (18). Insofar as our narrator will turn out to be representative of his generation (as the epigraph promised), then that generation is Makanin's own, composed of those who came of age in the Brezhnev era and who lived through late communism and postcommunism.

As we continue with the novel, we find out that the narrator is called Petrovich by all who know him. The use of a patronymic rather than a first or last name is, in everyday Russian life, a sign that the person so denominated is a simple sort, the salt of the earth. From a literary standpoint, any Russian reader would expect a connection between this narrator and the bluff, somewhat limited, and confused narrator of parts of Lermontov's *Hero of Our Time*. And indeed, the narrator of Makanin's novel does share some characteristics with Lermontov's Petrovich, particularly a penchant for grumbling more or less good-naturedly at his contemporary world. Unlike Lermontov's narrator, however, Makanin's Petrovich is the hero of the novel. And like Lermontov's hero Pechorin (or, even more important, some of Dostoevsky's heroes), he is obsessed with writing about himself and has a definite flair for the perverse.

Particularly perverse appears to be his refusal, in the new post-Soviet conditions, to achieve fame and fortune as a writer, as have so many of his former underground companions. Although he has had opportunities to "better himself," Petrovich continues to live the life of a demimonde bohemian, working occasionally at the quintessential communist-era job for persecuted writers, a watchman of apartments whose owners are on vacation in an enormous apartment building cum dormitory (a microcosm of Muscovite society). Much of the first half of the novel consists of his visits to various apartments in the building. Somewhat reminiscent of Chichikov's visits to the various landowners in the town of N. in Gogol's "poem," they allow Petrovich to provide sketches of their inhabitants and their successes and failures in the new society. In that same building, he has managed to stake out a Raskolnikov-like corner for himself: "A horrible little spot, but permanent: an anchor in the seaweed. All I have there is a cot. I attached my typewriter to it by a metal chain, a pretty strong one (having put the chain under the carriage so it couldn't be swiped). I don't write. I've given it up. But the typewriter is my old partner (actually a Yugoslav girl), and it gives me a bit of status" (33). Like Akaky Akakievich's overcoat in Gogol's famous story, the typewriter (gendered feminine in Russian) has apparently substituted for a wife, providing both companionship and a modicum of status to our contemporary little man.

But at least from the narrator's point of view the reason for being a writer disappeared as soon as it became possible for members of the former underground to publish. As a result, he not only refuses to have his work published; he also claims to have given up writing altogether in the present of the novel (that is, in the early to mid-1990s). Petrovich is well aware that this is a minority point of view, as can be seen in his report of the reaction of one of the now successful "democrats" when Petrovich refuses his offer to help him become a published writer: "'What?!'—he practically choked. This destroyed his entire understanding of the underground. He thought that the underground were those who had suffered under the communists and now wanted their cookie and glass of milk. 'I don't want to'—I repeated, not explaining anything because other words would just have confused him even more" (71).

To understand the central point of Makanin's novelistic analysis of his own generation we must carefully analyze Petrovich's seemingly absurd position. Why is it that a man whose entire life was wrapped up in being a writer does not have any desire either to publish his old work or to create new work when it becomes possible to reach an audience? To answer this question we need to discover what, from Petrovich's point of view, it meant to be a writer in communist times. In turn, this will allow us to grasp the essence of that society and the meaning of the transition to postcommunism.

Although he never says it in so many words, Petrovich recognizes that in the communist era the importance of being an underground writer had nothing to do with the literary work one produced. Instead, being a writer (that is, being identified and self-identified as one) had everything to do with the social and moral position implied by the activity. In a society that officially valued only the collective, writing (but, emphatically, not reading or publishing) became one of the few available ways to emphasize that a person had retained his individuality. A writer valued himself and was valued by others not so much for what he said (which in any case was pretty much unavailable) as because he represented the possibility of personal freedom within an oppressive world.

When that world disappeared in the wake of Gorbachev's reforms, most members of the underground rejoiced at the possibility of seeing their work

in print. They had, apparently, understood the essence of their activity as
protest against the Soviet state. With its demise they were free to come to
the surface, to take their rightful place in "normal" society. From Petrovich's point of view, however, this was an error. The true meaning of the
underground was that it allowed for an assertion of individuality as such
(the assertion of "my 'I'" as he puts it many times in the course of his
text). An underground writer was, therefore, not fighting the Soviet system but any system that oppresses the ego (and every system does). From
Petrovich's perspective, then, the main difference between the Soviet and
post-Soviet worlds is not that one oppressed the individual while the other
did not. Rather, it is that taking a principled stand in favor of one's own ego
was socially acceptable in Soviet times (because sanctioned by the larger
underground community), while now it seems perverse. The one flaw in
Petrovich's argument is his failure to acknowledge that the underground
was itself a system with its own strict code of laws, although, as I will argue
later, his tender concern with the life and work of his younger brother can
be seen as an implicit recognition of that fact.

Petrovich, then, remains true to the radical avant-garde belief that any
work acceptable to society is ipso facto tainted. This was a relatively easy
position to take in Soviet times, because society was willing to accept only a
very limited type of work. In the new conditions, however, it is far more difficult to maintain. Indeed, once society becomes willing to accept any work
of art, the only principled way to defend one's ego is to lapse into silence.
Precisely the battle between the expectation that an artist would want to
see his work in print and this particular artist's desire to defend his outsider, underground position at all costs constitutes the central theme of the
novel. We can see this desire thematized in the narrator's movement from
being "underground" (i.e., part of a communist-era movement) to going
"podpol'e" (also underground but now, in postcommunist conditions, a
much more solitary underground).

It is exceptionally significant that the Russian *podpol'e* connotes a particular kind of space, while (in Russian) *anderground* is a purely metaphor-
ical concept. As Régine Robin puts it, "To the Crystal Palace with its utopi-
ans, Dostoevsky opposes the underground or, more precisely, a podpol'e,
that is, the space between the floor and the joists in a wooden house."[6]
For actual physical space plays a major role in the novel. Petrovich is fascinated by "square meters" as he calls apartments ("lived-in odoriferous

6. Robin, 145.

meters, now make up the many-visaged face of the world for me" [32]). In particular he, along with other characters in the book, is fascinated by how these square meters come to be privatized, bartered, bought, sold, and stolen.

The old *obshchaga* (dormitory) in which he lives was in many ways a horrible place, but it was an inclusive one, as he notes near the very beginning of the novel: "By now the corridors are the only thing that remains of the connected space (and life) of the former dormitory" (17). Just as do many of the incidental characters in the novel, Petrovich himself manages on a number of occasions to acquire some square meters of his own. But he is constitutionally unable to hold on to them and loses them almost immediately to members of society who are better able to grab private space in the new conditions of bandit capitalism. Eventually, this leads to his being kicked unceremoniously out of the building he has called home for many years, and to his descent to an even more unsavory flophouse apartment. But Petrovich's inability to hang onto his own space, which might be seen simply as an inability to deal with post-Soviet reality, is, like his refusal to publish, actually one more "undergroundmanish" manifestation of his protest against the new society that compartmentalizes and individualizes. The spaces Petrovich prefers can be characterized as limited or closed collectives—the dormitory or apartment house, the insane asylum, the world of the communist era "anderground," the world of classical Russian literature. These are in opposition to the forced and false collective of Soviet society as a whole and the atomized society of postcommunism. As the former enemy has more or less vanished by the time of the narrative's beginning, however, the latter is more consistently attacked in Petrovich's text.

Just as Dostoevsky's narrator railed against the rationalist and optimistic views of progress so popular in the Russian society of his day, so does Petrovich go after the pieties of the post-Soviet world. For both heroes the possibility of and need for free choice far outstrip any benefits provided by a society or way of thinking that limits such choice. The only way to express that position, however, is to live almost completely outside the rules of society (or to break those rules whenever possible). Petrovich's podpol'e position is thematized in the novel through his treatment of those members of the former underground who have achieved success in the new world. We first see this attitude in his description of his relationship with an alcoholic poetess named Veronika. In the Soviet period, she was an equally underground writer (and a bad one, judged by the quality of the few verses that Petrovich reproduces in the text—incidentally, he never provides as much as a line of his own communist-era texts). In the perestroika period, however, Veronika joins the democratic forces and quickly becomes an important official. "And then, Veronika was doing something important and necessary. A person is always doing something important if he is on top. *I fell out of love with her immediately*" (51; emphasis mine). Petrovich appears to have internalized perfectly the logic of Dostoevsky's underground man. Any success is by definition a failure because it means sacrificing one's principles, no matter how idiosyncratic or perverse, to the collective. In this instance, however, we don't find out in great detail what Veronika thinks about her choice.

Toward the end of the novel, however, in a subsection with the Dostoevskian subtitle "Dvoinik" (The double), we get a fuller explication of the situation. At the offices of a new publishing house to which Petrovich goes for no reason other than to observe the collapsing relics of the former underground, he meets the now successful writer Zykov. Zykov is a member of an editorial board that rumor has it will organize the publication of an anthology of one hundred authors. As Petrovich puts it, "The book will, of course, be a fat one, a paper brick. The book will be set in tiny, tiny type. It will be published and immediately forgotten, unsold and fragile, with pages falling out, falling apart, friable like dried out clay. Like a little mound. Like a hump of dirt in a garden—a mass grave of writers who managed to drag themselves into the age of Gorbi. (But happiness even so. What can you say! Look at how their faces shone!)" (506–507), Zykov, however, ignores the other writers and immediately turns to Petrovich, who had, at one time, been seen as his competitor in the underground. Now Zykov has become famous in Russia and abroad, but he clearly misses the bad old days of communism. As Petrovich puts it, "In secret, I believe, he pined for the days when he was talented, hungry, and chronically drunk" (508). Zykov invites Petrovich to his house and, after a long, drunken conversation, admits to being worried that the underground (and Petrovich as its last and most perfect representative) does not fully respect him because one of his friends had once been a KGB major. He must know the opinion of the underground, "the unconscious of society" as Petrovich puts it, and this is more important to him than any literary fame he has achieved in the broader world. No such doubts assail the narrator, for he has succeeded in preserving the purity of his position, albeit at the cost of driving himself farther and farther underground.

Petrovich is not only haunted by the possibility of literary words appearing in the postunderground world. He is bothered by any and all verbal

signs, especially public ones, that have sprouted up in the post-Soviet jun-
gle. Thus, he sits in a subway car and looks at the advertisements (a fact
of life that had never existed in Soviet days). *"Protection against racke-
teers ... All kinds of security services ... Grates, Anti-thuggery ...* The world
was becoming filled not so much with new things as with new signs. The
things themselves weren't disgusting, but rather their burgeoning signs;
that's what is beyond any aesthetic system. A typical semiotic underground
(the underground after it has stepped out into the air). Perhaps I would
have become like that had I come out into the world. No. Forget it. The
ever-growing (and ever more irritating) novelty of life, or, to put it better,
my ego's quotidian kowtowing to that novelty, that is what made me a
person who was once a writer. Over twenty years had passed and my 'I'
demanded freedom from novellas and their stories; perhaps it wanted to
become both a story and a novella" (60).

The main point, then, is that writing and being a writer in the Soviet
days provided a peculiar vantage point that, at least from Petrovich's perspective, cannot be achieved through writing and publishing literary work
in the post-Soviet period. He needs to devise another method to assert
his ego now, one independent of the writing process. This does not mean
abandoning the world of literature altogether. Not surprisingly, given the
literary propensities of the narrator, his attempt to turn from writer to
character (from an observer of the world to an actor in the world) takes
place as a series of quotations. The first involves his murder of a Chechen
man who attempts to rob him one summer night while he is sitting outside
meditating. The Chechen sits down next to Petrovich, demands money
and cigarettes, and then attempts to lord it over him by pulling out a bottle
of vodka. The narrator asks for a gulp and the two sit drinking, side by
side. Their drinking eventually turns into a kind of surrogate duel, which
becomes real when the Chechen pulls out a knife. As it happens, the narrator also has a knife (something the Chechen did not expect), and, after
having been wounded, he kills the Chechen. The duel between a Russian
and a man from the Caucasus replays a host of clichéd scenes from Russian
literature of the nineteenth century, although its transposition to a park
bench in Moscow lends it a contemporary touch. The central literary theme,
however, is not the novel of the Caucasus or the duel, but rather the mind
of the killer after the act. As Petrovich puts it to himself, "When a man has
killed, he does not depend so much on the murder, but rather on all he has
read about murders or seen on the screen, that is my thought. A man who
has killed deals with virtual reality. He is pulled into a dialogue" (168).
Specifically, the narrator is pulled into a dialogue with Raskolnikov. Like

Dostoevsky's hero, he engages in self-examination after the fact and finds that he comes up wanting. Although he killed, at least in part, to prove to himself that he could be an actor rather than merely an observer, he finds that, far from being exalted by the deed, he becomes more like everyone else (his greatest fear), protecting himself, covering his tracks, and so forth.

He is taken in for questioning by the police (who employ tricks worthy of Dostoevsky's Porfiry Petrovich in an attempt to trap the killer into confessing), but he does not crack. Though he avoids becoming a prisoner of the state, he remains in thrall to Russian literature, as he recognizes after one of his interrogations. He asks himself whether the state and its organs could possibly elicit his respect, and recognizes that they could not. Instead, "the only collective judge before whom I feel (sometimes) the need to justify myself is precisely what my brain has been occupied with for the past twenty five years—Russian literature, not so much the texts themselves as their noble breeding, their exalted echo" (179). In its Dostoevskian variant the model of Russian literature should lead him to a public confession of his crime. But the narrator knows there is more to Russian literature than Dostoevsky and that to kill someone is not always a crime. As he puts it, "Literature is like a reproof. Like a great virus (literature is always working inside of us). But *thou shalt not kill* on the page is not the same as *thou shalt not kill* on the snow. And not to denigrate the authority of F.M., but a Russian has the right to go back three decades (just a single generation) from his days, from his martyr days, and bow to the authority of others" (186). Petrovich chooses to interpret the murder not as a Dostoevskian "crime" but rather as a duel in a work by Pushkin or Lermontov, either of whom would likely have approved of his actions given their own rich dueling history. As a result, there is nothing to expiate, and life can proceed. At the same time, the catharsis that could have been produced inside him by his willingness to transgress moral and ethical law fails to be achieved. According to the perverse logic of his underground position, a successful murder would have proved to Petrovich that his ego could assert itself in the post-Soviet period as strongly as it had (through writing) in the Soviet age. But a successful duel is not sufficient because it lacks any real element of transgression.

To recapture the self-esteem he lost together with the writer's prestige, Petrovich must turn to more extreme measures. One is to murder again, this time in far more morally questionable circumstances, and the other is to rescue a fallen woman. In both cases, the other protagonists are directly connected with the Soviet world that the hero is trying simultaneously to preserve and overcome. Although Petrovich describes numerous short- and medium-term sexual encounters in the course of his rambling narrative, the central one is his relationship with Lesia Dmitrievna Voinova. In the Soviet period Lesia Dmitrievna's martial last name (derived from the Russian word for "warrior") had, according to Petrovich, been entirely appropriate. Married to a professor at a literary institute and herself a scholar of sorts, she had made a career in the Brezhnev era by hounding unorthodox writers and thinkers (including Petrovich himself) out of official Soviet literary and cultural life. Now her husband has died and she herself has been pushed out of her job. Once elegant and beautiful, she is now fat, ugly, and decrepit. Like his Dostoevskian predecessor, Petrovich is attracted by failure and cannot resist the urge to "save" Lesia. After all, although she was a victimizer under the old system, she has now become a victim of the new. This urge becomes even stronger when she suffers a stroke and the hero forces himself to tend to her enormous, half-dead body until she recovers her strength. At the same time, his sexual relations with Lesia are by no means entirely altruistic. They can be viewed simply as a form of revenge taken by the underground man against a symbolic embodiment of Soviet power. This is true even though Lesia herself has forgotten her role in expelling the narrator from the literary institute and he makes no effort to remind her. By sleeping with this relic of the past, Petrovich asserts his ability to dominate and control it.

As was the case with the underground man, Petrovich's love affair with an "insulted and injured" woman does not prove salvific. Petrovich gives two reasons for this (the novel is written as a series of interrelated flashbacks, and it is not always easy to tell which events happened in which order). The first is that, with the help of old friends who eventually figure out new roles for themselves in the post-Soviet period, Lesia begins to crawl out of the deep hole into which immediate post-Soviet reality had cast her. As happened with Veronika earlier in the novel, as soon as the underground man's girlfriend achieves some degree of success or independence he must, by the logic of his position, stop loving her, for his love is precisely conditioned on her being in an utterly humiliated situation.

More crucial, however, is the narrator's realization that while he was attempting to use his relationship with Lesia to stand in for his attitude toward the entire Soviet past, she had had her own purposes. She, it turns out, was projecting her disgust with her past onto Petrovich, trying to atone for her past sins through their relationship. She was most disgusted with her role in firing someone who had gone on to become an alcoholic janitor at the institute. She wished at first to expiate this sin by giving her body to the old man himself but could not force herself to do so. Petrovich becomes a substitute. As he recognizes, "That old guy was just too much: she would have become nauseous. But with a downtrodden watchman from the underground (with me) her humiliation and repentance could be channeled into a much better outlined cultural stream. I (my self-esteem) could not not have been insulted. But I was able to do one other thing: I did not show that I was insulted. I just stopped visiting her" (250). As was the case with Dostoevsky's hero, the modern underground man can have only a sadistic relationship with a woman, one in which he, as low as he is, feels himself superior. As soon as he sees that she does not accept this superiority, the relationship is over.

Neither killing in a duel nor the sexual duel can allow our hero to escape the burden of his past and find a role for himself as an actor rather than an observer. His final attempt to do so is through a second murder, this time of Chubisov, a small-time KGB informer who is also a longtime hanger-on in underground circles. In the course of a long, drunken evening (one of many that dot the novel), Petrovich discovers that not only is Chubisov carrying a tape recorder in order to make recordings that will be handed over to the KGB, but also he has inserted a calumny against Petrovich on the tape— that is, he has made it sound not as if he invited himself to take part in the drunken conversation but as if Petrovich had invited him to do so. This attempt to besmirch Petrovich's honor ("the only thing an underground artist possesses" [271]) leads him to murder Chubisov. Interestingly, it is not merely the fact that Chubisov is working for the KGB that leads Petrovich to kill. As was usually the case in the Soviet Union, everyone in the circles in which Chubisov moved was aware of his KGB connections, although in the present of the novel some of the remaining underground artists appear convinced that he has given up this line of work. What is important is a literary fact. Petrovich sees his entire former writing career as having been neither more nor less than a matter of retaining his honor. He is no longer a writer, but he cannot stand to see the honor represented by his life and his texts besmirched by Chubisov's slander. "I have to. I can't give in. For two and a half decades I drummed on the typewriter keys. Should I throw away my 'I,' my texts (now I also insisted on the texts), just because he was also a person?" (281). Like Raskolnikov before him, Petrovich commits murder not for gain but for an idea, in order to retain his sense of having an independent and honorable ego. "There was nothing else to be done:

he was trying to destroy my 'I' that was so much greater than me and that I had been nurturing and protecting my entire life" (282). And like Raskolnikov, he can kill only by forgetting the humanness of his victim.

The murder, when it takes place, occurs exactly like that of the Chechen—Petrovich stabs his victim in the back. Again, no physical evidence links him to the crime. But, like Raskolnikov before him, he feels a strong need to turn himself in after the deed. In order both to do so and to avoid so doing he allows himself to be committed for a time to the same psychiatric hospital where his younger brother Venedikt has been a patient for many years. It is the mental hospital and the relationship of the two mental patient brothers, with all of their implied literary associations from Gogol's "Diary of a Madman" to Chekhov's "Ward No. 6," that we need to examine in order to understand the narrator's ultimate view of his society and its potential. Like the apartment building in which the narrator lived at the outset of the novel, the mental hospital forms a closed society that functions as a microcosm of the larger world. It has its own hierarchy, headed by psychiatrists and nurses and proceeding down through patients who can be quiet, out of control, or criminal. Readers of the novel have become familiar with the world of the mental hospital earlier through the narrative line connected with Petrovich's brother. According to him, his younger brother Venedikt was the true artistic genius in the family. As an inveterate prank player and naturally antiauthoritarian type, Venedikt, whose passion was for the visual arts, got into trouble with the Soviet authorities early on. His refusal to bend to their will eventually led to incarceration in the mental hospital where, as was frequently the case, he was treated with an aggressive series of injections of psychotropic drugs that eventually turned him into a harmless vegetable, a shell of his former self.

When the narrator finds himself confined to the same hospital, however, he is not taken to the wing with quiet patients like his brother, but rather to a section with a far more dangerous crowd. Initially, the psychiatrists suspect that Petrovich's illness is related to the current sociopolitical situation. The head psychiatrist asks: "Isn't your nervous breakdown linked to the overall changes? The status of the writer has fallen these days" (338). As they observe him, however, they begin to suspect something else (or else they always did—as Petrovich is the narrator, the reader is never entirely sure about the level of trustworthiness in his narrative). Eventually, in an attempt to worm a confession out of him, they transfer him to a unit for the criminally insane, which he, with his usual literary flair, names

"Ward Number One." The rogues' gallery of prisoners in this enclosed world resembles the inhabitants of Dostoevsky's "House of the Dead" more than those of Chekhov's story, and it is in this environment that our narrator almost cracks.

All around him, he and the various criminals are being given large doses of drugs that apparently encourage them to confess their crimes. And all around him the criminals give in, confessing to the psychiatrists and then disappearing from the unit, presumably taken off to prison. Petrovich cracks as well, but instead of confessing his crime to the psychiatrists and in the absence of a modern-day Sonia he confides his secret to a drugged-out fellow inmate, the contract killer Chirov. This nonconfession confession gives him enough breathing room (he simply could not keep the fact that he had killed entirely to himself) to resist the efforts of the psychiatrists to break him, and eventually he escapes the unit by attacking an orderly and getting beaten up badly enough to necessitate a long-term transfer to a medical ward. There he recovers both physically and mentally and apparently emerges with his "I" intact, no longer suspected of a crime but now fully recommitted to the podpol'e.

There is only one exception to the narrator's relentless efforts to defend his "I" at all costs against any and all incursions from the changing world. This is his treatment of his younger brother. Not only does he hold up Venedikt Petrovich as having been much more talented (this could be seen as a kind of "survivor's guilt" on the part of the narrator), but also he makes extraordinary efforts to identify and have published in the postcommunist era his brother's few remaining sketches. Given that this behavior is exactly the opposite of what he does with his own work, we might well wonder why. It appears to be because he views Venedikt's work as an example of pure art that has become completely detached from the creator's ego (because, in this instance, that ego has been completely destroyed). As opposed to his own work, which was created not with an eye to its artistic value but as a way to advance and protect his ego (and which is therefore worthless as soon as it can no longer fulfill that function), Venedikt's sketches continue to be pure expressions of undergound (as opposed to podpol'e) mentality, even after the destruction of that world. Therefore, although he is uninterested in accepting help to publish his own stories, Petrovich goes to great lengths to find an expert who authenticates Venedikt's work and publishes it in a German album devoted to Russian avant-garde art.

The final section of the novel, given the appropriately literary subtitle of "One Day in the Life of Venedikt Petrovich," describes how the narrator takes his brother on a one-day pass from the mental hospital to a gathering celebrating the publication of his drawings. Venedikt is unable to appreciate the meaning of the event, and his brother realizes this. Rather than spend the entire evening with the drunken artists who have organized a feast back in the apartment building to which the narrator has managed to return after his extended stay in the hospital, he takes Venedikt around to various friends in the building and to various apartments he is watching over, attempting both to give his brother a day of ease and plenty and to create the illusion that he himself is rich and happy. Even more important, he allows Venedikt to look at some art books and convinces his brother that he (Venedikt) had in fact painted all the work in them. It is this happy illusion that, presumably, remains in his brother's head as he returns to the mental hospital. The last lines of the work are exceptionally poignant, yet at the same time make clear Petrovich's vision of the hopeless position of the underground (that is to say, true) Russian artist in the modern world: "And he spoke quietly to the orderlies, to both of them in the end: 'Don't push me, I'll go myself!' And he even straightened up, proud, for just that moment—the Russian genius, beaten, humiliated, shoved, in shit, but just don't push me, I'll go *myself*" (556).

According to the narrator, in the brave new world of postcommunism, the artist, the only person who can truly have an "I" to defend, can do so successfully in one of two ways: remain an artist but give up any presence in the world (by allowing his ego to dissolve completely) or go podpol'e, defend his ego at all costs, but give up art in a world that has, finally, learned to live without literature. But, we may be justified in asking, does Makanin agree with his narrator? Is his view of post-Soviet Russian society in general, and of contemporary Russian culture in particular, as bleak as Petrovich's. There is, of course, no sure way to answer this question except to say that, like his Dostoevskian predecessor, Petrovich has been provided with a loophole. Despite his insistent claims to have given up writing, he has apparently written the enormous book we are reading. As opposed to Dostoevsky, Makanin does not provide any kind of "editor's introduction" to tell us how the work came into our hands. Nevertheless, its very existence testifies to the continued relevance of literature to postcommunist Russia, and particularly to the relevance of the most ambitious works of all: those that write themselves into the great tradition of Russian novels in an attempt to capture the essence of their times.

Whereas the overall tone of Makanin's novel is elegiac, somber, and pessimistic, Jáchym Topol's *Sister* is manic and upbeat, though not without

elegiac and even tragic moments. This difference might be seen as related to the differing experiences of the Russian and Czech societies in
the early 1990s, when both novels are set. After all, the shock of transition in the USSR after more than seventy years of disastrous communist
party rule was far more severe than was the case in Velvet Revolution
Czechoslovakia (and then the Czech Republic). It might equally be related to the generational difference between Makanin (born in 1937) and
Topol (born 1962). For while neither book is exactly autobiographical,
the first-person narrators of the two novels certainly belong to the same
generations as the authors. It is generally recognized that younger East
Europeans were better able to deal with postcommunist transition, so it is
perhaps not surprising that a narrator of Topol's age would be likelier to
focus on the positive aspects of this tumultuous period than would one of
Makanin's. At the same time, with only two novels under consideration, it
would be a mistake to draw global conclusions. Perhaps it would be better to examine them simply as two idiosyncratic attempts to capture the
essence of the immediate postcommunist period.

Topol's novel begins confusingly with the narrator describing a group
of which he was a member and which he categorizes as the People of
the Secret. Presumably, the novel will be their story, the story of a group
that thought (as described in the first few paragraphs), "We were going
forward, getting somewhere, but soon...lost all concept of which way
we were headed."[7] This description also characterizes the whole novel,
which moves in fits, starts, and circles, never following a single narrative
line for very long. If Makanin's novel was primarily concerned with space
(the loci of the apartment building, the insane asylum, the underground
in its various meanings, and the space of the Russian literary tradition),
Topol's novel is more focused on time, though it also has a significant
spatial component. Thus, to explain the group and its activities, the first-
person narrator announces a need to return to the beginning, to the "Stone
Age," the "era of the Sewer," that is, to the days in 1989 just before the
fall of the Berlin Wall when thousands of East Germans made their way to
Czechoslovakia and were allowed to leave from there for West Germany.
From what can be gathered from the extremely fragmented narrative, the
narrator, Potok by name, was an underground playwright and actor in the
Stone Age. He had his gang of bohemian artist friends and a girlfriend

---

7. Topol, 13. Further references to this novel will be in the main text by page number from
this edition.

whom he calls She-Dog. She-Dog's goal was to allow Potok to create a tribe, because "she knew we needed a tribe if we wanted to survive without giving away all our time, and she also knew how to save at least a piece of time for ourselves" (16).

Potok, however, is unable to follow She-Dog in every respect. In particular he is unwilling, or unable to live outside time because living outside time means being willing to give up on being in the world with its temporal mystery. What is more, it entails being willing to give up on the creative process. She-Dog, we are told, "wanted to free me of fear, but I didn't want to be free of it because without fear I couldn't act . . . without fear I could do anything except create . . . because the only way I can make up human characters and play around with them is if I know the wicked old horror of life and the horror of its ending. . . . I chose fear . . . so She-Dog cast me out of the community, cut me off from herself . . . she promised to send me a sister, though . . . to fulfill my future" (31). Rather than follow She-Dog's path he chooses to live in the present of postcommunism, "the years 1, 2, 3 after the explosion of time" (42), after the moment at which "human time had accelerated" (37). The entire plot of the novel can be seen as the narrator's quest to slow time down again, to find his "sister," to make himself whole in the brave new world of postcommunism. He does this through his writing, because to control language is to control time, especially at this point when "Czech had exploded along with time" (41).

This plot, which derives ultimately from the Platonic vision of a time before men and women were separated, operates on multiple levels in the text. On the personal, it refers to the narrator's desire to recreate the preadult wholeness he had achieved with She-Dog. As he puts it later, "Few mortals have experienced anything like it, she gave me strength . . . few men, when it comes time for Stary Bog [the Old God] to run the film, can find a couple of frames where they're with their sister. . . . I mean every guy, man or boy even the poor fucks everyone's written off, is searching for his sister, that's all there is, it's a possibility" (299). On the social level, the narrator searches for the sense of stability that was present, however much it limited personal and creative freedom, in the communist society of his youth. And on the level of literature, he tries to discover a language and a style capable of capturing society in all its complexity at a given moment.

As was true of Makanin's Petrovich, Potok never talks directly about writing the narrative we are reading. But he is highly conscious of his literary activity, and in particular of how his language has been changed and deformed by events. In his view, the very language he employs has within it something of the circular and complex structure of his narrative: "Coincidentally, the tongue I use is one of Czechs, of Slavs, of slaves, of onetime slaves to Germans and Russians, and it's a dog's tongue. A clever dog knows how to survive and what price to pay for survival. He knows when to crouch and when to dodge and when to bite, it's in his tongue. It's a tongue that was to have been destroyed, and its time has yet to come; now it never will. Invented by versifiers, spoken by coachmen and maids, and that's in it too, it evolved its own loops and holes and the wildness of a serpent's young. It's a tongue that often had to be spoken only in whispers. It's tender and cruel, and has some good old words of love, I think, it's a swift and agile tongue and it's always happening" (34).

Together with a new group of friends—Micka, Bohler, Sharky, and David—the same ones who were mentioned on the first page, our narrator decides that what is happening in postcommunist Prague is business because, as he puts it, "this was and still is the Klondike of the wild East" (70). That is, unlike Petrovich, who withdraws into himself and into the podpol'e, Potok forms a new society fit for the new world and attempts to grab what it has to offer. "Sometime in the dawning, in freedom, we decided to make money, to engage somehow in the changed world around us. What I liked most were the coins, the eyes of a wide-ranging organism, their gaze as cool as the distant stars, the cold wind blows over them too.... We soon realized that money wasn't the metal we used to buy our beer or red wine and the Northerners their rum, but that money was debts, stamped and unstamped papers, money grows from money, multiplying by division like cells.... Money is words, friendships, low blows, promises, money reacts magically when the right doorknobs are polished" (41).

The business of "byznys" on the one hand keeps the narrator and his friends occupied and in a certain amount of control over a surrounding landscape that is changing at warp speed. Yet on the other hand, the constant scams and rackets of the period prevent the narrator from achieving the inner stability he seeks, the stability that would be provided by the arrival of the Messiah (69) for whom the whole gang is waiting. Of course, this reference is by no means accidental; traditionally, with the arrival of the Messiah "there will be no more time."

There are, however, grave doubts in the minds of Potok and his friends regarding the possibility of the Messiah's hoped-for appearance. These become apparent during a horrifying dream sequence recounted by Potok that takes the form of a tour through Auschwitz guided by a Czech who had been both victim and victimizer in the camp. Not surprisingly, the group is unable to find meaning inside the dream, as we see when, having been led to the brink of despair by their guide, one of the group falls to his knees and pleads: "Mr. Novák, whoever you are, an especially if you're … if you used to be Czech, I beg you … tell us what all this means, why we're here, what happened … why us … what Stary Bog intends for us" (107). But Potok is able to find some meaning afterward, perhaps, he says, "cause I'm a dancer an an actor an therefore an artist, an as such've already got within me the proper dose of insanity" (121). The meaning he provides is horrifying particularly in the context of the narrative's overall desire to stop or at least control the flow of time. He uncovers a lump of twisted metal in the wreckage of Auschwitz which he interprets as the residue of a key that had once belonged to a young Jewish boy or girl who had been destined to become the Messiah but whose mission was aborted by premature death at the hands of the Nazis. As he puts it, "An space wasn't moving because time'd died with the Messiach in Auschwitz, an I grasped my enormous mistake. No time bomb exploded, brothers, an some of the acting an dancing I'd done was the dance of the dead, of a man without time, an that was a mistake, an arrogant mistake. Time died in the land of ashes, it hit me" (123). Apparently, the death of time in the ashes of the Nazi atrocities continued through the communist period, only to be followed by an uncontrollable acceleration of time in postcommunism.

While the narrator and his friends are obsessed with manipulating the system in ever more complex moneymaking scams, what has happened to culture? We discover something on this topic through the story of Jicha, once a leading samizdat poet. As recounted by Potok, Jicha's path lines up perfectly with the situation for writers and writing that we described in chapter 5. That is to say, he started out as a notorious samizdat poet, beloved by schoolgirls, but in the immediate postcommunist years (what the narrator calls "the years 1, 2, 3") he realized that poetry didn't mean much any more, so he turned to journalism. "I vaguely recalled some articles by him about attacks on *gastarbeiter* dormitories. They were the stepping-stones to his career as a post-revolutionary journalist. He infiltrated the Vietnamese, of which in those memorable bygone years 1, 2, 3 … after the explosion of time in Bohemia, there were tens of thousands" (162). But the writer as journalist also didn't pan out. "Most of the *gastarbeiters* either left Bohemia or fled to more desirable states. What's more, killing was an everyday thing and people got tired of Jicha's reports. He grew glummer and glummer. Just when he realized he could finally write whatever he wanted but nobody cared, the paper dumped him…. It went downhill from there. I'd heard he even began writing poems again. But meanwhile the high-school girls had turned old and gruff and lived their own poetry now. The new high-school girls didn't even read" (162).

That the narrator is telling the truth we discover from Jicha's own interpolated narrative (such interpolated narratives occur frequently in Topol's novel). "Surely you remember years 1, 2, 3, etc. when we came crawling outta the Sewer, slowly and cautiously, so the air wouldn't get us right away. But, O my brothers, before I struck out on my path I got tangled up in Kulchur . . . and maybe I ceased to be a slave, but instead I became a servant . . . to Kulchur sections . . . Kulchur sections, when I see you I keep my finger on the trigger! It's pulp and grit, and the Kulchur section servant's a flunky to the dwarf called Advertising" (169). We saw in chapter 2 the complaint that communist-era ideological censorship has been replaced in the postcommunist world by the censorship of money. Here we have that view instantiated in the fabric of a work of fiction. What we get from the discussion of Jicha, therefore, is not merely a description of culture's new role in the postcommunist age from the perspective of a former underground author, but a backhanded justification of Potok's own decision to give up playwriting and turn directly to "byznys."

Still, business and the group with which he does business cannot slow the mad pace of time, and eventually the group falls apart. As Potok's adventures continue in various places, some real, some that exist only in his dreams, he recognizes that space is an irrelevant category as long as time is out of control. And in the postcommunist period, time is out of joint. In the communist days time was definitely not money; it was one of the few things everyone possessed in abundance. In postcommunism, in the years 1, 2, 3, time sped up, which entirely changed the way in which the world was perceived: "Nowadays it's fashionable to say: I don't have time, it makes people feel tremendously important that they don't have time, that they're working, makes em feel almost American . . . Yeah, whenever I'm in a pub I ask: D'you read *War and Peace* an *Gilgamesh* yet, or how bout *The Man Without Qualities* or *Welzl the Eskimo*, you can get through it in a night. . . . Yeah you ought to see the look they get on their faces like: That's thick! I don't have time for that . . . these days! Isn't there a movie of it? Like the Bible? Yep, when someone tells me, all dignified and lofty, or with a drained look: I don't have time, I hear the rattle of the spit and shudder for the fate of humanity" (470).

After the collapse of the business enterprise and in order to gain control of time, Potok returns to writing. "While I wrote I thought a lot about Sister and the attic. This is my Firewater, I'd think to myself as I braked time with my writing, making it mine alone" (441). Earlier in the narrative, it seemed to Potok that a novel would be the appropriate form for describing, capturing, and thereby slowing down the speeding world: "It struck me, if a guy like Jicha can write a book, why not me. Only I'd write mine in Kanak. On the body of a changed world, in the ruins of the former time, I'd open the first glorious chapter of Kanak literature! I'll write the book in raw, post-Babylonian, the way I heard it on my wanderings through the past, present, an future" (243).[8] This book is, of course, precisely the one we are reading, although the narrator never directly mentions actually sitting down to do any writing. Kanak is his new universal language. Later in the novel, however, he switches to a kind of surrealistic poetry that is interpolated into the text of the narrative (441–447). The turn to poetry is cured by a stint working in a cheap snack bar near a writers' retreat with an aspiring poet named Kasel, who dreams of becoming the next great writer, "a crimson robe and the prince of poetry's lyre" (481). But the drunken babble of an established writer who comes to their kiosk for a beer and then the attacks of established writers on the work of the once up-and-coming Kasel apparently turn Potok back to stream-of-consciousness prose as the only way to slow time down.

Appropriately enough, the novel does not so much come to an end as simply break off in midstream. Potok is in the embrace of a woman who might or might not be the Sister he searched for through the entire text, that Sister who would provide the love, comfort, and stability that even more than writing would allow time to be slowed and perhaps stopped. Now she holds him as a bell rings calling him to leave, to move, to run again, and she tries to stop him: "Let's not open it, you said. Not anymore."

His answer is as ambiguous as the novel itself "No. Not now." Is this his final renunciation of accelerated time? Or is it merely a pause before he rushes off again into the maelstrom in his search for permanent love, a stable literary idiom, an Archimedean point from which the new society can be observed?

Makanin and Topol have chosen a risky strategy to remain relevant for their potential readers. Despite the instability of the times in which they wrote their work, they attempted to fix that very instability in narratives

8. Kanak is a Melanesian language that in Potok's mind appears to stand in as a kind of primitive pre-Babel universal language. See the excellent discussion of this point in Howell, 2002, 45–51.

that focus on their societies as seen through the eyes of a writer. Their success can be measured, perhaps, in the respect that has been granted to their works. Topol's novel, despite its stylistic and narrative complexity, not only won a major literary prize when it first appeared, but also is the only post-1989 book to be included in the writers' and critics' list of the hundred greatest Czech prose works of the twentieth century. As Yvonne Howell puts it, "It was recognized as a landmark literary achievement, destined to be read, studied and talked about as the point of departure for a new era in the development of Czech prose."[9] While Makanin's novel was not received with quite as great enthusiasm, the majority of critics nevertheless agree that it is a major achievement, perhaps the culminating novel of the Russian twentieth-century tradition, a classic worthy of comparison with the works of Dostoevsky and Lermontov. Because of their size and complexity, however, both novels are very much by and for the intelligentsia (Makanin's, for example, has almost certainly not sold more than ten thousand copies in Russia). Thus, within their countries, their relevance is limited to the highest echelons of the educated literary-oriented elites and does not reach a broad public. Topol's book has been translated into English, but it was published by the tiny Catbird Press, and it did not make a major impression. And while *Andergaund* was published recently in Dutch and French translations, it would be surprising if in today's literary market an American press would take a chance on Makanin's 550-page behemoth. Still, there is no doubt that these are both major works and that any future cultural historian trying to take the pulse of the unstable years of the 1990s in Eastern Europe will have to take them into consideration. What is more, as serious novels that write themselves directly into the mainstream high-cultural tradition, both are likely to have a longer shelf life than many of the more popular works I treat in the following chapter.

9. Howell, 2002, 45.

CHAPTER EIGHT

Learning to Love Popular Fiction

"Oh, come on, "I said, reassuring her, "you mustn't take literature so seriously."—Michal Viewegh

Communist regimes disliked Western popular culture. In his study of popular fiction, Clive Bloom lays out some of the reasons: "No really authoritarian states can stand pulp culture. It reeks of anarchy and nonconformity and subversion. Thus authoritarian states ban such corruption and condemn rock 'n' roll, alongside comic books, erotic literature, fast food, Levi jeans, James Bond, US soap operas and Coca Cola.... For Marxist-Leninism, spiritualism and rock 'n' roll were one and the same thing, not surprising that authoritarians can find themselves in Shakespeare and Dante but cannot tolerate Batman comics read by the lightning flashes of rock technology."[1] Bloom fails to mention a few exceptions to this rule, particularly when we are talking about the "softer" communist countries and/or about Western popular forms that became indigenous either before or in the early years of communism. Thus, for example, jazz and Hollywood-type movie musicals were domesticated by official Soviet culture in the 1920s and 1930s, homegrown rock and roll was more than tolerated in Yugoslavia, and certain kinds of intellectual science fiction flourished in both Poland and the USSR.[2] Still, there is no question that in general, communist governments were opposed to most forms of Western

---

1. Bloom, 15.
2. For books on various types of popular culture imported from the West in Eastern Europe, see Starr; Ziegfeld; Potts; MacFadyen, 2001; 2002, *Estrada*; 2002, *Songs for Fat People*; and, Howell, 1994.

popular culture, seeing them at best as worthless escapism and at worst as dangerous subversion.

Interestingly, they were not opposed to traditional folk culture (which by this period was no longer popular). As Dubravka Ugrešić puts it, "If anything in former Yugoslavia can be described as copiously *stressed* (rather than repressed), then it was folklore. For some fifty years, the Yugoslav peoples had pranced and capered, twirled and tripped in their brightly-coloured national costumes in various formations. . . . Indeed it seems to me now that they did little else."[3] The problem with truly popular culture was, it would seem, twofold. First of all it was spontaneous and therefore difficult, if not impossible, to control from above.[4] Perhaps even more important, the plurality of cultural values these forms implied went against the ideal of a single national culture that was the sine qua non of communist social and cultural engineering. As Jeffrey Brooks puts it in the conclusion to his study of prerevolutionary Russian popular literature, "The Bolsheviks had the active support of only a minority of educated people in their program to remake Russia, but both revolutionary and nonrevolutionary Russians who participated in cultural life often shared a conviction that cultural choices could be curtailed in the name of high ideals."[5]

Like all forbidden fruit, however, many products of Western popular culture acquired an aura of attractiveness. For the most part, the best-known such products were musical, at least in part because music needed little or no translation. This was true even in the tightly controlled USSR, as Nicholas Glossop notes: "For almost as long as rock and roll has been played in the West, it has been heard in Russia. Soviet youth received its first large infusion of Western styles and sounds during the Seventh International Festival of Youth and Students which took place in Moscow in 1957. . . . Signs of black-market traffic in rock recordings appeared immediately thereafter. While imported original recordings were traded and peddled, music appeared more often on a unique format known as *rentgenizdat*, or 'ribs,' that was borrowed from the jazz scene. Equipment needed to fashion a facsimile of an LP could easily be found, but the requisite vinyl could not, so the grooves were cut into used x-ray plates. . . . The festival of

3. Ugrešić, "Balkan Blues," in Labon, 8–9.

4. According to Katerina Clark, the conflict between spontaneity and control, with ultimate victory going to the latter, was the central theme of the socialist realist novel. See Clark, 15–24.

5. Brooks, 356.

1957 also contributed to the appearance of a new youth subcultural form on the streets of Moscow and Leningrad. Small circles of urban youth took to wearing sneakers and—whenever possible—blue jeans, and dancing to American rock and roll and the music of the 'British invasion,' which they referred to as *Bit* or *Big bit*."[6] And manifestations of Western sounds were even more apparent in the freer East European countries such as Poland, Czechoslovakia, and Yugoslavia.

Popular literature, by contrast, was less accessible to East European readers. As was noted in chapter 2, communist and dissident authors alike agreed on a number of things, one of which was that literature should provide a system of values for the public at large. Western popular literature, which either aggressively denies the need to propagate values through literature or propagates values that neither communists nor dissidents would have approved of, simply had no space in the mental universe of East European elites. Official state publishers could not accept popular literature for the ideological reasons enumerated by Clive Bloom above. What is more, they had little financial incentive to publish books that the general public might have wanted (as most of their books were sold to other state organizations). So they did not publish translated popular literature even in periods of liberalization when such writers J. D. Salinger, John Updike, and Kurt Vonnegut were released in the communist world. Nor could dissidents accept the seeming frivolity and lack of moral purpose in popular literature. While music could be smuggled in on LPs and reproduced by local musicians on improvised instruments, popular literature needed to be translated and published before it could reach an audience.[7] And although some dissidents may have been willing to work for years to translate a forbidden classic like James Joyce's *Ulysses*, no one wanted to translate, say, romance novels, and so these never appeared in samizdat (which also did not function according to market mechanisms). As a result, the public that might have wished to read these works, less sophisticated East European readers who did not know foreign languages, in most cases never even knew of their existence.

6. Nicholas Glossop, "On the Peculiarities of Soviet Rock and Roll," in Wachtel, *Intersections and Transpositions,* 1998, 275.

7. Even in the realm of popular music, litero-centricity reigned in Eastern Europe. Thus, one of the characteristics of homegrown Soviet and East European rock and roll and pop when they appeared was the comparatively great attention paid to the lyrics, which were often, in the cases of such Russian bardic poets as Vladimir Vysotsky and Aleksandr Galich, serious and difficult poems in themselves.

All of this changed swiftly in the 1990s. Censorship disappeared, publishers needed to sell books, and they quickly discovered that there was an enormous pent-up appetite for Western popular culture. One of the characteristic new sights in this period, remarked by natives and visitors alike, was the profusion of kiosks and tables selling hundreds of new titles in genres like criminal fiction, detective stories, horror, and romance that had never existed before. Mostly pirated, translated from English by teams of hacks, these books rapidly overwhelmed the local cultural production and, to the dismay of former communists and dissidents alike, became the reading matter for the masses. More than a decade later, although some continue to decry the popular culture invasion, more and more writers and publishers in Eastern Europe are realizing that it is better to switch than fight. Thus, while the big imported names continue to sell well, local writers have busily begun to carve out their own market share, producing works that naturalize the genres of popular literature in their own languages. This is particularly true in countries where the book market is large—Russia and Poland, for example. But the phenomenon has increasingly trickled down to smaller markets such as the Czech Republic, Hungary, and Croatia. In this chapter we will examine the phenomenon of Aleksandra Marinina, who has sold tens of millions of copies of detective novels in Russia over the past decade. However, if one wanted to find and analyze works in other popular genres, one could find plenty of authors to talk about in almost every East European country.

Marinina's novels can be classified as pulp fiction, which, for the purposes of this chapter, can be defined as literature that does not pretend to offer the reader anything beyond the plot. I am not using the term pejoratively here. Such books may be (and in the case of Marinina are) well constructed with believable characters and suspenseful situations. They lack, however, any elements that would interfere with the reader's enjoyment of the story line—complex or difficult language, self-conscious irony, allusions to other literary works that require effort to decode, and so forth. As such, they do not reward close analysis, and therefore I will not spend a great deal of space on them, even though, whether translated or locally produced, these are the most widely read books in Eastern Europe today.

A more interesting phenomenon for the literary critic studying this region is the appearance of works that make use of the genres of Western popular fiction but that simultaneously lend them new and interesting twists. This seems to occur in part because "classically trained" writers who turn to popular genres can still draw on a broad range of literary culture even as they produce books for a mass market. They possess the cultural resources do so because their own literary training, which took place before the end of communism, was heavily litero-centric. And, even more important, they know that their potential readers went through this same educational system and can thus appreciate a certain level of literary sophistication. Furthermore, they know that many readers want to enjoy the pleasures of popular fiction but would be embarrassed to be seen buying a Harlequin romance or a novel by Stephen King. Exploiting this niche, if they are sufficiently clever, writers of this new breed can satisfy the hunger of many East European readers for popular and exciting genres while cloaking their writing in a halo of respectable literariness. Ultimately, the best of them produce works that blur the boundaries between popular and highbrow literature to create strangely attractive, extremely self-conscious hybrids.

To be sure, stretching back to the days of Dostoevsky there is a tradition of high-cultural writers in Eastern Europe who take advantage of lowbrow genres to create more serious work. In some sense the writers discussed here are followers of that tradition, one that for the most part was not exploited during the communist period. The main difference, however, is that while Dostoevsky fully subsumed the original genres into his work, the writers discussed here display the low genre more openly. Thus, rather than creating a synthesis that raises the low genre to highbrow status, they create works that are in fact low- or middlebrow but that also contain a layer of metageneric commentary: postmodern pulp, in a word. Such books sell remarkably well, though in the majority of cases the literary critics, who remain the last bastion of traditional cultural taste all over Eastern Europe, are not impressed. In this chapter we will look carefully at three popular authors—Michal Viewegh of the Czech Republic, Boris Akunin of Russia, and Andrzej Sapkowski of Poland.

First, however, let us examine the phenomenon of Aleksandra Marinina. According to her official biography on the Web site http://www.marinina.ru/, Marina Anatolyevna Alekseeva was born in 1957 into a family that had strong ties with the legal professions.[8] Her grandfather and mother were specialists in law and her father was a police detective. She herself worked for the police of the Ministry of the Interior between

8. The complex and sophisticated Web sites of authors of East European popular fiction are a characteristic feature. They combine clever marketing with various information in numerous languages.

1980 and 1998, when she retired (the royalties on her crime fiction had, by that time, begun to bring in more than a comfortable living). Since publishing her first crime novel in 1994, she had produced some twenty-seven more novels by 2005, and her Web site claims that she has sold more than 21 million copies. Her books are available on tape, a television serial has been made based on some of them, and they have been translated into many languages. Even foreign academics have gotten involved: a conference in Paris was devoted to her work in 2001, and articles about her have appeared in leading publications concerned with Russian literature and culture.

At first glance, it is not easy to see what all the fuss is about. The novels are decently written, well plotted, and filled with the requisite murders and suspense. Part of their attraction is their heroine, understood by readers to be more or less autobiographical, although there is no reason to believe that the crimes solved were actually handled by the author herself. "Marinina's 'heroine' is Anastasiia Kamenskaia, like her creator a police lieutenant colonel who works as an analyst (*analitik*). Kamenskaia, however, works not in an institute, but at 38 Petrovka, the central police headquarters in Moscow. Kamenskaia's character is based on the premise that she remain in her Petrovka office, drinking cup after cup of coffee and chain smoking, while her male colleagues do all the legwork of gathering evidence and interviewing suspects. She then solves what are generally devilishly complex crimes by subjecting the material the men gather to cold, machinelike logic combined with an extraordinary imagination, which allows her to (re)construct multiple narratives based on the evidence and ultimately arrive at the 'correct' story."[9] It has been pointed out that Marinina's fiction owes debts to such Western detective-story writers as Sidney Sheldon, Georges Simenon, Rex Stout, Ed McBain, and Charlotte Armstrong, as well as late-Soviet-era writers such as Arkady Adamov, Leonid Sloven, and the two-brother team of Georgy and Arkady Vainer.[10] But although all of these writers have been popular in Russia, none approached the level of popularity achieved by Marinina.

Anthony Olcott explains the appeal of homegrown Russian detective novels in general and those of Marinina in particular (as opposed to other

9. Catharine Theimer Nepomnyashchy, "Markets, Mirrors, and Mayhem: Aleksandra Marinina and the Rise of the New Russian *Detektiv*," in Barker, 169.
10. See Nepomnyashchy, "Markets, Mirrors, and Mayhem"; and Olcott.

genres of popular literature" such as romance, which is still dominated by translated works), by claiming that they provide Russian readers with a specifically Russian definition of crime, qualitatively different from Western ones. On this view, every nation has its own conception of justice and normality, and Russian readers prefer Marinina and her ilk because their books draw on specifically Russian concepts which are naturally absent in translated detective fiction: "Much of what the west calls 'crime,' the Russian genre finds to be simply human weakness, or an inescapable part of an imperfect world. Conversely though, many of the relations between people that the west accepts as a matter of course seem so barbaric to Russians as to become a kind of crime. The unit of measurement that the western genre finds supreme—the individual—is to the Russian genre, at best, a solipsism and, at worst, a criminal, actively working to destroy the Russian basic unit, an amorphously defined but acutely felt larger community (the *mir* or *obshchestvo* or *narod* or *Rodina*)."[11] While this relativistic and simultaneously ultra-Slavophile account of the popularity of specifically Russian detective fiction has some appeal, it cannot be the entire story. After all, do not Russians have their own ideas of romance as well? And, in the specific case of Marinina, if this work is so directly connected with Russian conceptions of crime and justice, why is it being successfully translated and sold in numerous other countries that, presumably, do not share these rather specific Russian values?

Catharine Nepomnyashchy is probably closer to the truth when she notes that, at least in the specific instance of Marinina, popularity is tied specifically to advertising and to the commodification of her person. She quotes a Russian journalist's description of a Marinina presentation organized by her publisher Eksmo (see chapter 2 for more about them) as follows: "By a remarkable coincidence, Marinina's presentation to journalists took place in the 'Tolstoy' hall, and the buffet afterward—in the 'Pushkin' hall. Probably, the Eksmo people have the idea that the fashionable detective lady should take her place in those ranks, not in the sense of the classic quality of her prose, but by automatic association: fruit-apple, detective fiction–Marinina."[12]

Juxtaposing the two photographs presented in figure 6, taken from unrelated pages of her official Web site, allows us to see how Marinina's image

11. Olcott, 185.
12. Nepomnyashchy, "Markets, Mirrors, and Mayhem," 169.

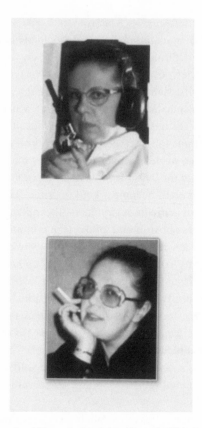

FIGURE 6. Two photographs of Alexandra Marinina. (From the Web site http://www.marinina. ru/rus/personal. Top photograph, with revolver, by V. Zavjalov.)

is being used. The top picture depicts her in the role of police lieutenant. The phallic pistol at the ready reinforces the idea of her role as woman in a man's world and hints at the lurking danger in her fiction. The picture below, posed identically, presents her in a somewhat bohemian mode, the suave best-selling author in Russian history.

A quick look at the "Forum" section on Marinina's Web site confirms the idea that, at least by now, the phenomenon of Marinina has outgrown any texts that might be connected to an author. To be sure, on the site one can find discussions of the texts themselves among readers who agree or disagree about the relative merits of one book or another. One can also find statements of the type "The walls of my room are papered with portraits of her [Kamenskaia] and portraits of Aleksandra Marinina. [She is] a great writer without whom many people's lives would lose all meaning."[13] Even more important, however, is the fact that readers and participants have begun to use the forum almost outside the books and their author. This is how someone writing in using the pseudonym "Ice Girl" asked for advice on September 30, 2002: "How should I react when people who see a book by Marinina in my hands turn away scornfully? How can I explain to people who have not read Marinina that this is not light reading but thought-out, serious work. I argued with my classmates, I practically came to tears over this, that Marinina is a modern classic." Naturally, given what has been said up to this point, it is not surprising that many fans are unwilling to admit that they read her work merely as entertainment. Rather, their Soviet and Russian education remains in force and they cannot and do not say, "I want to read something fast-paced and mindless."

Instead, they defend these books as serious literature and their author as a modern classic. But it is the responses that "Ice Girl" received that are most revealing. "Grey Mouse" replying on October 1 cited an anecdote from her youth in Soviet Russia when she was required to write about Western popular literature (negatively of course) despite never having read those unavailable works in order to illustrate how stupid it is for people to judge things they haven't read. "Ant" replied, also on October 1, with a plea for tolerance. You just have to realize that some people like one thing, and others another, she insists. Finally, "Yucatan" weighed in on October 4 with a plea for "Ice Girl" to reorder her priorities: "Don't react at all. Don't let them jangle your chain. And, basically, why fight with friends over idols. Idols come and go but friends remain. Ice girl, make it up with your friends." Clearly, discussions of this sort are far from literary.

If Aleksandra Marinina can be considered a Russian translation of popular Western genres (albeit based on a hybrid of various Western crime novelists and with some specifically Russian touches), the other authors to be considered in this chapter are literarily more ambitious. Each of them makes use of genres of popular fiction that were more or less unknown during the communist period. It is possible to read their works straightforwardly, and their broad popularity leads one to guess that many readers do indeed read them in this way. But at the same time, each of these authors makes sure that at least the educated reader is aware that he is playing with the popular genre. Thus, the works in question are in some sense simultaneously genre fiction and metagenre fiction.

13. "Dionis," "Lutchche pisatel'nitsy net" [There is no better writer], Nov. 17, 2002.

Michal Viewegh, one of the most popular Czech authors of the postcommunist period, could just have easily been considered in chapter 7.[14] Indeed, his *Bringing Up Girls in Bohemia* (*Výchova dívek v Čechách*, 1994)[15] is in certain ways quite similar to the novels of Topol and Makanin. The main character and first-person narrator is a middle-aged writer who ekes out a living as a novelist and schoolteacher in the postcommunist Czech Republic. Like his counterparts, Petrovich in Makanin's novel and Potok in Topol's, Viewegh's narrator is self-conscious, well attuned to the changes that have occurred in his society, and himself a writer. However, what sets this novel apart is its aggressively middlebrow, sometimes even lowbrow aesthetic. The narrator, in conversation with the daughter of the nouveau riche Czech whom he is supposed to be instructing in creative writing and with whom he is having a steamy affair, captures beautifully the essence of Viewegh's balancing act, characterizing himself as "a sort of voluntary liaison officer between scorned reading matter that people bought and literature that was respected and read by almost no one" (112).

We can discern Viewegh's strategy from the novel's first page. It opens with a quotation from the respected and eminently serious Czech author Věra Linhartová. The quotation focuses on the act of writing and points to the self-conscious approach of the narrator and implied author who will sprinkle his text with a large quantity of pithy quotes from high literature. "The oddest thing of all, the thing that mostly strikes us when we embark on a story is the total void spreading out before us" (5). Such out-of-context quotations form a kind of postmodernist background pastiche, against which the narrator's own lower-brow literary efforts stand out in high relief. The main narrative begins in the next paragraph with the narrator's own straightforward prose. "When I returned home from school that Wednesday with my daughter, the letter-box was literally full to bursting:

---

14. Viewegh was born in Prague in 1962. He graduated from the philological faculty of Charles University with a major in Czech language and pedagogy and subsequently worked as a teacher. He is the author of *Názory na vraždu* (1990), *Báječná léta pod psa* (1992), *Nápady laskavého čtenáře* (1993), *Výchova dívek v Čechách* (1994), *Účastníci zájezdu* (1996), *Zapisovatelé otcovské lásky* (1998), and *Povídky o manželství a sexu* (1999). Two of his novels have been turned into films. A recent work, a political satire entitled *Báječna léta s Klausem*, has caused much controversy in the Czech Republic. His works have been translated into most of the major European languages, though he is popular primarily in Eastern Europe. For more on Viewegh, see Segel, 585–586.

15. The novel, translated by A. G. Brain (the pseudonym of the British couple Gerald and Alice Turner) was published in English in 1996. All quotations are from this edition, noted in the main text by page number.

apart from the usual *Lidove noviny*, it contained a large brown envelope with the page proofs of my novel plus a white envelope also addressed to me, and finally that controversial blue cellophane packet containing an advertising sample of a Proctor and Gamble product . . . The white envelope contained a brief letter from Kral, our local millionaire, offering me *a lucrative part-time job with easy hours.* In other words, the beginning of *this* story did not lie in a formless mass in a total void, but in a white envelope in our letter-box on 16th June 1992" (5).

It is important to consider who the implied reader of such a text might be. Clearly, he or she is expected to be a Czech or Slovak with a reasonably high level of literary education, otherwise the interpolated quotations from Linhartová—and later from Jan Mukařovský, Shakespeare, Karel Čapek, Alain Robbe-Grillet, and others—would pass unappreciated. Nevertheless, as the quotes are presented completely out of context, there is no need for a deep knowledge of the authors in question—rather, it is important that the reader be able to register the names and recognize that their texts come from a world of high culture mostly absent from the regular narration. As such, they can be attributed to the narrator, who can be seen as trying to jazz up his, for the most part, lowbrow text with such references. In short, the novel could perhaps not be appreciated by a high-school dropout, but anyone who had finished school in communist-era Czechoslovakia could be expected to register the high-cultural references, if not to appreciate them fully. As for the main narrative, what strikes us immediately—and this is in sharp contrast with the narratives of Makanin and Topol—is its simplicity and straightforwardness. We find no neologisms, no complex sentence structures, and no experiments with space and/or time. Rather, the narrator reads the standard newspaper and is clearly a regular guy, well aware of the nuances of everyday life (able and willing, for example, to register a Procter and Gamble ad campaign for tampons, it turns out—a brand new feature of postcommunist reality). Furthermore, the narrator reveals here his strategy for dealing with the high literary material that he sprinkles through the text: deflation. Whereas someone like Linhartová confronts the void, our narrator deals with everyday reality, registered by the specific date of the story's beginning.

Although in many respects Viewegh's writing is a new phenomenon in Czech literature, it is not entirely without precursors. We find a similar strategy of combining a relatively simple love story with more highbrow material in Kundera's celebrated 1984 novel *The Unbearable Lightness of Being.* That novel begins with a discussion of Nietzsche's idea of eternal

return. This is quickly followed by a consideration of the French Revolution and the Nazi period. However, these and other philosophical and
historical digressions by the narrator exist as window dressing to gussy up
the love story between the main characters, Tomas and Tereza, which plays
itself out against the backdrop of the Prague Spring and its aftermath. It
is interesting to speculate on why Kundera's novel is considered a major
literary work, while Viewegh's is relegated to the category of popular fiction. Most likely, the explanation can be found not in the text of the novel
itself, but in the position that Kundera was able to make for himself in
the context of the cold war, as well as the literary reputation he achieved
with the books he published during the liberal period of the mid-1960s
(his novel *The Joke* in particular). Viewegh, who came of age in the 1980s,
would have been unable to publish serious fiction before 1989 and so had
no literary reputation to point to when he became popular with Czech
readers.

Be that as it may, as Viewegh's *Bringing up Girls* continues, we realize
that it is in a sense a chronicle of the narrator's changing literary ambitions.
At the beginning of the book his wife notes that he had been planning to
write "a post-modern novel" (6). In literary terms this would clearly be a
step up from what he had published earlier, most likely a detective novel
(as we can guess from its title—*Views on a Murder*), the book whose success
had led the completely Král to engage the narrator to teach his daughter
in the first place. Toward the end of the novel, the narrator, now working
in an editorial office, asks his colleagues to reserve a pink cover for his
upcoming book, presumably this one, because it will be "a *love story* with
all the trimmings" (113). But romance is not the only genre of which the
narrator is capable. He shows his versatility by interpolating into the text
a short story that he purports to have written and published in the Czech
edition of *Playboy*. The story, a rather feeble effort at erotic prose, registers
the presence on the Czech scene of an entirely new outlet for writers,
one that is particularly valued because its large circulation allows for the
payment of a reasonable royalty. As is typical of his style, the narrator is
incapable of merely presenting the story. Instead, he finds it necessary to
demonstrate that he is fully self-conscious about his writing. In this way,
in theory at least, he can present the kind of lowbrow story many readers
want while cloaking it in an extra layer of respectability. He prefaces the
story as follows: "I thought long and hard about whether to include it in
this book—for one thing, it bears the marks of having been written to cater
to the requirements of a specific readership, and for another the casting

of myself in the role of a *divorced playboy* must needs have a comic effect after everything I've said about my marriage so far, and thirdly, even I find that such transitions to quite a different story are generally disruptive" (156). Nevertheless, include it he does. Readers, presumably, are titillated; Czech literary critics, predictably, are outraged.

In the end, then, the narrator is too self-conscious to write a straightforward romance novel, for after all, as another of his interpolated quotes notes, "romance novels can be thrilling. But do they provide a healthy outlook on life and marriage?" (183) His pulling away from the low genre of romance recalls the narrative tactics of writers of picaresques who, after providing the reader with hundreds of pages devoted to the immoral acts of their hero, allow him or her to confess all sins on the last page and so turn the narrative from a source of prurient interest into a warning against sinful behavior. Insofar as this book is a love story, it is a bittersweet one, for the affair ends and on the last pages the narrator's former love commits suicide by smashing her Volkswagen Golf into a bridge support at high speed (a very postcommunist method, by the way).

The novel concludes with a line that sums up everything Viewegh stands for, and I mean that both positively and negatively—"Oh, come on," I said, reassuring her [his wife], "you mustn't take literature so seriously" (185). In the context of a culture that has precisely taken literature extremely seriously, this ending can be seen as a moment of literary terrorism. An author who is well-enough educated and sufficiently facile to write a serious postmodern work has instead used a number of postmodern structural clichés to produce a novel that appeals to a middle- and lowbrow audience while simultaneously winking leeringly at those remaining highbrow writers and critics whose work is no longer in demand.

Not surprisingly, Czech literary critics have taken at best a dubious stance toward Viewegh. While they grudgingly admire him for his ability to sell books to a wide range of Czech readers, they excoriate him for his bad taste and for pandering to the lowest common denominator. This appears to bother the author, as an interview in the Czech magazine *Reflex* reveals. Describing and defending his work, Viewegh says, "I have an essential need for, let's say, my mother, my father, and people who aren't in the trade to understand it [my writing]. My concept of the writer's craft encompasses this as well.... [But] the idea that I sit down at the computer and write for some previously determined target audience isn't even technically realizable. How would one do that? Always write one joke for the intellectual, then one for the salesgirl.... The problem is that I manage to get the salesgirls, but have a tougher time with the intellectuals." Interviewer: "And that irritates you?" "It does. Because of course I have higher ambitions than to write just for salesgirls."[16]

Viewegh is disappointed that Czech critics do not consider him to be a serious writer, but the equally popular Russian Boris Akunin (pseudonym of Grigory Chkhartishvili) is less conflicted, even if at least some of his novels have a greater pretension to high literature than anything Viewegh has produced. Asked by a reporter from the Moscow newspaper *Argumenty i fakty* "Don't you have a complex, like Chekhov's Trigorin, of an author who writes worse than Turgenev? A writer whose work can be read only once?" Akunin replied: "No, because I don't consider myself a writer. I am a belletrist and I don't try to write better than Turgenev. My goal is to amuse the reader."[17] And there is no question that in this he has succeeded. Writing with almost unbelievable speed, Akunin has produced more than fifteen novels since 1998 in three separate cycles. At first relatively obscure, they have hit a nerve among the Russian reading public, and the author has now been raised to cult status. What is more, foreign translations have appeared in quantity, as have television series, movies, and Web sites devoted to the author and his work. There is no question then, that Akunin has become relevant to a broad spectrum of readers. Simultaneously, however, as opposed to a writer like Marinina, who for all her sales is generally dismissed by intellectuals as hopelessly trashy, Akunin is also popular with the Russian intelligentsia and has received (though not universally) excellent reviews. He manages to straddle the line between popular and serious literature in an unusual way. How does he do it?

First, let us answer this question in relation to the popular audience. If we examine the novels of Akunin's best-known series, the so-called Fandorin cycle linked by the actions of the detective hero Erast Petrovich Fandorin, we can find the keys to the author's success among the mass public. First there is the time period in which the novels are set. Rather than the nitty-gritty world of post-Soviet excess favored by Marinina, Akunin sets the novels of this series in Russia in the second half of the nineteenth century. They are thus both detective novels and historical novels. And the period they describe is one that Russian readers have come to see as

16. Interview with Alena Jezkova entitled "Vieweghova krev," *Reflex* June 12, 1997.

17. *Argumenty i fakty* Internet version #44 (1045) Jan. 11, 2000 (http://www.aif.ru:86/aif/1045/12_02.php).

a kind of golden age—the years just before the Bolshevik revolution. The novels project a definite nostalgia for a lost world of manners, aristocratic privilege, and order. Within this world, Erast Fandorin acts as a detective magician. With his knowledge of all world languages, his phenomenal physical strength and ability to disguise himself (i.e., his perfect control of his own body), his Sherlock Holmes–like logical capacity, his personal charm combined with aloof independence, and his dogged determination, Fandorin embodies a number of the qualities that post-Soviet Russians admire and wish to emulate. What is more, the novels in this series are written in a style that, while by no means primitive, is readable for anyone with a Soviet high-school education (i.e., the majority of adult Russians). And of course, as all good detective novels do, Akunin's feature exciting plots, situations of high drama and intrigue, and the pleasant challenge of figuring out whodunit.

At the same time, the novels and their author offer a great deal more to the well-educated member of the intelligentsia, and this helps to explain their impressive "crossover" potential. To see what else they offer, we must turn to the category of intellectual and literary play, for primarily this aspect of Akunin's work makes him so captivating for the Russian intelligentsia. The play begins with the chosen pseudonym, which can be interpreted in a number of ways. When the novels first appeared almost no one knew who was behind this name, but it must have been clear that it was indeed a pseudonym. After all, the first Fandorin novel (and the first published) was characterized by the author as a "conspiratorial detective" and chronicles Fandorin's attempts to solve a series of terrorist bombings in Moscow in 1876.[18] Given that one of the inspirations for Russian terrorist organizations of the nineteenth century was the famous anarchist philosopher Mikhail Bakunin, it would have been hard for readers to ignore the fact that the author's first initial and last name spell B. Akunin.

When the author's real identity became known, however, a second possible interpretation appeared, for it turns out that in Japanese *akunin* means an evildoer. While that language would not normally be relevant for Russian readers, the author of these books, Grigory Chkhartishvili, is in fact an expert on Japanese literature and the editor of the well-known

---

18. One of Akunin's desires in the Fandorin series is to write a novel in every possible detective fiction genre. Thus, he writes *The Turkish Gambit* (a spy novel), *Leviathan* (a hermetic detective story), etc. Again, the casual reader may or may not care that each novel is in a different genre, but for the intellectual "literary collector" this is rewarding.

journal *Inostrannaia literatura* (Foreign literature), the leading and vener-
able periodical outlet for the publication of translated works into Russian.
This double pseudonym game is typical of Akunin's work in general, where
a surface clue turns out to be the key to a more complex and challenging
intellectual game, one that by no means all readers are expected to play.
It should be added at the same time that Akunin, unlike the other authors
discussed in this chapter, has impeccable intelligentsia connections, and
this, too, helps to explain why the critics who normally disparage popular
literature are willing to praise him.[19]

In order to see how this game works and why it is so successful, it is
best to analyze a single work a bit more carefully. Here, we will examine
Koronatsiia, ili Poslednii iz romanov (The coronation, or The last of the
novels, 2000). Set just before, during, and after the coronation of Nicholas
II, the novel is characterized by Akunin as a "high-society detective."
The game begins with the title, which is a pun based on the fact that the
genitive plural of the word "novel" in Russian (*roman*, as in French) is
romanov, which is also the family name of the last Russian dynasty in
the nominative singular. Thus, the subtitle, which reads "The last of the
novels," could also (almost) mean "The last of the Romanovs," which,
of course, is precisely what Nicholas was. The game with history will, it
turns out, continue through the entire novel. As is the case with any good
historical novel, Akunin's manages to weave real historical characters with
invented ones. In this case, the plot revolves around the kidnapping of one
of the archdukes by a vicious and completely unscrupulous British criminal
just before the coronation of Nicholas. By threatening to embarrass the
Romanov family before the international audience gathered for the events,
the kidnapper manages to collect a ransom that includes practically all of
the most famous Russian crown jewels. Naturally, the tsar's own police as
well as those of the Moscow governor general are unable to solve the crime,
and so, much against their own will and inclinations, they turn to Fandorin.

After many twists and turns, Fandorin recovers the jewels and kills
the kidnapper and his band, but the archduke is also killed. The events
are entirely invented, although along the way the narrative does provide
the reader with scenes of the Romanov family (most of whom appear
under easily decoded pseudonyms), their behavior, and surroundings that

---

19. In this sense the Akunin phenomenon can be seen as a successor to the Andrei Sini-
avsky/Abram Tertz phenomenon. Russian intellectuals could accept Tertz's "Fantastic Tales"
much more easily when it was clear that he was the same person as the literary critic Siniavsky.

are based on careful historical research. Thus, those who wish to get a titillating glance at the life of the last tsar (a popular topic in historical and pseudohistorical post-Soviet literature) in addition to a mystery story are satisfied. What is more, cognoscenti of Russian history will appreciate the fact that the novel provides an explanation for the famous tragedy at the Khodin Fields outside Moscow, where more than a thousand people were trampled to death in a stampede to get free trinkets that were to be given out in honor of the coronation. No one knows exactly what set off the stampede, but here we "discover" that it happened when the novel's villain, Dr. Lind, in a successful attempt to avoid capture by Fandorin, told the surrounding folk that the trinkets were being given out a short distance away. This led them to charge off in that direction and begin the uncontrollable melee. Most readers, of course, are expected not to remember this tragedy and certainly not to care very much about its cause. But those intellectuals who want more than just a detective story can be counted on here to appreciate Akunin's historical footnote.[20]

The Web site Akunin has created to accompany his novels (http://www.akunin.ru) serves to deepen and extend the pleasant historical mystification of the works. It opens with a page that appears to have come from the library of Fandorin himself (see figure 7). The paper scanned here looks old, and the typeface, though in contemporary orthography, is nevertheless not a modern one. The stamps are made to look as if the book has passed through the hands of many readers, and the Fandorin ex libris in the upper-right-hand corner adds a level of seeming authenticity to the central character. When the reader opens the site he can find not only the full electronic text versions of many of the novels (not the most recent releases, naturally) but also much material that can add to the pleasure and enlightenment of the historically minded reader. These include materials created specifically for this site, such as a full listing of the tsarist table of ranks, various old maps, information about weights and measures in use in the nineteenth century, and so forth. In addition, there are links to other sites related to Russian history, as well as to an

---

20. A detective novel that is simultaneously a historical novel is a new genre in Russian literature. It is not without precedent in world literature, however. Apparently, Akunin's inspiration is the Dutch Sinologist Robert Hans van Gulik (1910–1967) who wrote, in English, a series of detective novels set in eighteenth-century China. His invented hero, Judge Dee, solves complex murder cases the keys to which lie in a sophisticated knowledge of Chinese culture. At the same time, even without the author's encyclopedic knowledge of the subject, the normal reader can enjoy the mystery.

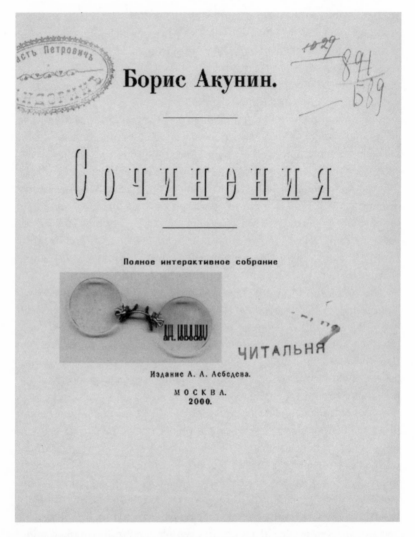

FIGURE 7. Title page of Boris Akunin's *Works: Full Interactive Edition*, showing Erast Petrovich Fandorin's ex libris at upper left. (Graphic design by Artemy Lebedev; from the Web site www.akunin.ru.)

"unofficial" site devoted to Fandorin (http://www.fandorin.ru/main.html), which includes a lively forum on which readers can discuss burning issues relating to the novels and their author. Thus, for example, one group of readers considered the possibility of visiting the bridge on which the final and fatal meeting of Fandorin and Dr. Lind takes place in the novel we have been discussing. In the end, they did not agree on whether there had ever been such a bridge or whether it had been preserved, but the participants in other forums have gotten together to walk through Fandorin's places in Moscow and to experience the atmosphere of the novels at first hand.

In addition to their plot elements, Akunin's novels are noteworthy from the point of view of style. As noted above, the novels come in three cycles, the one devoted to Fandorin comprising, for the moment at least, the largest number of books. There are, however, at the time of writing, three novels in the cycle "Provincial detective novels," in which the hero is a woman named Pelagiia, and two in the series "The adventures of a master," in which the hero is Fandorin's grandson, Nicholas Fandorin. Each series is distinguished not only by the hero and place of the action, but also stylistically. In fact, what Akunin has done is to recreate Mikhail Lomonosov's theory of three styles and apply it to the detective genre.[21] The Fandorin series is in middle style and directed primarily at middlebrow readers (although, as we have noted above, it provides reading pleasure for better-educated readers as well): these novels provide a fair amount of action, do not require a high level of education, and stylistically mimic the discourse of unchallenging nineteenth-century prose. The Pelagiia series, on the contrary, is written in high style, demands quite a bit of knowledge of Russian nineteenth-century culture and literature, and mimics the writing of classic highbrow Russian literature. Finally, the modern-day adventures of Nicholas Fandorin are presented in the manner of contemporary pulp fiction, with bodies littering the ground, fast cuts from scene to scene, and little psychological development, and are written in an accessible modern style.

The phenomenal crossover success of Boris Akunin has not been achieved in the detective genre in other East European countries by any writer. In Poland, however, Andrzej Sapkowski (born 1948) has managed to create a best-selling and, for the most part, critically well-received series of novels in another genre that was almost unknown in Eastern Europe before 1989: fantasy. Indeed, according statistics provided by the newspaper *Rzeczpospolita*, in 2001 Sapkowski's novels (none of which had actually been released during 2001) accounted for eight of the top fifteen best

21. Lomonosov proposed three stylistic levels for Russian literature in his *O pol'ze knig tserkovnykh* [On the Use of Ecclesiastical Books] (1757), in Lomonosov. The high style was reserved for solemn odes, epic poems, and sermons. The middle style was for tragedies, epistles, and satires. And the low style, which employed almost exclusively Russian words, was reserved for fables and comedy.

sellers in the category "Polish literature." In all, Sapkowski sold 265,000 copies of his novels in Poland in 2001.[22] Statistics are not available from other countries, but his novels have been translated into Russian, Czech, Ukrainian, Lithuanian, German, and Spanish.

At the center of Sapkowski's oeuvre is the figure of the warlock (*wiedźmin*) Geralt. This character, a mutant and hired killer (mostly of monsters of various kinds), appeared in Sapkowski's first fantasy novella, "Wiedźmin," published as early as 1986. This was followed in the early nineties by two collections of loosely connected novellas devoted to Geralt in the early 1990s. Sapkowski's real breakthrough, however, occurred when he published a five-part saga (the novels appeared between 1994 and 1999) in which he succeeded in creating his own mythological world, complete with its own languages and geography. These five volumes (almost 1,900 pages) tell a more or less coherent story about Geralt, his beloved witch Yennefer, and their adopted daughter Ciri. This plays itself out against a series of wars between human beings and describes the efforts of the humans to rid their world of all nonhuman elements (including the main heroes as well as assorted elves, gnomes, monsters, magicians, and mutants). The novels are well plotted and filled with action scenes which make them eminently readable by a large public. Simultaneously, however, they are, like the novels of Akunin and Viewegh, literarily sophisticated, filled with allusions to earlier works of fantasy as well as to the high literary tradition.

In order to give a feeling for what Sapkowski does, I will provide a short analysis of the final novel in the cycle, *Pani jeziora*.[23] Before doing so, however, it is necessary to discuss the reasons for the absence of fantasy in Eastern Europe before 1989. This is important because the related genre of science fiction was perhaps the only popular literary form that was widespread during the communist period. It is beyond the scope of this book to explore in detail why science fiction was acceptable; however, it is worth noting that Lenin saw science fiction as a method of popularizing scientific and technological progress. During the 1920s, the Soviet Union produced a great deal of science fiction, most of which was utopian in its

22. This made him the third-best-selling author in Poland for the year, after J. K. Rowling, whose four Harry Potter books sold approximately 1.5 million copies in 2001, and Helen Fielding, whose novel *Bridget Jones's Diary* sold more than three hundred thousand copies. See http://www.rzeczpospolita.pl/dodatki/ksiazki_020202/ksiazki_a_9.html#1.

23. Sapkowski. References to this novel will be made in the main text by page number from this edition.

outlook. At the same time, Evgeny Zamiatin's dystopian science fiction novel *We* laid the foundations for such works as *1984* and *Brave New World*. During the Stalinist period, science fiction was generally taboo, but it made a comeback after Stalin's death. It could be digested even by more or less orthodox Marxist critics primarily because its scientific and future-oriented attitudes were seen as pointing the way toward the ultimate perfection of mankind (naturally in keeping with communist ideas in this regard). As a result, many of the leading works of Western science fiction were translated into East European languages (it did not hurt that many Western science fiction authors were overtly or covertly critical of their own countries), and a number of major East European practitioners of the genre appeared, Stanisław Lem in Poland and the Strugatsky brothers in Russia being the most prominent.

Fantasy, however, was not treated in the same way. Most likely this was because fantasy novels tend to be set in the past rather than in the future, and this past is usually seen nostalgically as a kind of golden age that has been lost in the present. Given the Marxist teleological view of history as moving ever forward toward communist perfection, such an attitude is simply unacceptable. Thus, works of fantasy were seen as escapist, attempts to avoid the challenges of life today and tomorrow by sinking into an idealized past.[24] In this sense, they were considered to be the direct opposite of science fiction. The result was that very few works of fantasy were translated into East European languages (J. R. R. Tolkien was an exception, but even his work was published in small editions and remained obscure), and no native practitioners of the genre appeared. Since 1989, a number of homegrown fantasy writers have come onto the scene, primarily in Russia and in Poland, but Sapkowski is clearly the star.

Sapkowski has been forthright about naming the works he found most important for his own development as a writer of fantasy. These are, as he pointed out in a long interview in the Polish magazine *Nowa Fantastyka*, almost all from the Anglo-Saxon literary world.[25] The list does not include many surprises—Thomas Malory's *Morte d'Arthur*, Robert Howard's contributions to *Weird Tales*, J. R. R. Tolkien's *Lord of the Rings*, C. S. Lewis's *Chronicles of Narnia*, T. H. White's *The Once and Future King*, and Ursula

24. Fantasy was considered acceptable for children at various times and in various East European countries. But I am speaking here about fantasy pitched at an adult market.

25. "Pirog albo Nie ma zlota w Szarych Gorach" [The pirogue, or There is no gold in the Grey Mountains], *Nowa Fantastyka*, vol. 5 (1993). I quote here from the Russian translation as it appears on the Web site http://lib.ru/SAPKOWSKIJ/pirog.txt.

Le Guin's corpus. In this same article, Sapkowski argues that the reasons for the boom in fantasy in the 1960s in the West can be traced to a desire on the part of readers to escape from the modern consumerist, destructive world into a nonexistent never-never land "in order, together with the true companions, to battle the Forces of Darkness, because those Forces of Darkness, that very Mordor which threatens the fantastic world on the pages of the book, in fact threatens individuality and, even more, the possibility of dreaming" (5). These comments on the one hand provide further evidence about why fantasy was so strongly discouraged in communist societies that were officially based on a future-oriented utopian ideology. On the other hand, they help us to understand why fantasy should be appealing in postcommunist Eastern Europe, in countries in which much of the populace has lost faith in utopian promises about the future (be they those of communism or free-market capitalism) and in which the possibility of dreaming seems to have been undermined. Nevertheless, there are many writers of fantasy in Eastern Europe, and such general comments do not help to explain why Sapkowski in particular has succeeded in capturing the attention of a broad reading public.

A consideration of the novel *Pani jeziora* (The lady of the lake), the fifth and final volume of the Geralt saga, may perhaps help us to understand Sapkowski's appeal. From the title, of course, we recognize that his work is connected to the wellspring of many fantasy novels, the King Arthur cycle, particularly as popularized by Thomas Malory. In most of the interviews he has given about his work, Sapkowski notes the importance of Malory, not just to himself but to the entire genre. The connection to the Arthurian legends is underscored by the work's second epigraph, which is taken directly from Malory, specifically the scene in which Arthur and Merlin see the Lady of the Lake walking on water and approaching them. The book's other epigraph, by the way, is from *The Tempest* ("We are such stuff as dreams are made on"). Given that a fair amount of the narrative is said to be based on a series of dreams, this makes thematic sense, while at the same time it clearly establishes Sapkowski's credentials as a serious writer able to quote a highbrow predecessor like Shakespeare.

The novel's short opening chapter reads almost like a spoof of fantasy novels, rather than the beginning of an actual exemplar of the genre. We see a knight who comes to the shore of what he takes to be an enchanted lake. He drinks its water and hears sirenlike singing. What goes through his mind (and the way it is presented to the reader) indicates the self-consciousness typical for Sapkowski's text: "The knight was like every knight who had been brought up on the songs of bards and courtly romances. He knew that nine times out of ten a girl's singing or moaning was a trick and that the knight who hurried to save her would certainly fall into a trap. Often a fatal one" (6). The knight, who turns out to be none other than Sir Galahad himself, nevertheless makes contact with the unknown woman. Their dialogue can only be perceived as comic. Sir Galahad takes the woman, who identifies herself as Ciri (readers of Sapkowski's earlier novels know her as one of the main heroines of the saga), to be the Lady of Lake and expects to receive the sword she is carrying. She, however, does not know the legend. "'I am truly worthy to receive the sword from your hands, O Lady of the Lake.' 'I don't get it.' 'The sword. I am ready to receive it.' 'This is my sword. I won't let anyone touch it.' 'But . . .' 'But what?' 'The lady of the lake, when . . . She always comes out of the waters and bestows a sword.' The girl was silent for a moment, then she said: 'I get it. As they say, each country has its own mores. Sorry, Galahad, or whatever your name is, but you've found the wrong Lady. I don't give out anything, don't bestow anything, and I don't let anyone take anything. Let's be clear on that'" (9).

After the confusion has been dispelled, Galahad asks Ciri to tell her story. She tries to avoid doing so but eventually agrees, saying that it appears to have no beginning or end, but is rather like a serpent that eats its own tail. Given that the final pages of the book will see Ciri agreeing to go with Galahad to Camelot, the reader can see that the serpent metaphor is apt, because the novel itself forms a kind of circle in which the outer ring is formed by the meeting of Ciri and Galahad. The intervening 475 pages, however, form the inside of the circle, one in which Galahad and the Arthurian knights are not directly present.

The circle formed by the first and last chapter is not the only frame surrounding the main story. Instead, the novel's second chapter concerns a sorceress named Nimue, who is also identified by her visitor, a young sorceress in training by the name of Condwiramurs, as the "Lady of the Lake." Nimue has invited the young woman to stay with her in order to examine old manuscripts and paintings devoted to the main characters in the saga's central story. Condwiramurs has won prizes for her ability to conjure vatic dreams, and Nimue hopes that, on the basis of what she sees, the young adept will be able to discover the truth about certain unclear portions of the ancient legends. Thus, the events of the saga described in the chapters that follow are presented not as unmediated narrative, but rather as stories filtered through the dreams and visions of Condwiramurs. As was the case with the Galahad frame, however, the reader who wishes merely to get to the central story (and of course, readers who had gone through the first four volumes of the series could be expected to want to get precisely back to the story of characters who had captivated them before) can be counted on to skip quickly through the frame. This is not as easy as it sounds, at least not at first, because the novel's second chapter cuts back and forth between the conversations of the two sorceresses and dream narratives that present little and intriguing bits and pieces devoted to the lives of some of the saga's main characters.

Beginning with chapter 3, the frame narrative falls away and the book's remaining four-hundred-odd pages are devoted almost exclusively to the actions of Geralt, Yennefer, and Ciri on the one hand and the clash of human ambitions on the other. Even here, however, the narrative is by no means simple. Sapkowski does not provide a straightforward narrative in which *fabula* and *sjuzhet* are closely aligned. Rather, he favors an MTV-like approach marked by fast cuts, sudden flashbacks, and flash-forwards, and his prose is saturated with visually striking imagery. Furthermore, although the adventures of his three main heroes are not completely unconnected to the wars between the men of Nilfgaard and the United Kingdoms (all of them have to do, at some level or other, with a desire to control, protect, or possess Ciri, who is seen as the key figure who may be able to save the world), the narratives of the heroes exist more in parallel than in connection to each other.

It would be unnecessarily complicated to attempt to provide readers with a plot summary of this novel, dependent as it is on what took place in the previous four volumes. Readers of Polish or Russian can find enormous amounts of material on the semiofficial Sapkowski Web site at http://www.sapkowski.pl (smaller amounts of material can be found in Spanish and Czech on the same site), including a full chronology of the events of the books, a detailed map of the geography of the imagined world, genealogies of the main characters, and so forth.[26] Instead, I will point out a couple of the main lines here.

Perhaps the central desire embedded in the novel is to force the heroine, Ciri, to have a child. Because Ciri's genes are said to stretch back to one of

26. In one tongue-in-cheek article entitled "Advice to Authors Who Would Write Fantasy," Sapkowski says: "Before writing a book in the fantasy genre the author must create a world. But the creation of a world is not an easy thing and requires a devilishly large amount of work.... Fortunately, in place of a world we can simply create its equivalent, namely, a map. And we not only can, we must. In a book of fantasy a map is an obligatory element, a sine qua non." See http://lib.ru/SAPKOWSKIJ/map.txt.

the most important early sorceresses, her child is believed, by any number of characters, to be predestined to save the world. In the course of the novel, three different and unrelated people or groups of people attempt to use Ciri's body as the means to produce a savior. The evil sorcerer Vilgeforts keeps her imprisoned in his castle and proposes to artificially inseminate her, remove the placenta as soon as the embryo is formed, and presumably kill her in the process. The goal of the book's superheroes (Geralt and his small troop of friends, which includes a vampire) is to rescue Ciri from Vilgefort's evil clutches. Simultaneously, the emperor of Nilfgaard, who also happens to be Ciri's own father in disguise, intends to bring Ciri back to his capital and marry her there in order to produce a child who will save the kingdom and the world from destruction. Finally, in another world and a parallel time a group of elves hold Ciri prisoner and expect that she will become pregnant by their king in order to save the elves still living in the world of humans, which will be destroyed by "an ecological catastrophe of colossal proportions" (168). In the end, however, Ciri manages to escape from all of these dangers with, apparently, her virginity intact. Her preservation from these perils is what allows her to fall into the frame with Sir Galahad at the beginning and end of the novel.

One especially interesting fact about Sapkowski's epic is its occasional, seemingly anachronistic references to problems facing the world of the late twentieth century—ecological catastrophe, genocide, refugees and displaced persons, discrimination on the basis of ethnic identity (figured here as various degrees of humanness), totalitarianism, and so forth. In various interviews Sapkowski vigorously denies that his novels should be read as in any way allegorical or as coded descriptions of the contemporary world. Indeed, they do not provide any coherent encoding of our world. Nevertheless, there is equally no question that Sapkowski includes references to contemporary problems precisely in order to induce readers to try to make such connections, and it would appear that part of his popularity can be explained precisely by the tendency of his readership to find coded references to issues of concern to them. Simultaneously, they are perhaps equally attracted by the comic-book violence of the superheroes who, for the most part, overcome these problems, as well as by the relatively frequent erotic scenes. Finally, as was the case with most of the other writers discussed in this chapter, Sapkowski includes in the text of his novel many metatextual and ironic references that, at least to an extent, undermine the illusion of the fantasy world. Because of this, he has been dubbed the first postmodern fantasy writer by Polish critics and readers and has been compared by some to Jorge Luis Borges and Gabriel García Márquez (comparisons the validity of which Sapkowski tends to deny, by the way). This allows more sophisticated readers to receive his work not merely for its plot elements but also as serious literature. Such a reading is made even more possible by Sapkowski's deft deployment of a variety of stylistic registers as he tells his story from multiple narrative perspectives.

After having finished the Geralt cycle, Sapkowski embarked on a new type of novel which explicitly combines history with fantasy. His 2001 novel *Narrenturm* is set during the Hussite Rebellion in neighboring Bohemia, but is not without elements of witchcraft and sorcery. It remains unclear, at the time of this writing, whether Sapkowski will be able to turn himself into a twenty-first-century Sienkiewicz (with a dose of fantasy), but that appears to be the direction in which he is headed.

The appearance of popular Western literary genres was certainly one of the most shocking results of the fall of communism to writers in Eastern Europe. Suddenly, they were confronted with the specter of enormous numbers of translated books that people were eager to buy. Many writers simply hoped that the taste for such literature would disappear after an initial fascination. Their more perspicacious colleagues, however, recognized that the phenomenon was here to stay. Some responded by producing translations and adaptations directly from the originals. Their works are now widely available but their authors are unknown outside their own countries and will remain so. Some, like Aleksandra Marinina, perfected a given genre and fully nativized it, without adding significant new elements. They have become immensely popular at home and are beginning to be translated into Western languages as well. Finally, a group of authors, including those we have focused on here, have learned to exploit the relatively high level of literary sophistication of their target readership to produce works that at one and the same time incorporate genres of popular fiction and provide an ironic metacommentary on them. These works and authors, too, have become popular in their home countries. Whether such writing can be successfully exported to Western countries, where the audience for popular fiction is probably not as literarily sophisticated as the current generation of East Europeans, remains to be seen.

Conclusion

Russian author Viktor Pelevin is an exception to many of the trends described in this book. His novels belong squarely in the tradition of high literature, yet they sell well to the Russian public (not as well as those of Marinina or Akunin, but well nevertheless). Simultaneously, they have generally been praised by Russian critics and have found an audience in Western Europe and the United States. The hero of his 1999 novel *Generation P* is Vavilen Tatarsky, a writer of slogans for the post-Soviet advertising industry. In the waning days of the Soviet Union, the young Tatarsky had dreamed of a different career: he had hoped to become a poet, writing for "eternity." By the early 1990s, however, he had come to understand that "the eternity in which he formerly believed could exist only through state subsidy—or, and this was the same thing, as something forbidden by the state.... He stopped writing poems: with the collapse of Soviet power they had lost all meaning and value. The last words he wrote just after these events were shot through with influences from a song by the group DDT ('What is fall—it is leaves...') and allusions to the late work of Dostoevsky. The poem ended as follows: 'What is eternity—it is a jar. / Eternity is a jar of spiders. / If some simple Masha / forgets about the jar / What will happen to our Fatherland and to us?'"[1]

The question posed by this jejeune poem echoes the thoughts of Vladimir Makanin's hero that I used as the epigraph to chapter 7: "What would happen if, in our days, people were really to learn to live without literature?" Living without literature would mean no longer using it as

---

1. Pelevin, 15–16 (translation mine). This novel has appeared in English under the title *Homo Zapiens,* trans. Andrew Bromfield (New York: Viking, 1992). The translation, however, omits the last sentences of this section.

the basic medium for asking existential questions. It would mean that the Mashas of this world would no longer be likely to use allusions from classic works like *The Brothers Karamazov* to formulate their answers, and it might lead would-be Dostoevskys to realize that literary work had lost its centrality as the motor of meaning creation in their societies.

Pelevin's hero abandons literary writing in response to this realization, choosing to exercise his creativity in an area to which his contemporary society pays more attention, not to mention money. But—and this is of crucial importance—Pelevin himself has not chosen this path. What is more, the success of his work with Russian and foreign critics and with various reading publics indicates that it remains possible in the postcommunist period to produce literature that, to return to the formulation proposed by Mihailo Pantić, "in a synthetic way recapitulates the general truths of people's experience and deepens their understanding of reality." Surely, the belief that this is still possible animates Pelevin and many of the writers described in this book. Still, Pelevin's choice of a writer who has given up literature as his hero betrays an ambivalence toward his own position and, more generally, toward the role of the writer in Eastern Europe. For Pelevin, like the vast majority of writers in contemporary Eastern Europe, must be aware that the changes since the end of communism all but preclude the possibility that a writer can be as relevant to his society as, say, Solzhenitsyn was in the 1960s and 1970s. The reasons for this, as I hope has become clear in the preceding pages, have little or nothing to do with some difficult-to-define quality called literary talent. Rather, they have to do with how East European societies were organized under communism and how they are organized today.

Perhaps the most salient feature of actually existing socialism was its limitation of choice. The constitutions of communist states enshrined monopoly political control in the hands of the communist party. And the party *nomenklatura* worked diligently to limit or eliminate choice in a vast number of social, cultural, and economic arenas. Consumers had to make do with a single brand of detergent (if that was available). All writers were to belong to a single association. Economic activity was to be controlled by a single state planning organization. Unquestionably, on the ground it proved impossible for the communist party to control society to the degree envisioned. But efforts on the part of citizens to escape that control were usually disorganized and spontaneous and did not pose a challenge to the system as a whole, and the overall possibilities of choice were an order of magnitude less than in Western societies.

While the limitation of choice in the political and especially in the economic realm proved enormously problematic, its effects on literature were more mixed. The system curtailed the choice of cultural consumers, limiting their exposure to popular literature and presenting them with a steady diet of classic works and contemporary writing that fitted within state-sponsored canons. At the same time, it provided support for a large group of producers, such that, as Hungarian sociologist Miklós Haraszti noted when the system was still in place, "artistic production has boomed under communism."[2]

Outside the official cultural realm, a cultural black market grew up, but at least as far as literature was concerned, this market did not behave according to normal economic laws. The black market for consumer goods was driven primarily by consumer tastes: if socialist citizens wanted blue jeans, blue jeans would be found. If their tastes shifted to leisure suits, black marketers did not force them to keep buying jeans. Dissident writers, however, were not producing their work for a broad market, at least in part because for ideological reasons their activity was more heavily policed than that of economic entrepreneurs. Instead, they tended to produce in opposition to the state rather than in response to reader demand. As Pelevin's Tatarsky came to realize, this meant that the literary world was split between those who received state subsidies and those who struggled against the government. And, as I indicated in chapter 1, these worlds overlapped to a surprising extent. Solzhenitsyn and Kundera, for example, began their careers as officially accepted writers. I doubt that one could find an example of a socialist-era state planner who, disgusted with the inefficiency of the system, became the operator of a black market retail operation.

Precisely because of the complex interdependence of official and nonofficial literary culture, the collapse of communism and the advent of choice posed particularly difficult challenges to writers. For there is no question that the public's right to make a variety of choices, even bad choices, was the most striking feature of the postcommunist environment. If during the communist period one could either go along with the system or opt out (recall the stark choice that Havel presented his grocer with in "The Power of the Powerless"), East Europeans now had multiple options. In the political realm, these manifested themselves in a plethora or new parties. In Lithuania, for example, a country with a population of

2. Haraszti, 9.

approximately 3.5 million, more than forty different political parties contested elections in the 1990s. And throughout the region political parties grew up to cater to the needs and interests of a wide variety of voting blocs (the Czech Beer Drinkers Party being a comic example). In the economy, small and medium-sized business flourished, and consumers were suddenly confronted with ten brands of detergent, none of which they could afford.

Pluralism has been the mark of literature in the postcommunist period as well, as this book has attested. As I illustrated statistically in chapter 2, one constant across all postcommunist countries has been a sharp increase in the number of book titles published combined with an even sharper decrease in the number of copies per title. This indicates that the once almost monolithic audience has segmented very rapidly and that, as a result, the possibility that a single author could dominate public attention has diminished or disappeared. Publishers, if they are to survive, must behave more like clothes manufacturers than like arbiters of taste, and they can afford to support only those authors whose works reach a broad market.

In this environment, the concept of relevance in relation to literature takes on a new meaning. The reason that a great work of literature could once "recapitulate the general truths of people's experience" had to do, it turns out, more with the structure of communist-era societies than with the talent of a given author (though talent was always required as well). Now that there is no longer a single society with a single shared experience, an author or work can be relevant only to a segment of the population.

What I have tried to do in this book is to illustrate a number of ways in which authors have adapted, attempting to remain relevant to segments of their formerly more or less unified publics. Turning to politics, a number of writers managed to convert the broad name recognition they had achieved in earlier times into political capital. It is unlikely, however, that this route will be open to writers who began their careers after the collapse of communism. For those who would continue to write, it has become necessary to choose an audience, be it readers who are groping for a sense of national identity, those who want to know "the truth" about their societies, those who wish to interact with the cultures of the outside world, those who want to focus on how their societies have transformed, those who want to experience the joys of popular literature, or populations I have not dealt with, including gay and lesbian readers, those nostalgic for the "good old days under communism," and so forth. Making predictions is always a dangerous business, but it is safe to say that in this new environment the appearance of another Miłosz, Solzhenitsyn, or Kundera is all but impossible.

Throughout this book it has been my claim that in the literary realm the experience of postcommunist countries has been exceptionally similar. The same basic processes have characterized developments from Russia to Hungary, from Croatia to Estonia, although each country has its own fascinating peculiarities. Recent events, however, indicate that this period of broad postcommunist similarity might be coming to an end. For those countries that have joined or will join the European Union, the processes of cultural fragmentation will probably continue, though as these states become more wealthy we can expect that they will make efforts, like their West European counterparts, to support high-cultural writing, thereby mitigating some of the side effects of fragmentation that have been described here. As Russia drifts back into authoritarianism (and Belarus remains there), however, the likelihood of a reimposition of censorship and a strong limitation of choice grows. In such an environment, it is possible that individual writers and their work will again have the opportunity to become broadly relevant. An old saying has it that a lucky people is one whose history is boring. Based on what I have presented here, that saying might be rewritten: Lucky is the people whose literature need no longer be universally relevant.

Bibliography

Aczél, György. "Poet and Revolutionary." *New Hungarian Quarterly* 14, no. 50 (Summer 1973).

Akunin, B. *Koronatsiia, ili poslednii iz romanov.* Moscow: Zakharov, 2000.

Albahari, David. *Svetski putnik.* Belgrade: Stubovi kulture, 2001.

———. *Tsink.* Evanston: Northwestern University Press, 1997.

Ali, Rabia, and Lawrence Lifschultz, eds. *Why Bosnia?* Stony Creek, CT: Pamphleteer's Press, 1993.

Aralica, Ivan. *Četverored.* Zagreb: Znanje, 1999.

Avins, Carol. *Border Crossing: The West and Russian Identity in Soviet Literature, 1917–1934.* Berkeley: University of California Press, 1983.

Ballinger, Pamela. *History in Exile: Memory and Identity at the Borders of the Balkans.* Princeton: Princeton University Press, 2003.

Banac, Ivo. "Yugoslavia: The Fearful Asymmetry of War." *Daedelus,* Spring 1992.

Barker, Adele Marie, ed. *Consuming Russia: Popular Culture, Sex, and Society since Gorbachev.* Durham: Duke University Press, 1999.

Bełza, Władysław. *Katechizm polskiego dziecka.* Lvov: self-published, 1912.

Bloom, Clive. *Cult Fiction: Popular Reading and Pulp Theory.* New York: St. Martin's, 1996.

Bogert, Ralph. *The Writer as Naysayer: Miroslav Krleža and the Aesthetic of Interwar Central Europe.* Columbus, OH: Slavica, 1990.

Bozóki, András, ed. *Intellectuals and Politics in Central Europe.* Budapest: Central European University Press, 1999.

Braham, Randolph L., ed. *The Tragedy of Romanian Jewry.* New York: Columbia University Press, 1994.

Brooks, Jeffrey. *Thank You, Comrade Stalin: Soviet Public Culture from Revolution to Cold War.* Princeton: Princeton University Press, 2000.

Brown, Edward J. *Russian Literature since the Revolution.* Cambridge, MA: Harvard University Press, 1982.

Brown, J. F. *The Grooves of Change: Eastern Europe and the Turn of the Millennium.* Durham: Duke University Press, 2001.

Brubaker, Rogers. *Nationalism Reframed: Nationhood and the National Question in the New Europe.* Cambridge: Cambridge University Press, 1996.

Brudny, M. *Reinventing Russia: Russian Nationalism and the Soviet State, 1953–1991*. Cambridge, MA: Harvard University Press, 1998.

Chaloupka, Otakar. *Takoví jsme my: čeští čtenáři*. Prague: Adonai, 2002.

Chitnis, Rajendra A. *Literature in Post-communist Russia and Eastern Europe: The Russian, Czech and Slovak Fiction of the Changes, 1988–1998*. London: RoutledgeCurzon, 2005.

Clark, Katerina. *The Soviet Novel*. Chicago: Uuniversity of Chicago Press, 1981.

Cohen, Lenard. *Serpant in the Bosom*. Boulder, CO: Westview Press, 2001.

Cooper, Henry J. "The Baptism on the Savica as Romantic Program." In *Obdobje romantike v slovenskem jeziku, književnosti in kulturi*, ed. Boris Paternu, 215–225. Ljubljana: University of Ljubljana, 1981.

Cornis-Pope, Marcel, and John Neubauer, eds. *History of the Literary Cultures of East-Central Europe: Junctures and Disjunctures in the 19th and 20th Centuries*. Amsterdam: John Benjamins Publishing Co., 2004.

Ćosić, Dobrica. *Into the Battle*. Trans. Muriel Heppell. New York: Harcourt Brace Jovanovich, 1983.

———. *Reach to Eternity*. Trans. Muriel Heppell. New York: Harcourt Brace Jovanovich, 1980.

———. *Sabrana dela*. 8 vols. Belgrade, 1966.

———. *A Time of Death*. Trans. Muriel Heppell. New York: Harcourt Brace Jovanovich, 1978.

Crnković, Gordana. Review of *The Culture of Lies*, by Dubravka Ugrešić. *Slavic and East European Journal* 43, no. 3 (Fall 1999).

Dabrowski, Patrice Marie. "Reinventing Poland: Commemorations and the Shaping of the Modern Nation, 1879–1914." PhD diss., Harvard University, 1999.

Davies, Norman. *God's Playground: A History of Poland*. New York: Columbia University Press, 1982.

———. *The Heart of Europe: A Short History of Poland*. Oxford: Oxford University Press, 1984.

Debeljak, Aleš. *Nedokončane hvalnice*. Ljubljana: Založba Mladinska knjiga, 2000.

Deleuze, Gilles, and Félix Guattari. *Kafka: Toward a Minor Literature*. Trans. Dana Polan. Minneapolis: University of Minnesota Press, 1986.

Desplatović, Elinor Murray. *Ljudevit Gaj and the Illyrian Movement*. Boulder, CO: Westview Press, 1975.

Doder, Duško, and Louise Branson, *Milošević: Portrait of a Tyrant*. New York: Free Press, 1999.

Drakulić, Slavenka. *Café Europa*. New York: Penguin, 1999.

———. *How We Survived Communism and Even Laughed*. New York: Norton, 1992.

Erofeev, Venedikt. *Moscow Circles*. Trans. J. R. Dorrell. London: Writers and Readers Publishing Cooperative, 1981.

Gabrič, Aleš. *Socialistična kulturna revolucija*. Ljubljana: Cankarjeva založba, 1995.

Garrard, John, and Carol Garrard. *Inside the Soviet Writers' Union*. New York: Macmillan, 1990.

Garton Ash, Timothy, ed. *Freedom for Publishing, Publishing for Freedom: The Central and East European Publishing Project*. Budapest: CEU Press, 1995.

———. *The Magic Lantern: The Revolution of '89 Witnessed in Warsaw, Budapest, Berlin, and Prague.* New York: Random House, 1990.

Gordy, Eric. *The Culture of Power in Serbia.* University Park, PA: Pennsylvania State University Press, 1999.

Goscilo, Helena. *The Explosive World of Tatyana N. Tolstaya's Fiction.* Armonk, NY: M. E. Sharpe, 1996.

Haraszti, Miklós. *The Velvet Prison.* London: I. B. Tauris, 1988.

Harris, Jane Gary, ed. *Autobiographical Statements in Twentieth-Century Russian Literature.* Princeton: Princeton University Press, 1990.

Havel, Václav. *The Art of the Impossible: Politics as Morality in Practice: Speeches and Writings, 1990–1996.* Trans. Paul Wilson et al. New York: Knopf, 1997.

———. "A Farewell to Politics." Trans. Paul Wilson. *New York Review of Books,* Oct. 24, 2002, http://www.nybooks.com/articles/15750.

———. *The Power of the Powerless. Citizens against the State in Central-Eastern Europe.* ed. John Keane. Armonk, NY: M. E. Sharpe, 1985.

———. *Temptation.* Trans. Marie Winn. New York: Grove Press, 1989.

———. *Three Vanek Plays.* London: Faber, 1990.

Hawkesworth, Celia, ed. *A History of Central European Women's Writing.* New York: Palgrave, 2000.

Higley, John, and György Lengyel, eds. *Elites after State Socialism.* Lanham, MD: Rowman and Littlefield, 2000.

Higley, John, Jan Pakulski, and Wlodzimierz Wesolowski, eds. *Postcommunist Elites and Democracy in Eastern Europe.* New York: St. Martin's, 1998.

Howell, Yvonne. *Apocalyptic Realism: The Science Fiction of Arkady and Boris Strugatsky.* New York: Peter Lang, 1994.

———. "'Where's the Velvet?' Jachym Topol's *Sestra* and the Reception of Alex Zucker's translation *City, Sister, Silver.*" *Translation Review* 63 (2002): 45–51.

Hroch, Miroslav. *Social Preconditions of National Revival in Europe: A Comparative Analysis of the Social Composition of Patriotic Groups among the Smaller European Nations.* Trans. Ben Fowkes. New York: Columbia University Press, 2000.

Jančar. Drago, *Mocking Desire.* Trans. Michael Biggins. Evanston: Northwestern University Press, 1998.

Jones, Malcolm, and Robin Miller, eds. *The Cambridge Companion to the Classic Russian Novel.* Cambridge: Cambridge University Press, 1998.

Keane, John. *Václav Havel: A Political Tragedy in Six Acts.* New York: Basic Books, 2000.

Kemp, Walter A. *Nationalism and Communism in Eastern Europe: A Basic Contradiction?* New York: St. Martin's Press, 1999.

Konrád, György. *Antipolitics: An Essay.* Trans. Richard E. Allen. San Diego: Harcourt Brace Jovanovic, 1984.

———.*The Melancholy of Rebirth: Essays from Post-communist Central Europe, 1989–1994.* Trans. Michael Henry Heim. San Diego: Harcourt Brace Jovanovic, 1995.

Konrád, György, and Iván Szelényi. *Intellectuals on the Road to Class Power.* New York: Harcourt Brace Jovanovich, 1979.

Krleža, Miroslav. *The Return of Philip Latinowicz*. Trans. Zora Depolo. London: Prager, 1959.

Kundera, Milan. *The Farewell Party*. New York: Penguin, 1977.

———. *The Unbearable Lightness of Being*. Trans. Michael Henry Heim. New York: Harper and Row, 1984.

Kustec, Aleksander. "The Poetry of a Nation: France Prešeren, Slovene Literature's *Pater Patria.*" *The Wordsworth Circle* 30, no. 1 (Winter 1999).

Kuzin, N. P., and M. N. Kolmakova, eds. *Sovetskaia shkola na sovremmennom etape*. Moscow, 1977.

Kuzminsky, Konstantin, and Gregory L. Kovalev, eds. *The Blue Lagoon Anthology of Modern Russian Poetry*. 9 vols. Newtonville, MA: Oriental Research Partners, 1980.

Labon. Johanna. *Balkan Blues: Writing out of Yugoslavia*. Evanston: Northwestern University Press, 1994.

Lednicki, Wacław, ed. *Adam Mickiewicz in World Literature*. Berkeley: University of California Press, 1956.

Levitt, Marcus. *Russian Literary Politics and the Pushkin Celebration of 1880*. Ithaca: Cornell University Press, 1989.

Limonov, Eduard. *Eto ia, Edichka*. New York: Index Publishers, 1982.

———. *Moia politicheskaia biografiia*. St. Petersburg: Amfora, 2002.

———. *Po tiur'mam*. Moscow: Ad Marginem, 2004.

———. *Russkoe*. Ann Arbor, MI: Ardis, 1979.

Lomonosov, M. *Izbrannye proizvedeniia v dvukh tomakh*. 2 vols. Moscow, 1986.

Lyotard, Jean-François. *The Postmodern Condition: A Report on Knowledge*. Trans. Geoff Bennington and Brian Massumi. Minneapolis: University of Minnesota Press, 1984.

MacFadyen, David. *Estrada?! Grand Narratives and the Philosophy of the Russian Popular Song since Perestroika*. Montreal: McGill-Queen's University Press, 2002.

———. *Red Stars: Personality and the Soviet Pop Song, 1955–1991*. Montreal: McGill-Queen's University Press, 2001.

———. *Songs for Fat People: Affect, Emotion, and Celebrity in the Russian Popular Song, 1900–1955*. Montreal: McGill-Queen's University Press, 2002.

Makanin, Vladimir. *Andergaund, ili Geroi nashego vremeni*. Moscow: Vagrius, 1999.

Makine, Andrei. *Dreams of My Russian Summers*. Trans. Geoffrey Strachan. New York: Simon and Schuster, 1997.

Masson, Sophie. "An Interview with Andrei Makine." *Quadrant,* Nov. 1998.

Mandelstam, Nadezhda, *Hope against Hope*. Trans. Max Hayward. Harmondsworth: Penguin Books, 1975

McConnell, Lauren. "Gray Zones and Black Holes: The Effects of Normalization Censorship on Czech Playwriting." PhD diss., Northwestern University, 2004.

Mihailovich, Vasa. "Faction or Fiction in *A Tomb for Boris Davidovich*: The Literary Affair." *Review of Contemporary Fiction* 14, no. 1 (1994).

Miller, Nicholas J. "The Children of Cain: Dobrica Ćosić's Serbia." *East European Politics and Societies* 14, no. 2 (2000).

———. "The Nonconformists: Ćosić and Popović Envision Serbia." *Slavic Review* 58, no. 3 (Fall 1999).

Miłosz, Czesław. *The Captive Mind.* New York: Vintage, 1990.

Morris, Meaghan. *The Pirate's Fiancée: Feminism, Reading, Postmodernism.* London: Verso, 1988.

Negrici, Eugen. *Literature and Propaganda in Communist Romania.* Trans. Mihai Codreanu. Revised by Brenda Walker. Bucharest: Romanian Cultural Foundation Publishing House, 1999.

Nemec, Krešimir. *Povijest hrvatskog romana od 1945 do 2000.* Zagreb: Školska knjiga, 2003.

Olcott, Anthony. *Russian Pulp: The Detektiv and the Russian Way of Crime.* Lanham, MD: Rowman and Littlefield, 2001.

Pantić, Mihailo. "Promena društvene funkcije književnosti u Srbiji, 1988–2000." Unpublished article, 2000.

Peković, Ratko. *Ni rat ni mir: Panorama književnih polemika 1945–1965.* Belgrade, 1986.

Pelevin, Viktor. *Generation P.* Moscow: Vagrius, 1999.

Potts, Stephen W. *The Second Marxian Invasion: The Fiction of the Strugatsky Brothers.* San Bernardino, CA: Borgo Press, 1991.

Prešeren, France. *Poems by France Prešeren.* Trans. J. Lavrin. Lljubljana: DZS, 1997.

Prokhanov, Aleksandr. *Gospodin Geksogen.* Moscow: Ad Marginem, 2001.

Pynsent, Robert. *Questions of Identity: Czech and Slovak Ideas of Nationality and Personality.* Budapest: CEU Press, 1994.

Ramet. Sabrina P., and Gordana P. Crnković, eds. *Kazaaam! Splat! Ploof! The American Impact on European Popular Culture since 1945.* New York: Rowman and Littlefield, 2003.

Robin. Régine. *Socialist Realism: An Impossible Aesthetic.* Trans. Catherine Porter. Stanford: Stanford University Press. 1992.

Rostoskii, B. I., et al., eds. *Genezis i razvitie sotsialisticheskogo iskusstva v stranakh tsentral'noi i iugo-vostochnoi evropy.* Moscow, 1978.

Sapkowski, Andrzej. *Pani jeziora.* Warsaw: SuperNOWA, 2001.

Segel, Harold B. *The Columbia Guide to the Literatures of Eastern Europe since 1945.* New York: Columbia University Press, 2003.

Shentalinsky, Vitaly. *Arrested Voices: Resurrecting the Disappeared Writers of the Soviet Regime.* Trans. John Crowfoot. New York: Free Press, 1996.

———. *Donos na Sokrata.* Moscow: Formika-S, 2001.

———. *Pereletnye snegi.* Moscow, 1983.

———. *Raby svobody: V literaturnykh arkhivakh KGB.* Moscow: Parus, 1995.

———. *Za chto? Proza, poeziia, dokumenty.* Moscow: Novyi kliuch, 1999.

Sholokhov, Mikhail. *At the Bidding of the Heart.* Trans. Olga Shartse. Moscow: Progress Publishers, 1973.

Skilling, H. Gordon. *Samizdat and an Independent Society in Central and Eastern Europe.* London: Macmillan, 1989.

Slovenska hronika XX stoletja, 1900–1941. Ljubljana: Nova revija, 1997.

Šmejkalová, Jirina. *Kniha: K teorii a praxi knizní kultury*. Brno: Host, 2000.

Smith, Gerald S., ed. *Contemporary Russian Poetry: Bilingual Anthology*, Bloomington: Indiana University Press, 1993.

———. "On the Page and on the Snow: Vladimir Makanin's *Andergraund, ili Geroi nashego vremeni*." *Slavonic and East European Review* 79, no. 3 (July 2001).

Solzhenitsyn, Alexander. *Nobel Lecture*. Trans. F. D. Reeve. New York: Farrar Straus and Giroux, 1970.

Starr, S. Frederick. *Red and Hot: The Fate of Jazz in the Soviet Union, 1917–1980*. New York: Oxford University Press, 1983.

Steinberg, Mark D. *Proletarian Imagination: Self, Modernity and the Sacred in Russia, 1910–1925*. Ithaca: Cornell University Press, 2002.

Stokes, Gale, ed. *From Stalinism to Pluralism: A Documentary History of Eastern Europe since 1945*. New York: Oxford University Press, 1991.

Stritar, Josip. *Izbrana delo*. Ljubljana: Mladinska knjiga, 1969.

Suny, Ronald Grigor. *The Revenge of the Past: Nationalism, Revolution, and the Collapse of the Soviet Union*. Stanford: Stanford University Press, 1993.

Tismaneanu, Vladimir. *Fantasies of Salvation: Democracy, Nationalism, and Myth in Post-communist Eastern Europe*. Princeton: Princeton University Press, 1998.

To Honour Roman Jakobson: Essays on the Occasion of His Seventieth Birthday. 3 vols. The Hague: Mouton, 1967.

Tolstaya, Tatyana. *Dvoe*. Moscow: Podkova, 2001.

———. "Russkii chelovek na randevu." *Znamia* 6 (1998): 200–209.

Topol, Jáchym. *City Sister Silver*. Trans. Alex Zucker. New Haven, CT: Catbird Press, 2000.

Ugrešić, Dubravka. *The Culture of Lies*. Trans. Celia Hawkesworth. University Park: Pennsylvania State University Press, 1998.

———. *Have a Nice Day: From the Balkan War to the American Dream*. Trans. Celia Hawkesworth. London: Jonathon Cape, 1994.

Ursu, Liliana. *Angel Riding a Beast*. Trans. Bruce Weigl and the author. Evanston: Northwestern University Press, 1998.

Verdery, Katherine. *National Ideology under Socialism*. Berkeley: University of California Press, 1991.

———. *What Was Socialism and What Comes Next?* Princeton: Princeton University Press, 1996.

Vidmar, Josip. *Kulturni problem slovenstva*. Ed. Aleš Debeljak. Ljubljana: Cankarjeva založba, 1995.

Viewegh, Michal. *Bringing Up Girls in Bohemia*. Trans. A. G. Brain. London: Readers International, 1996.

Wachtel, Andrew Baruch. *The Battle for Childhood*. Stanford: Stanford University Press, 1991.

———, ed. *Intersections and Transpositions*. Evanston: Northwestern University Press, 1998.

———. *Making a Nation, Breaking a Nation: Literature and Cultural Politics in Yugoslavia*. Stanford: Stanford University Press, 1998.

———. *An Obsession with History: Russian Writers Confront the Past*. Stanford: Stanford University Press, 1994.

————. "Translation, Imperialism and National Self-Definition in Russia." *Public Culture* 11, no. 1 (1999): 49–73.

Walicki, Andrzej. *The Slavophile Controversy: History of a Conservative Utopia in Nineteenth-Century Russian Thought*. Oxford: Clarendon Press, 1975.

Wolff, Larry. *Inventing Eastern Europe*. Stanford: Stanford University Press, 1994.

Zabuzhko, Oksana. *Pol'ovi doslidzhennia z ukraïns'kogo seksu*. Kiev: Zgoda, 1996.

Ziegfeld, Richard E. *Stanislaw Lem*. New York: F. Ungar Publishing Company, 1985.

Zlobina, Maia. "Zarubezhnaia kniga o Rossii." *Novyi mir*, 1996, no. 10.

Index

Page numbers in italics refer to illustrations

Aczél, György, 29
Adamov, Arkady, 194
Aksenov, Vasily, 38
Akunin, Boris, 193, 202–207, 208
Albahari, David, 111, 136–138
Andrić, Ivo, 107
Angier, Natalie, 160
Anpilov, Viktor, 162
Aralica, Ivan, 107–110
Ardis, 40
Arkan, 93
Armstrong, Charlotte, 194
Ash, Timothy Garton, 3n3
Atwood, Margaret, 159

Baader, 95
Babel, Isaac, 156, 157, 158
Bakunin, Mikhail, 95
Balzac, Honoré de, 26
Baudrillard, Jean, 122
Beckman, John, 123n4
Beethoven, Ludwig van, 25
Beránek, Ivan, 55
Berezovsky, Boris, 115
Beria, Lavrenty, 156
Bitov, Andrei, 54
Bleiweis, Janež, 17n14
Bloom, Clive, 189
Bloom, Harold, 25
Blue Lagoon Anthology of Modern Russian Poetry, 37, 40
Borges, Jorge Luis, 130, 214

Botev, Christo, 15
Bourdieu, Pierre, 43
Bowlt, John, 38
Boyle, T. Coraghessan, 7
Bozóki, András, 75
Brezhnev, Leonid, 168
Brodsky, Joseph, 42
Brooks, Jeffrey, 141, 190
Brown, Edward J., 91
Brubaker, Rogers, 106n14
Bulgakov, Mikhail, 157
Bunimovich, Evgeny, 92
Bunin, Ivan, 131–132

Cankar, Ivan, 17n14
Caranfil, Nae, 167
Carden, Patricia, 96
Ceauşescu, Nicolae, 103, 104–106, 163–165
Čapek, Karel, 199
Chekhov, Anton, 169, 179, 180, 202
Chernyshevsky, Nikolai, 96
Ćosić, Dobrica, 73, 76, 84–89, 96, 107, 119
Chuprinin, Sergei, 53, 66
Clancy, Tom, 8
Clark, Katerina, 190n4
Crnković, Gordana, 151, 152
Csurka, István, 73, 102, 103

Daniil, Yuli, 42
Dante, 17, 25
Debeljak, Aleš, 19n16, 139
Deleuze, Gilles, 7

DeLillo, Don, 8, 57
Diaghilev, Sergei, 133
Dobrovský, Josef, 14n7
Domokos, Mátyás, 57
Dostoevsky, Feodor, 95n45, 116, 168, 169,
    170, 172, 173–181, 188, 193, 216
Drakulić, Slavenka, 106–107n15, 144,
    149–151
Drašković, Vuk, 108n19
Druzhba narodov, 40
Dunin, Kinga, 158–161

Eastern Europe, definition of, 3–5
Editura Fundaţiei Culturale Române,
    50
Eksmo, 53, 195
Eminescu, Mihai, 15, 140n1, 163
Engels, Friedrich, 26
Ensler, Eve, 160
Erofeev, Venedikt, 40
Erofeev, Viktor, 149

Fichte, Johann Gottlieb, 14
Fielding, Helen, 208n22
Florensky, Pavel, 157
Fonvizin, Denis, 124

Galich, Aleksandr, 191n7
Garibaldi, Giuseppe, 25
Garrard, John and Carol, 32–33, 39
Gazeta Wyborcza, 159, 161
Glossop, Nicholas, 190
Gogol, Nikolai, 169, 170, 171, 179
Göncz, Árpád, 73, 87
Gorbachev, Mikhail, 66, 115, 141, 171
Gorky, Maxim, 157
Górnicki, Wiesław, 144
Goethe, Johann Wolfgang von, 17, 25
Goscilo, Helena, 145, 146
Grynberg, Henryk, 143fn
Guattari, Felix, 7
Guevara, Che, 95
Gulik, Robert Hans van, 205
Gusinsky, Vladimir, 115

Hankiss, Elemér, 42n48
Haraszti, Miklós, 30, 32, 33n37, 217
Havel, Václav, 4, 8, 38, 42, 73, 76–84, 87, 96,
    217
Hegel, Georg Wilhelm Friedrich, 25

Heidegger, Martin, 169
Heilbrun, Carolyn, 152
Hemingway, Ernest, 57
Herbert, Zbigniew, 38
Herder, Johann Gottfried von, 13
Hildegard of Bingen, 159
Hitler, Adolph, 162
Howard, Robert, 209
Howell, Yvonne, 188
Hribar, Ivan, 17
Hroch, Miroslav, 15n10

Iliescu, Ion, 164
Ilnitsky, Mykola, 66
Inostrannaia literatura, 39, 204
Iveković, Rada, 106–107n15
Izvestiia, 65, 141

Jančar, Drago, 42, 111, 133–136
Jong, Erica, 111
Joyce, James, 120, 191

Kant, Immanuel, 25
Kapuściński, Ryszard, 8n9, 140n2
Karadžić, Radovan, 73
Karadžić, Vuk, 14n7
Karamzin, Nikolai, 124
Keane, John Reuter, 78, 83
Kemp, Walter A., 99
Kerouac, Jack, 168
Kertész, Imre, 101, 102, 103
Kesić, Vesna, 106–107n15
King, Stephen, 8, 57, 193
Kiš, Danilo , 1, 100, 103, 157n23
Klaus, Václav, 77
Klima, Ivan, 168
Kliuev, Nikolai, 157, 158
Kolesnikov, Mikhail, 66
Konrad, György, 10, 25, 30, 36, 42, 70
Kontinent, 40
Kopitar, Jernej , 14n7
Kościuszko, Tadeusz, 24
Koštunica, Vojislav, 88
Kotlowitz, Alex, 8
Kraigher, Boris, 85
Krasiński, Zygmunt, 23–24
Krleža, Miroslav, 125, 126
Kultura, 40
Kundera, Milan, 1–4, 38, 67, 128, 129, 135,
    199–200, 217, 219

Kutik, Ilya, 39, 53
Kutik, Vitaly, 66

Le Guin, Ursula, 209–210
Lem, Stanisław, 8n9, 209
Lenin, Vladimir, 28, 95, 116, 162, 208
Leontiev, Konstantin, 95
Lermontov, Mikhail, 168, 169, 170, 176, 188
Lewis, C. S., 209
Limonov, Eduard, 73, 76, 89–97, 114,
    161–164
Lincoln, Abraham, 23
Linhartová, Věra, 198
literature: definition of in this book, 7–8;
    and nationalism under communism,
    98–106; role of in communist regimes,
    26–32; role of in nation building, 14–26;
    role of in postcommunism, 66–68
Literatura na świecie, 39
literary journals, Polish, 60–61, 68–69
literary prizes, 65–66
Literaturnaia gazeta, 65
Lomonosov, Mikhail, 14, 207
Lovrić, Jelena, 106–107n15
Lynch, David, 160
Lyotard, Jean-François, 127

Makanin, Vladimir, 54, 133, 166, 167, 168,
    169, 170, 171, 180, 182, 183, 187, 188, 199,
    215
Makine, Andreï, 130–133, 146–149
Malory, Thomas, 209, 210
Mandelstam, Osip, 37, 157
Marinina, Aleksandra, 48, 192–197, 202,
    214
Márquez, Gabriel García, 214
Marx, Karl, 26, 28
Masaryk, Tomáš, 82
Mažuranić, Ivan, 15
Mazzini, Giuseppe, 25
McBain, Ed, 194
McPhee, John, 8
McVeigh, Timothy, 95
Meri, Lennart, 73
Michnik, Adam, 159, 161
Mickiewicz, Adam, 4, 8, 15, 21, 22, 23, 31,
    124
Miller, Henry, 111
Miller, Nicholas, 86, 88
Milošević, Slobodan, 84, 87, 88, 89

Miłosz, Czesław, 4, 8, 10, 30, 31, 32, 141,
    219
Molodaia gvardiia, 53
Morris, Meaghan, 160
Morrison, Toni, 7
Movchan, Paulo, 66
Mukařovský, Jan, 199
Mussolini, Benito, 95

Nabokov, Vladimir, 131, 132
Němcová, Božena, 5n5
Nepomnyashchy, Catherine, 195
New York Review of Books, 37, 77, 145, 146,
    147, 148, 149
Nicholas II, Romanov, 204
Norwid, Cyprian, 53
Novyi mir, 39, 40, 155
Njegoš, Petar Petrović, 15, 124

Ogonek, 155
Olcott, Anthony, 194
Osojnik, Iztok, 123n5
Ovid, 121

Pál, Závada, 57
Panić, Milan, 88
Pantić, Mihailo , 2, 66
Păunescu, Adrian, 104–106
Pécsi, Györgyi, 57
Pelevin, Viktor, 167n2, 215–217
Petőfi, Sándor, 15, 29, 30, 31
Petrushevskaia, Liudmila, 54
Phillips, Arthur, 123n4
Pilniak, Boris, 157
Pirjevec, Dušan, 85
Platonov, Andrei, 157, 158
Pochoda, Elizabeth, 67
Pope, Alexander, 39, 53
Popov, Nebojša, 84
Popović, Danko, 108n19
popular literature, communist attitudes
    toward, 31–32, 189–191, 208–210
position of writers: after communism, 45–52,
    69–72, 73–75; under communism,
    31–42
Pravda, 65, 141
Prešeren, France, 4, 15, 16, 17, 18, 19,
    20, 21
Prigov, Dmitry Aleksandrovich, 46
Prokhanov, Aleksandr, 113–117

protochronism, 103
publishing industry: Czech, 54–55, 141–142;
    ex-Yugoslavia, 64; Hungarian, 55–58;
    Moldavian, 50–51; Polish, 60–63;
    Romanian, 49–50, 58–59; Russian,
    39–40, 48–49, 52–54, 59, 63–64;
    Ukrainian, 50
Pushkin, Alexander, 3, 4, 15, *16*, 17, 21, 27,
    29, 169, 176
Putin, Vladimir, 66, 95, 114, 115, 116
Pynchon, Thomas, 8
Pynsent, Robert, 14n9

Ranković, Aleksandar, 85
Robbe-Grillet, Alain, 199
Robin, Régine, 172
Roman, Constantin, 104
România literară, 49
Romaniuk, Viktor, 66
Roth, Philip, 37, 67
Rowling, J. K., 208n22
Rusu, Nicolae, 50, 51

Salinger, J. D., 191
Samizdat, 37–42
Sapkowski, Andrzej, 193, 207–214
Schuster, Rudolf, 73
Selenić, Slobodan, 108n19
Selimović, Meša, 107
Šabach, Petr, 55
Shakespeare, William, 17, 25, 84, 199,
    210
Shafir, Michael, 163
Sheldon, Sidney, 194
Shelley, Mary, 84
Shentalinsky, Vitaly, 142, 154–158
Shevchenko, Taras, 15
Shevchuk, Valerii, 66
Škvorecký, Josef, 40
Sholokhov, Mikhail, 127
Štayner, Karlo, 101n7
Shteyngart, Gary, 123n4
Štúr, L'udovit, 13
Sienkiewicz, Henryk, 214
Simenon, Georges, 194
Siniavsky, Andrei, 42, 116, 141, 204n19
Sloven, Leonid, 194
Smith, Hedrick, 144
Solzhenitsyn, Alexander, 1, 4, 8, 37–38, 43,
    67, 95n45, 127–128, 156, 216–217, 219

Sovetskii pisatel', 39
Sovremennik, 52, 53
Stalin, Iosef, 30, 116, 156
Steel, Danielle, 8, 57
Stout, Rex, 194
Stritar, Josip, 17
Strugatsky, Boris and Arkady, 8n9, 209
Stubovi kulture, 64
Suny, Ronald, 98
Szelényi, Iván, 10, 25, 30, 36, 42, 70
Szymborska, Wisława, 1, 38

Tito (Josip Broz), 85, 108
Tiutchev, Feodor, 133
Tolkien, J. R. R., 209
Tolstoy, Lev, 13, 27, 100, 131
Tolstaya, Tatyana, 144–149
Topol, Jáchym, 133, 167, 168, 181, 182, 187,
    188, 199
Topol, Josef, 167n1
Tuđman, Franjo, 106, 107, 108, 110, 152
Tudor, Corneliu Vadim, 73, 161–165
Turgenev, Ivan, 202
Trubar, Primož, 16n11

Ugrešić, Dubravka, 73, 106–107n15, 144,
    149, 151–154, 190
Updike, John, 7, 191
Ursu, Liliana, 119–122, 125, 129, 135

Vagrius, 53
Vainer, Georgy and Arkady, 194
Vazov, Ivan, 15
Verdery, Katherine, 10, 35, 36, 41, 103
Verdi, Giuseppe, 25
Veselinov, Jovan, 85
Vidmar, Josip, 19n16
Viewegh, Michal, 111, 189, 193, 198–202, 208
Vlad, Maria, 66
Vladimov, Georgy, 38, 41
Voiculescu, Dan, 106
Vonnegut, Kurt, 191
Vraz, Stanko, 19
Vysotsky, Vladimir, 191n7

White, T. H., 209
Whitman, Walt, 8
Winterson, Jeanette, 159
Wolfe, Thomas, 120, 126n14
Wolff, Larry, 3

Woolf, Virginia, 159
writers' unions, 32–34; Bulgarian, 68;
    Hungarian, 68; Romanian, 68;
    Slovenian, 68n9

Yeltsin, Boris, 66, 95, 115, 162

Zabuzhko, Oksana, 111–113, 118
Zagajewski, Adam, 38
Zamiatin, Evgeny, 209
Zhirinovsky, Vladimir, 94
Znamia, 53, 66
Zorin, Valentin, 144